How to become the person you want to be

How to become the person you want to be

Norman E. Hankins

 Nelson-Hall/Chicago

Library of Congress Cataloging in Publication Data

Hankins, Norman E.
  How to become the person you want to be.

  Includes bibliographical references and index.
  1. Success.   2. Behavior modification.   I. Title.
BF637.S8H22   158'.1   78–21596
ISBN 0–88229–297–8

Dedicated to my Father

Contents

Preface

All of us find ourselves not doing enough of some things that we should and doing too much of other things that we shouldn't. Too frequently we attempt to excuse or justify our actions by attributing them to some form of control beyond ourselves. How often have you heard or used excuses such as these: "I just can't resist the urge," "I'm a victim of circumstances," "There's nothing I can do," "I could not have done otherwise," "What's to be will be," or "The devil made me do it." After reading this book it is my hope that you never again use such statements as these and that you learn not only to accept responsibility for your behavior but also to manage it more effectively.

The purpose of this book is first to provide you with a thorough discussion of the nature of learning and principles of behavior modification and then to present specific programs designed to render assistance in changing specific kinds of overt behavior patterns and internal emotional states including smoking, overeating, quarrels with family members, depression, anxiety, anger, and impulsive behavior, problems which we all encounter from time to time. Enough concrete information will be presented so that you will find specific recommendations that should help you experience success without the necessity of purchasing expensive consultative services. This book is for those who believe that we do have the power and the techniques to change our behavior and, to some extent at least, to control our destinies. It is definitely not for those seeking instant and painless success nor for those who prefer to place the blame on fate or circumstances instead of coming to grips with the problem at hand.

This book is arranged in two parts. Part I consists of three chapters designed to provide insight into the nature of human behavior and to acquaint you with some of the accepted techniques of behavior management. In Part II separate chapters are devoted to what are for some people behavior problems. Problem areas include overeating, smoking, time management, study behavior, anxiety control, anger control, and dating skills, to mention only a few. Each chapter in Part II begins with a review of some research findings relevant to the specific area. Following this review of scientifically validated techniques, specific suggestions and recommendations for coping with this behavior are presented. It should be emphasized that the suggestions contained in each chapter are based on techniques that have been scientifically tested, usually in a clinical setting. You should be able to apply these suggestions in regulating your behavior. If you find the techniques do not work for you, please seek professional assistance.

You may want to read the entire book or you may want to focus your attention only on the chapters that are of particular interest to you. In either case you should read Part I before delving into any chapter in Part II. By so doing, you should have sufficient background to comprehend the material in any chapter in Part II.

I owe a special debt of gratitude to Marvine Rich, who wrote Chapter 13, and to G. E. Myles Genest, who wrote Chapter 14. I also wish to thank Sandra Miller and Joyce Larimer for their assistance in the preparation and typing of the manuscript.

Part 1
The Nature
of Behavior

1/The Nature of Behavior: Why you behave as you do

Have you ever wondered why we behave as we do? Why do we, for example, watch a ball game or movie on TV, go visit a neighbor, bathe in the spring sunshine, or smoke a cigarette? After all there are hundreds of alternative activities which could occupy our time. Does one light up a cigarette because he willfully chooses to do so or because he has become a slave of habit and cannot resist the urge when confronted with appropriate cues, such as the completion of a meal or the sight of a friend lighting a cigarette, which trigger the smoking response? An even more important question might be: Could he stop smoking if he wanted to?

Answers to the preceding questions reflect one's conception of the nature of behavior. One view is that man is basically a passive creature who responds to cues in his environment. Those with this concept of the nature of man see behavior as a series of mechanistic stimulus-response retionships in which the individual has little, if any, control of his behavior. They see man as a product of and at the mercy of environmental factors both external and internal. One behaves as he does because he cannot do otherwise. It is often argued that criminals are not really responsible for their conduct because of the detrimental influences of their environment. D. T. Lunde (1975) observes that during the depression of the 1930s there was an increase in suicides, while during the economic decline of the mid-1970s the

homicide rate increased. He attributes this reversal largely
to one's perception of the source of his or her difficulties.
During the thirties people tended to blame themselves for
their hardships but during the seventies they had an increased tendency to project the blame onto other persons.
Too frequently we hear comments such as "Anyone in my
situation would have done the same thing I did," or "I am
a victim of circumstances." The comedian Flip Wilson uses
a variation of this theme with his classic excuse for unacceptable behavior, "The devil made me do it." Whether we
attempt to excuse our behavior by attributing its cause to
external environmental factors or to "devils" within us, we
are, in effect, implying that we do not have control of our
actions.

The opposing view is that man has conscious control of
his behavior and acts upon the environment in such a manner as to fulfill his needs and desires. People holding this
view see man as having freedom of choice in choosing environmental changes and the ability and power to operate
on the environment in a manner that will produce those
changes. They see man as the dominant force and the environment responding to this force rather than vice versa.
From this position it might be argued that given sufficient
desire or "willpower," behavior is under conscious control
and subject to modification.

Neither of these views offers adequate explanation for
most behavior. It is true that all of us respond to numerous
environmental stimuli but probably not in the mechanistic
way that some seem to believe. It is also true that none of
us has complete control of our surroundings. Rather than
merely responding to environmental cues or acting upon the
environment so as to completely control it, our behavior is
a process of interaction between ourselves and our environment. For example, suppose a man is waiting at the airport
for his plane when a woman with a beautiful face and
luscious lips smiles at him, crosses her legs in an enticing
manner, and invites him to join her for a cup of coffee. The
stimulus has been presented; what is his response? Given

the biological appetites of most young virile males, our man is likely to accept the invitation. Not only is he likely to respond to the invitation by joining her for coffee but, as his ego is flattered and his confidence boosted, he may initiate romantic conversation, hold her hand, and suggest that they have a meal, see a movie, or meet on some future occasion. The point is that our man is no longer merely responding to flirtatious overtures but making advances and initiating some of the action. Not only is he being acted upon; he is also doing some of the acting. In other words the two of them are interacting with each other. Each responds to the other and in turn serves also as a stimulus for the partner's response. In the interaction process the environment is changed. It is possible that our man becomes infatuated to the point that he suggests missing his plane and spending the evening with his new acquaintance. On the other hand, she may well have ideas to the contrary.

What I have been attempting to illustrate with this example is that behavior is not determined solely by the individual nor by his environment, but by both. While behavior theorists used to view man as a respondent to environmental influences which shaped and controlled his actions, he has proved to be more active and the environment less autonomous than they believed. The manner in which environmental events are perceived by the individual determines his behavior. In commenting on the influence of the environment on behavior Albert Bandura sees it this way:

> The environment is not an operator that inevitably impinges upon individuals. Rather, it is only a potentiality until actualized through appropriate actions. Fires do not burn people unless they touch them. Rewards and punishments remain in abeyance until the relevant performances occur. Through their conduct people play an active role in producing the reinforcement contingencies that impinge upon them. Thus, behavior partly creates the environment, and the environment influences behavior in a reciprocal fashion. It is first as important to analyze how man shapes environmental conditions as it is to assess how conditions

modify his actions. A distinguishing feature of man is that he is capable of self-regulative influences. By functioning as an agent as well as an object of influence, man has some power of self direction (*Thoresen and Mahoney*, 1974, pp. v-vi).

What is the relationship between behavior and learning? Learning includes any changes in our behavior that develop as a result of interaction with the environment. Thus, the vast majority of our behavior is learned, although it is true that some kinds of behavior can be learned much more quickly than others depending on prior experience and perhaps even genetic or biological predispositions. Even our inherited tendencies are modified by person-environment interaction. Beautiful people, for example, may behave differently from those who are not beautiful, or a short person may behave differently from one who is tall because they perceive themselves differently and others may treat them differently. Inherited biological characteristics interact with the environment to produce learned behaviors. Since it is so difficult to isolate behavior from learning, let us now look at some of the basic principles of behavior.

Principles of Behavior

From observation of the interaction of many kinds of organisms, including man, with their environment, certain principles of behavior have been derived. A study of these principles can help us to understand how behaviors become associated or connected with certain situations.

Psychologists make a distinction between behavioral antecedents and behavioral consequences. These antecedents and consequences are called stimuli because they stimulate us to act or respond in some way. Antecedents are stimuli that precede some behavior (response) and either naturally possess or develop the power to elicit that behavior. When the knee tendon is gently tapped, the extension of the leg occurs automatically. If you place food in your mouth, salivation is involuntary. A sudden unexpected loud noise may produce a startled response accompanied by increase in heart beats and breathing rate. These are examples of reflexive behaviors.

Respondent Conditioning

Although it is easy to see how the previous examples could elicit or trigger certain responses the first time they occur, how can we account for the fear or anxiety that may be elicited by such antecedents as tests in school, standing before a group to speak, or approaching the boss with a request for a raise? How do these stimuli gain control over our behavior? Our responses to these situations are learned by a process that psychologists call respondent conditioning. The classic example of respondent conditioning is Pavlov's 1927 experiment in which a dog learned to salivate at the sound of a tuning fork. The procedure involves finding some stimulus (meat powder in this case) that has a natural relationship with salivation response. Pavlov found that when he placed meat in the dog's mouth, the dog salivated. The meat powder served as an unconditioned stimulus and salivation was the unconditioned response. This is reflexive behavior. Respondent conditioning involves pairing the original stimulus (meat powder) with a second one (tuning fork) so that the subject (dog) reacts automatically to the meat in the presence of the sound of the tuning fork. After a number of these occurrences, the dog responded (salivated) to the sound of the tuning fork (conditioned stimulus) alone in nearly the same way that he had responded to the meat powder (unconditioned stimulus).

A baby will salivate automatically when milk enters his mouth. This is merely reflexive behavior in which the milk serves as an unconditioned stimulus and salivation as an unconditioned response. Milk is the antecedent event that controls salivation. Will the baby also salivate automatically at the sight of the bottle? Probably not, because this stimulus-response relationship is not innate. Can the baby learn to salivate when he sees the bottle? Yes, if every time that he sees the bottle he is fed milk from it; he will reach a point where he salivates at the sight of the bottle regardless of whether milk follows. The bottle has become a conditioned stimulus. This learning process is called respondent conditioning. Respondent conditioning, then, is a process in which a previously neutral cue or cues, through association with unconditioned stimuli that have control over some reaction themselves, come to possess that same power of control.

Figure 1.1 Classical Conditioning Paradigm During and After Training

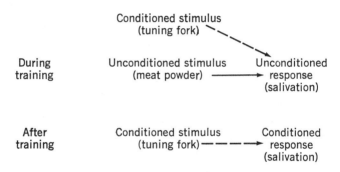

Why, then, might a person experience anxiety over tests in school, asking the boss for a raise, or standing before a group to speak? The most likely explanation is that these kinds of situations have become associated with such anxiety-arousing acts as teacher disapproval and refusal of a boss to grant requests. By being associated with teacher disapproval and humiliation, the test alone can acquire the power to elicit anxiety. Merely thinking of such a situation may be followed by the anxiety response. Later in the book respondent conditioning will be given further consideration with emphasis on how we can exert greater self-control by learning to control the antecedent stimuli that accompany various response patterns.

Operant Conditioning

There are many behaviors for which no specific antecedent stimuli can be identified. These behaviors are called
operants because their purpose is to operate on the environment in order to produce some desired result. Operants are
not elicited by antecedent stimuli and neither are they auto-
matic. Operant behaviors are largely under conscious or
voluntary control and include such activities as walking,
talking, driving an automobile or any other behavior subject to our own volition. Operant behaviors are strengthened by the consequences rather than the antecedents of the
behavior. If a behavioral act is followed by a pleasant or desirable consequence that behavior is likely to be repeated;
if it does not result in a desired consequence, it is less likely
to occur again.

Recent investigations (Miller, 1969; Herendon and
Shapiro, 1971, 1972) have demonstrated that rather than
being completely independent, respondents and operants are
intimately interrelated. It was once believed that the physiological functions of blood pressure, rate of heart beat, and
glandular processes were under the control of the autonomic
nervous system, but under recent experimental procedures
some persons have learned to regulate activities such as
heart beat and blood pressure, at least to some degree,
through operant conditioning procedures.

My behavior as I write this book, which includes much
cognitive activity, can be considered primarily operant behavior. I have the option of writing what I want to write
and I am also free to choose when I work on the manuscript
as long as I meet the deadlines set by the publisher, although I am more likely to engage in writing behavior when
the appropriate cues (seated at my desk with pencil, paper,
and thoughts of writing) are present. To the extent that my
behavior is under stimulus control it would be classified as
respondent; therefore, we are actually talking about a combination of operant and respondent behavior. Whether or
not I write another book when this one is completed depends

to a great extent on the outcome or consequences of this effort. If readers find this book useful and create a demand for it that would be a gratifying experience for me, I would be more likely to try another one in the future. If this effort is not sufficiently appreciated and rewarded, I will be less likely to attempt another manuscript. Most human behavior is of this nature; it is either strengthened or weakened depending on the consequences.

Positive and Negative Reinforcement

When a consequence strengthens behavior, that behavior is said to be reinforced. Reinforcers strengthen behavior by adding something to or taking something away from a situation. A positive reinforcer is a consequence that strengthens behavior by adding something to the situation. A student's study behavior may be strengthened by verbal praise, a pat on the back, or a smile from the teacher. A factory worker may labor at his station all week for his check on Friday afternoon. A kiss from a fellow's sweetheart may make the long drive to see her worth the effort. The reward of teacher attention, the pay check, or the kiss in these situations strengthens the behaviors preceding them, provided each of these persons perceives the consequences to be satisfying.

A negative reinforcement is a behavior or agent that strengthens the response by removing something from the situation. Negative reinforcers are usually unpleasant or aversive stimuli, the removal of which strengthens behavior. The husband who finds his nagging wife unbearable may drive to a local tavern for a cool brew. The removal of the aversive stimulation, i.e. his wife's nagging, may strengthen the behavior of leaving the house. Suppose middle-aged parents are chaperoning a group of teenagers at a dance where there is a rock band playing very loud music. The chaperones may choose to wear ear plugs or to stay away from the band, thereby avoiding or reducing the deafening noise. In other words, reduction of the intolerable noise will strengthen the act of inserting the ear plugs into the ears.

There are some cases in which positive reinforcement and negative reinforcement would appear to be opposite sides of the same coin. Consider this example. You come home on a midsummer evening after a hard day at work and enter a hot and stuffy house. You immediately turn on the air conditioner. What is it that strengthens the response of turning on the air conditioner? Is it the fact that hot air is removed (negative reinforcement) or that cool air is produced (positive reinforcement)? In this particular case, regardless of how the consequence is stated, the response pattern of turning the knob to switch on the air conditioner is strengthened. In a great majority of instances the difference between positive and negative reinforcement is a real difference and not merely two ways of looking at the same thing. An important point to remember is that all reinforcers, whether positive or negative, strengthen the behavior which they follow and become associated with.

Punishment

A third agent acting on behavior—most likely weakening it—is punishment. Punishment occurs when a response produces aversive or undesirable results. It is the direct opposite of negative reinforcement. Negative reinforcement occurs when the response *removes* aversive stimulation whereas punishment occurs when the response *produces* aversive stimulation. If I go outside on a cold day without a coat, I chill; this is punishment. When I step back inside a warm room the cold is removed; this is negative reinforcement.

Effects of Behavioral Consequences on Behavior

The consequences of our behavior may be desirable or undesirable. Behavior may either *produce* or *remove* those desirable and/or undesirable agents from our immediate environment. Thus we have four possibilities: (a) desirable consequences may follow a behavior (behavior is strengthened); (b) desirable consequences may be removed from a situation as a result of our behavior (behavior is weakened); (c) undesirable consequences may arise from behavior (behavior is weakened); and (d) undesirable consequences may be removed by our behavior (behavior is strengthened).

Each of the possibilities with the exception of extinction has been discussed. Extinction of behavior occurs when desirable consequences do not result from that behavior. For example, the factory worker will not continue indefinitely at his work station without his check on Friday afternoon, nor is the fellow likely to continue to drive long distances to see his girl friend unless the kiss or some happy consequence is forthcoming. Behavior which produces no consequence serves no purpose and eventually ceases to occur. After all, what's the point of squeezing the cow's teats if you are getting no milk?

This simple example can be used to illustrate each of the four preceding possibilities. Suppose you walk into a dark room and need to see your way around. You flip the light switch and the lights enable you to see. This desirable consequence strengthens your response of flipping the switch (positive reinforcement). Let's now assume that the brilliance of the lights and the glare from them causes you to have a headache. You now flip the switch to either turn them off or lower their intensity, and your headache disappears. In this case you have removed something unpleasant and the response of flipping the switch is again strengthened (negative reinforcement). Now let us assume that you flip the switch and nothing happens one way or the other. Very quickly you will cease this behavior and try something else—another switch or the bulb, in which case the response of flipping the switch is weakened (extinction). Finally let us suppose that there is a faulty connection and when the switch is flipped you receive a shock. In this case your response has produced an undesirable consequence (punishment) and your behavior is weakened.

Practically all behavior can be explained by respondent and operant conditioning. We can associate certain behavior patterns with antecedent events and/or with the consequences. How we behave is determined by the nature of the situation. The fact that behavior is learned does not mean that when you become an adult all you do is to repeat behaviors that you learned when you were growing up. It is true that many behaviors learned during youth do persist into old age; these are called habits. But new or changed situations may require new behaviors; old response patterns may become inadequate or even detrimental in helping one cope with different situations. A parent might learn effective techniques of managing a young child, but as the child grows into adolescence, the situation is quite different and new methods of interaction must be learned, i.e., less direct control by the parent and greater independence of the adolescent become necessary. The parent who cannot adjust to these changed conditions must eventually pay a price for his inability or refusal to learn new behaviors as the need arises. Learning is a continuous and never ending process.

Making Effective Environmental Adjustments

Behavior is essentially an attempt of the individual to maintain a satisfying relationship with the environment. All of us are constantly in the process of adjusting to some situation or condition. Our needs must be met on a daily basis; none of us can do without life's necessities for very long. In addition, we all have psychological needs such as love, security, significance, purpose, and so on. Some people learn to meet these needs effectively while others never do. At times all of us find ourselves behaving in ways that we do not want. We may wish we did not smoke or eat so much or did not feel so tongue-tied around attractive members of the opposite sex, or did not spend so much time drinking beer with the boys. These are kinds of behavior that we would like to decrease. Sometimes we may find ourselves not behaving in a way we wish we could. In this case we want to increase some behavior that is not occurring frequently enough. We may feel the need to study more, to spend more time in the gymnasium or on the track shedding those extra pounds. Regardless of whether we are attempting to increase some behavior or decrease it, the goal is the same—that of attaining a higher level of adjustment to our environment.

Persons who have some understanding of the many environments (including their own internal ones) which influence them and who manage these environments consistent with their personal values are manifesting not only self-control and a certain level of self-sufficiency, but considerable dignity as well. As has been previously stated, not only is behavior a function of the environment, but environments are a function of the individual's behavior, i.e. man's relationships with his many environments is not one of reaction but interaction. Mahoney and Thoresen (1974) phrase it this way:

> ...the truly "free" individual is one who is in intimate contact with himself and his environment (both internal and external). He knows "where he's at" in terms of the factors influencing both his actions and his surroundings. Moreover, he has acquired technical skills which enable him to take an active role in his own growth and adjustment. He is no mechanical automaton, passively responding to environmental forces. He is a personal scientist, a skilled engineer capable of investigating and altering the determinants of his actions. He is free to exert countercontrol on his environment, free from the resignation and inadequacies of a totalitarian existence, and free to draw upon a repertoire of effective behaviors. His happiness and development are not restricted by incapacitating fears of disabilities. Hence, the person with more freedom is the one with skills of behavioral self-control. (B. 71-72.)

A major concern of many humanists, including theologians and other religious backers, is that the individual person must assume responsibility for his or her actions. The technique for developing self-control discussed in this book can clearly be used to encourage humanistic actions.

That brings us to the primary purpose of this book. It is intended to help you establish programs for modifying your behavior by helping you eliminate undesirable habits or behavior patterns and acquire more desirable ones. This book is based on the assumption that most behavior is under voluntary control, and that with increased knowledge and information regarding the nature of behavior, it can be modified and desirable results achieved. After having read this book I hope you will never again rationalize your behavior with such standard comments as: "I just can't help myself," "I am a victim of circumstances," or "The devil made me do it." When you have completed this book you should have sufficient understanding of learning principles and specific suggestions regarding behavioral self-control that you can proudly and truthfully proclaim, *"The devil can't make me do it, without my consent and cooperation."* Your behavior can truly come under your control if you are willing to systematically and conscientiously apply the principles and techniques described in the following chapters.

2/Principles of Behavior Management: How to break the chains of habit

You will recall that in the previous chapter it was emphasized that new behaviors are acquired through learning. Behavior can be modified or changed through the same processes by which it is acquired. In this chapter, we will discuss some of the fundamental learning principles, not covered in the previous chapter, which are prerequisites to effective behavior management—one's own or that of others.

Before proceeding with our discussion let us briefly review the principles of learning discussed in Chapter 1 with which you should now be familiar. They are summarized as follows:

1. Respondent behavior is a function of the antecedent events associated with that behavior.
2. Operant behavior is a function of its consequences; the consequences may either strengthen or weaken the behavior.
3. Positive reinforcement strengthens behavior by adding something pleasant or desirable to the situation.
4. Negative reinforcement strengthens behavior by removing something undesirable or unpleasant from the situation.
5. When behavior occurs without reinforcement (no consequence one way or the other) that behavior is weakened. This process is called extinction.

6. When behavior is followed by punishment that behavior is also weakened or eliminated.

Kinds of Reinforcers

Positive reinforcers may be tangible or intangible ranging from food to personal satisfaction for a completed task. Reinforcers such as food, water, sex, and so on are called primary reinforcers because they satisfy or reduce some physiological need. Food will reinforce food-seeking behavior. Many other stimuli or events can also be reinforcing although they do not satisfy any physiological need. These stimuli include money, pins, certificates, some symbols of status, good marks or grades; they are called conditioned or secondary reinforcers because they are desired not so much for their inherent value as what they represent. People desire and are willing to work not so much for money itself but for the goods or services that money will buy. This is reflected in the often asked question, "What good is money unless you can spend it?" It is not so much the grade or mark that a student receives but what that mark represents that is of most importance. High marks represent success and progress toward goals. The high mark is reinforcing but only because it is associated with the achievement of success. Military personnel may work hard for another stripe or bar or for an eagle rather than an oak-leaf cluster because these symbols represent increased authority, power, achievement, status, and money.

A third kind of reinforcer, being less tangible than either primary or secondary reinforcers might be called extrinsic reinforcement. This category includes a pat on the back from a superior, a smile, a compliment, or the opportunity to converse with other people. A fourth kind of reinforcement might be called intrinsic reinforcement because it comes from within the individual rather than from without. Intrinsic reinforcement includes the satisfaction one gets from knowing that one has given a good performance or achieved a deserved goal. It also includes the pleasure one gets from engaging in an activity for its own sake such as reading, collecting antiques, doing crossword puzzles, bird watching, and so on. Mere participation in the activity provides its own reinforcement.

Motivation and Reward

Abraham Maslow (1953) has listed in hierarchical order what he considers to be man's basic needs. They may be listed in pyramid form with those at the base being most basic and concrete and those near the apex being most abstract.

Figure 2.1. Maslow's Hierarchy of Needs

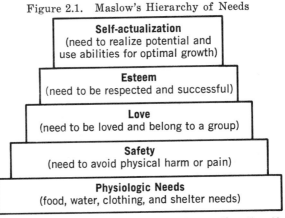

Adapted from: Maslow, A.H. **Motivation and Personality**. New York: Harper and Brothers, 1954.

From Figure 2.1 it can be seen that man's most basic needs are physiological, including the need for food, water, clothing, and shelter. Next in order is physical safety; most people have a need to avoid physical harm or pain. These needs are largely innate. Higher in the pyramid are the learned needs of a psychological nature including the need to be loved and to belong to some group, need for esteem such as that to be successful and respected, and self-actualization needs. Self-actualization includes the need to use one's abilities and to realize potential—to become that which one is capable of becoming. The implicit assumption in this hierarchy is that man's most basic needs (those lower in the pyramid) must be satisfied, at least to some degree, before one can be very effective in attaining any of the higher-level needs.

This analysis would imply that physiological needs can best be satisfied directly through primary reinforcers and indirectly through some secondary reinforcer, namely money. It is very likely that the higher level needs (psychological) could best be satisfied through secondary, intangible-extrinsic and intangible-intrinsic reinforcers.

Deci (1971) recommends that in reinforcing behavior we make a distinction between intrinsic and extrinsic motivation. Intrinsic motivation includes those motives that cause one to engage in certain behaviors for the sheer pleasure of the activity. Extrinsic motivation includes those incentives and pressures applied by external forces. As a result of his research, Deci has concluded that tangible-extrinsic reinforcement such as money or candy may be effective in strengthening extrinsically motivated behavior but should not be used to reinforce intrinsically motivated behavior. For the latter behavior intangible-extrinsic (smile, compliment, pat on the back) and intangible-intrinsic (personal satisfaction) reinforcement are more effective. As illustrated in the following case, tangible-extrinsic reinforcement may actually destroy intrinsic motivation. Suppose that a father has a teenage son who enjoys mowing the lawn on Saturdays as he assumes responsibility for keeping the grass cut. The father then decides to reward his industrious son with a couple of dollars each week. Will this strengthen grass-cutting behavior? What is likely to happen is that the son will continue cutting the grass but for a different reason; he previously did it for personal enjoyment but he learns to keep doing it because he is being paid to do so. He now associates lawn mowing with money rather than with pleasure. He reasons that mowing must be labor because his father pays him to do it. What happens if there comes a time when lawn-mowing behavior no longer produces money? That behavior is likely to cease. Now that mowing the lawn is associated with pay, the behavior stops when the pay stops. The intrinsic motivation has been destroyed by the application of tangible-extrinsic reinforcement. Deci feels that, in a case such as this, verbal praise given the son by the father would have been the effective act to encourage the son's pleasure in the work.

Relativity of Reinforcement

Until Premack's (1959) assertion that not all reinforcers are equally effective in strengthening behavior, it was generally assumed that they were. Behavioral consequences which sustain or strengthen behavior in some individuals or under some conditions are less effective with other people or with the same person under different circumstances. The effectiveness of a reinforcer depends to a great extent on how it is perceived by the person receiving it. Money, for example, does not automatically strengthen behavior. If an employee labors all day for his employer and at the end of the day the employer gives him a five-dollar bill, the work behavior of the employee is not likely to be strengthened. In fact, he may not even report for work on the following day because his expectations were not met. If one completes a task expecting twenty dollars in remuneration and receives only ten, then that money may be perceived as punishment (and produce the same effect) rather than as reinforcement.

Premack believes that the opportunity to engage in a highly preferred activity can reinforce participation in a less preferred activity. In order to apply this technique, commonly called the "Premack Principle," we would observe the behavior of an individual when given an opportunity to do whatever he wishes, and make a list of activities from highest preference to lowest preference. When it has been determined what the most preferred activities are, they are then made contingent on less preferred activities.

One must complete the less enjoyable task in order to engage in a more pleasurable activity.

A working mother may have difficulty getting her daughter to help with the dishes. She decides to take measures to rectify this problem situation and starts by observing the daughter to determine the activities she seems to enjoy most. She lists the activities in order of her preference, as follows:

A. Talking to boyfriend on the telephone
B. Listening to records
C. Reading the newspaper
D. Washing the dinner dishes

According to Premack, Activity A should reinforce B, C, and D; B should reinforce C and D. How does our tired mother solicit her daughter's assistance with the dishes? She permits that daughter to talk to her boyfriend only after she has washed the dishes. Activities B and C could also be used as reinforcers. For this technique to be effective in this case, we must assume that the mother has sufficient control of the situation so that the daughter does not have access to the phone until the dishes are washed. If she can engage in A, B, or C without first engaging in the less preferred behavior, it is not likely that D will be accomplished.

A child in school may prefer eating candy and watching movie cartoons to doing his arithmetic. According to the Premack principle, also known as Grandma's law, the child should do arithmetic if he or she is reinforced by being permitted to eat candy or watch a cartoon afterward. Incidentally Grandma's law states, "You cannot have dessert until you clean your plate." This, of course, is a behavioral contingency.

Shaping Behavior

Many behaviors occur so infrequently, are so complex, or require so much effort that we cannot wait until the final behavior pattern is established before reinforcement is presented. Animal trainers are very familiar with behavioral shaping. Suppose a dog trainer wants the dog to turn twice to the right, turn a somersault, and jump through a firey ring. The dog learns this sequence in small steps. The trainer begins by reinforcing any movement to the right, then a complete turn, two complete turns, until the entire sequence has been mastered.

A friend of mine decided to lose some weight and after analyzing the situation, he discovered that he had learned to eat all the food on his plate at every meal. He decided to teach himself not to eat everything on his plate and started by placing a very small portion of food to the side of the plate. This small portion was not to be eaten. He gradually increased the size of the portions not to be eaten until he was soon eating only about half the food on the plate. Another technique would have been to have gradually reduced the amount of food he put on the plate. Either of these examples illustrates the shaping process and numerous other examples will be presented later in this book.

Up to this point in our discussion of reinforcers, it has been implied that reinforcement was experienced on a continuous basis, i.e. after every response. We have also learned that when behavior is not reinforced extinction occurs. Between these extremes of continuous reinforcement, where every behavior of a certain kind is reinforced, and extinction, where there is no reinforcement, there are many situations where behavior is only occasionally or partially reinforced.

Scheduling Reinforcers

The frequency with which various behaviors are reinforced seems to produce different response patterns. People behave differently when their behavior is reinforced only occasionally than they do when a specific behavior is reinforced every time that it occurs. A pattern or system for administering reinforcers is called a reinforcement schedule. This schedule is a method of arranging reinforcement contingencies with respect to the number of responses, the passage of time, or both. It seems reasonable to expect that intermittent reinforcement would produce an effect somewhere between continuous reinforcement and no reinforcement, but such is not the case.

Schedules based on the passage of time are called interval schedules and those based on the number of responses that occur are called ratio schedules. Either ratio or interval schedules may be fixed or variable. A fixed interval schedule is one in which no reinforcement will be received regardless of the number of responses that occur until the passage of some predetermined period of time. Employees who work for an hourly or weekly wage or a monthly salary are on a fixed interval schedule. Variable interval schedules are also based on time except that reinforcement follows various time intervals fluctuating around a mean or average time period. If a fixed interval schedule of one week were converted to a variable interval schedule the employees would be paid on the average of once per week but their pay could come at any time. A fixed ratio schedule is one in which reinforcement may follow every response, every other response, every tenth response, or some similar pattern. A variable ratio schedule is one which is less predictable. If one were converting a fixed ratio of every tenth response to a variable schedule, he would arrange for 10 percent of the responses to be reinforced but the learner would have no way of knowing which response would be followed by the reward.

Different schedules exert different influences on behavior, especially in a laboratory setting. When a fixed interval schedule is used, response rate decreases immediately following reinforcement and then increases near the end of the interval just prior to the time for the next reinforcement. In practical applications of the principles, results are not always so clear-cut. It is doubtful, for example, if an employee paid on a monthly basis works any harder at the end of the month than he does at the beginning. The rate of responding on a variable schedule is usually higher and relatively constant over time.

Since the amount of reinforcement is dependent upon the number of responses, the rate is usually higher under a ratio schedule than under an interval schedule. Industrial piecework is an example of a fixed ratio schedule. Since the worker is paid according to the work produced, there is a premium for a high rate of activity. Sales work would represent behavior based on a variable ratio schedule. Most sales people receive a commission on their sales. Naturally, they do not make a sale on every attempt so the commissions received are intermittent or sporadic. The salesman never knows when he is going to make a sale, but the greater the number of people he approaches, the greater is the likelihood of his being successful. Salespersons who get a base salary plus commission operate on a combination fixed-interval variable-ratio schedule. Variable ratio schedules are noted for the persistence of the behavior associated with them. Most of us know how difficult it is to get rid of some salesmen. Gambling behavior is based on variable ratio schedules. The poker player does not expect to win every hand he plays, but he knows that if he plays long enough he will have a winner and, who knows, the very next deal may be the one. This temptation is irresistible for many gamblers. Many of them are unable to quit until they have lost everything. Both variable interval and ratio schedules produce behavior that is highly resistant to extinction.

Desensitization

Systematic desensitization is a technique for producing behavior change that is based on the principles of respondent conditioning. It is aimed specifically at the alleviation of maladaptive anxiety. One of the first studies utilizing something similar to desensitization was that of Jones (1924) in which a young boy who feared objects having the characteristic of "furriness" was shown a rabbit which elicited the fear response. Over a number of days while the child was engrossed in some of his favorite activities such as sitting in his high chair, eating favorite foods, and playing with desired toys, he was shown a rabbit briefly and from a distance. On successive days the rabbit was gradually brought a little closer to the boy while he was preoccupied with eating and playing. Through the very gradual pairing of this fear-arousing stimulus (rabbit) with pleasant activities, the boy learned to tolerate the rabbit's presence and eventually overcame his fear of it. This situation might be diagrammed as follows:

Figure 2.2. Desensitization of a Young Boy's Fear
Responses to a Rabbit

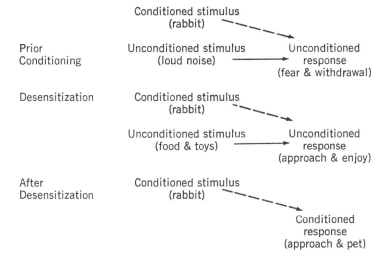

Whereas the rabbit was previously associated with fear, the boy has now learned to associate it with relaxation and approach rather than fear and avoidance responses. This process is called counter-conditioning.

Guthrie (1935) believed that one way of changing behavior was to introduce a formerly aversive stimulus in such mild degrees that it did not elicit the fear response. Pleasantness and relaxation rather than fear become associated with what was formerly aversive stimulation. An example of this principle is that of allowing one who is afraid of water to first become relaxed and then start wading in water at the shallow end of the pool. Although it may take several days the learner will gradually learn to move farther and farther into the water without becoming afraid until he is able to put his head under water. When this is accomplished he should be relaxed and confident enough to begin swimming. As you can see, this is essentially the same technique used by Jones in extinguishing the boy's fear of the rabbit.

Systematic desensitization, as developed by Wolpe (1958), is aimed specifically at the reduction of anxieties resulting from various kinds of fears and phobias. The technique involves the pairing of complete relaxation with imagined scenes depicting situations that the person feels anxious about. The assumption is that if one can learn to experience relaxation, rather than anxiety, while imagining such scenes, the real-life situation that the scene depicted will produce much less discomfort. These imagined scenes are usually arranged in a hierarchy beginning with situations that are only mildly associated with anxiety and proceeding to scenes associated with high anxiety. Usually betweeen ten and fifteen such scenes are depicted.

Rimm (1974) used this method with a forty-year-old male who had developed a fear of heights shortly after his discharge from the Army Air Force during World War II. He was a navigator, had flown a large number of combat missions, and he attributed this phobia to these wartime experiences. The items used were in order of increasing anxiety as follows:

1. You are beginning to climb the ladder leaning against the side of your house. You plan to work on the roof. Your hands are on the ladder, and your foot is on the first rung.
2. You are halfway up the ladder, and you happen to look down. You see the lawn below you and a walkway.
3. Driving with the family, road begins to climb.
4. Driving with family on California coastal highway, with dropoff to the right.
5. On California seashore cliff, approximately thirty feet from edge.

6. On California seashore cliff, approximately six feet from edge.
7. Driving with family, approaching mountain summit.
8. In commercial airliner, at the time of takeoff.
9. In commercial airliner, at an altitude of 30,000 feet.
10. In airliner, at an altitude of 30,000 feet with considerable turbulence.
11. On a California seaside cliff, approximately two feet (judged to be a safe distance) from the edge and looking down.
12. Climbing the town water tower to assist in painting, about ten feet from ground.
13. Same as above, but about twenty feet from ground.
14. On the catwalk around the water tank, painting the tank. (p 58)[1]

More information regarding the use of this technique will be presented in later chapters.

Stimulus Narrowing

Behavior does not occur in a vacuum but, as you learned in Chapter 1, it is under lawful stimulus control. Since behavior is under stimulus control, it is possible for us to weaken or eliminate undesirable responses and strengthen desirable responses by changing the stimulus environment. If a college student had difficulty studying in the library because he found the girls distracting, he might try studying alone in his dormitory room.

Some maladaptive behavior patterns are especially troublesome because they occur in such a wide variety of situations. Obese individuals may have formed a habit of eating while watching TV, reading the newspaper, studying, or talking with friends. An example of stimulus narrowing would be restricting eating behavior to the dinner table and then only at certain times of the day and without the TV or newspaper. The number of cues associated with the troublesome behavior are greatly reduced.

---

1. Rimm. D., & Masters, J. *Behavior Therapy: Techniques and Empirical Findings.* New York: Academic Press, Inc., 1974. Reprinted with permission of Academic Press.

Competing Responses

The competing responses technique can be used in conjunction with stimulus narrowing. When the cues associated with the troublesome behavior occur, one may engage in competing or incompatible behavior. When the obese person finds himself desiring food while reading the newspaper, he may go for a walk, or drink a large glass of water or diet soda. Or every time he reads the paper he may think how slender and attractive he wants to become. These thoughts are incompatible with eating.

Undesirable behavior is usually the termination of a sequence of responses chained together, i.e., one response produced another stimulus which in turn encourages the next response. The alcoholic may decide to stop getting intoxicated but continue to drink socially. At a party he accepts his first drink only to find that he needs another and another. Before long he has lost all control and is drunk once more. This situation is actually the termination of a chain of behaviors. The earlier in the chain a competing response is introduced the greater the likelihood of success in producing a behavioral change. One competing response would have been that of refusing the first drink. If this proves unsuccessful he may find it necessary to refuse invitations to gatherings where drinking occurs and do something else on those evenings. This point seems rather obvious but many persons with self-control problems seem oblivious to it. Some people behave as if they believe the mark of self-control to be the ability to withstand any and all temptations. It is, in fact, far more correct to say that the mark of self-control is the ability to minimize temptation by early interruption of such behavioral chains.

Contingency Management

Contingency management consists of making behavioral consequences contingent upon the behavior preceding those consequences. This is usually accomplished through the presentation and withdrawal of reinforcement and punishment. In the early applications of contingency management procedures, a therapist, teacher, or other person would observe the target behavior of an individual and administer appropriate rewards or punishment depending on the behavior that occurred. While these techniques are still effective, it has since been demonstrated that one can learn to manage his own behavior. He does this by establishing a set of contingencies and following the occurrence of target behaviors, both desirable and undesirable, with the consequences set forth in the contingency.

Contingency management involves more than the mere dispensation of rewards and punishments. The first step is to clearly define the problem behavior which can be either some behavior which *does* occur and *should not* or some behavior which *should* occur and *does not*. The target behavior should be so clearly described that there is no question that it has or has not occurred.

A second step consists of an analysis of conditions surrounding the occurrence of the behavior in an attempt to identify the cues which seem to trigger or set the stage for the behavior and the consequences which seem to maintain it. This analysis becomes possible only after several observations are made, and records are kept, describing in detail the frequency of the behavior and the context. Although procedures for collecting and presenting baseline data are discussed in some detail in the next chapter, the following examples are illustrations of the value of analyzing the situation in which the behavior occurs. An acquaintance of the author who was interested in weight reduction began to keep a record of her eating habits. After a few days of record-keeping it became apparent that her major difficulty stemmed from the fact that she was eating the leftover food from her four children. She explained that she had always made an effort to reduce waste, but she was not aware of how much food she was eating until she began to make and record these observations. She was able to overcome most of her problem by simply giving the children smaller portions of food and throwing away what they left. Without an analysis of the situation, it is unlikely that she would have discovered the source of the problem. Penick, Filion, Fox, and Stunkard (1971) report the case of a thirty-year-old housewife who, after two weeks of record-keeping, recognized that anger stimulated her eating. Following this discovery, whenever she began to get angry she left the kitchen and wrote down how she felt. This action not only decreased her anger but also stopped her eating.

It cannot be overemphasized that an integral part of the problem of behavior analysis is the identification of the particular stimuli, situations, and conditions that consistently precede the target behavior and those that consistently follow it. To determine the eliciting stimuli can be an aid in the identification of reinforcers and also in discovering the kinds of stimuli which could be used as reinforcers for more desirable behavior. For example, if watching television triggers eating behavior, a contingency could be established whereby television watching is permitted only when the appropriate amount of food has been consumed. What was formerly the eliciting stimulus for the undesirable behavior can be made to function as a reinforcer for desirable behavior. This analysis is also beneficial in determining and describing the social and physical environment that elicit the troublesome behavior and into which more adaptive behaviors must be programmed. The third step is the development and implementation of the program for behavioral change. This step, along with a more complete discussion of each step in contingency management will be presented in the following chapter.

Summary

At the beginning of this chapter you reviewed six principles of learning discussed in Chapter 1. Let us now extend that list by reviewing the additional principles and generalizations presented in this chapter.

7. Reinforcers may be classified as tangible or intangible

and as extrinsic or intrinsic. Some kinds of reinforcers are more effective than others depending on the circumstances.

8. Tangible rewards are usually more appropriate for lower-level need (physiological) while intangible reinforcers may be more effective in strengthening higher-level (self-actualization) needs.

9. The effectiveness of a particular reinforcer depends on the environmental conditions and also on the perceptions and internal state of the particular individual. What is reinforcing to one person may not be to another. What is reinforcing to a person at a given time may not be at another. The effectiveness of a reinforcer is relative to several variables.

10. Complex behavior patterns are usually acquired via the shaping process, i.e., through the reinforcement of small steps or successive approximations to the desired behavior.

11. There are four basic reinforcement schedules and each of these schedules may produce different effects on behavior.

12. Systematic desensitization is a procedure based on respondent conditioning procedures designed primarily to reduce anxieties, fears, and phobias.

13. Contingency management is a procedure for modifying behavior by making behavioral consequences contingent upon the behavior preceding those consequences. These consequences may be positive or negative.

3/**Self-Control Techniques:**
Planning for change

Now that you are somewhat familiar with the nature of behavior and principles of behavior modification, you are ready for exposure to some of the techniques and procedures by which you can learn to modify your own behavior. The primary purpose of this book is to help you, the reader, learn the secret of and develop skills in self-control.

Although the desire to change our behavior is a prerequisite to self-control, *desire* in and of itself is not enough, as Benjamin Franklin long ago discovered. In setting out on a "bold and arduous project of arriving at moral perfection" Franklin made these observations:

> As I knew, or thought I knew, what was right and wrong, I did not see why I might not *always* do the one and avoid the other. But I soon found I had undertaken a task of more difficulty than I had imagined. While my attention was taken up in guarding against one fault, I was often surprised by another. Habit took the advantage of inattention. Inclination was sometimes too strong for reason. I concluded, at length, that the mere speculative conviction that it was our interest to be completely virtuous, was not sufficient to prevent our slipping; and that contrary habits must be broken and good ones acquired and established, before we can have any dependence on a steady uniform rectitude of conduct.

Franklin made a list of thirteen virtues (temperance, silence, order, frugality, industry, sincerity, and so on) which he regarded as desirable, and developed a plan for shaping his behavior in the direction of these virtues.

I made a little book in which I allotted a page for each of the virtues. I ruled each page with red ink, so as to have seven columns, one for each day of the week, marking each column with a letter for the day. I cross'd these columns with thirteen red lines, marking the beginning of each line with the first letter of one of the virtues, on which line, and in its proper column, I might mark by a little black spot every fault I found upon examination to have been committed respecting that virtue upon that day.

Form of Franklin's Page

TEMPERANCE							
Eat Not to Dullness Drink Not to Elevation							
	Sun	Mon	Tue	Wed	Thu	Fri	Sat
Temperance	*						
Silence	**	*		*		*	
Order	**	*	*		*		*
Resolution			*			*	
Frugality		*					
Industry			*		*		
Sincerity							
Justice							
Moderation							
Cleanliness							
Tranquility							
Chastity							
Humility							

I enter'd upon the execution of this plan for self-examination, and continu'd it with occassional intermissions for some time. I was surpris'd to find myself so much fuller of

faults than I had imagined, but I had the satisfaction of seeing them diminish. To avoid the trouble of renewing now
and then my little book, which, by scraping out the marks
on the paper of old faults to make room for new ones in a
new course, became full of holes, I transferr'd my tables
and precepts to the ivory leaves of a memorandum book, on
which the lines were drawn with red ink that made a dur-
able stain, and on those lines I mark'd my faults with a
black lead pencil, which marks I could easily wipe out with a
wet sponge. After a while I went thro' only one course in a
year, and afterward only one in several years, till at length I
omitted them entirely, being employ'd in voyages and business abroad with a multiplicity of affairs, that interfered,
but I always carried my little book with me.

My scheme of *Order,* gave me the most trouble, and I found,
that tho' it might be practicable where a man's business was
such as to leave him the disposition of his time, that of a
journeyman printer, for instance, it was not possible to be
exactly observ'd by a master, who must mix with the world,
and often receive people of business at their own hours.
Order too, with regard to places for things, papers, I found
extremely difficult to acquire. I had not been early accustomed to *Method,* and having an exceeding good memory, I
was not so sensible of the inconvenience attending want of
method. This article therefore cost me so much painful attention, and my faults in it vexed me so much, and I made
so little progress in amendment, and had such frequent re-
lapses, that I was almost ready to give up the last attempt,
and content myself with a faulty character in that respect,
like the man who, in buying an ax of a smith, my neighbor,
desired to have the whole of its surface as bright as the
edge. The smith consented to grind it bright for him if he
would turn the wheel. He turn'd while the smith press'd the
broad face of the ax hard and heavily of the stone, which
made the turning of it very fatiguing. The man came every
now and then from the wheel to see how the work went on;
and at length would take his ax as it was without further
grinding. "No," says the smith, "turn on, turn on; we shall
have it bright by and by; as yet tis only speckled." "Yes,"
says the man; "but—I think I like the speckled axe best."

I determined to give a week's strict attention to each of the
virtues successively. Thus in the first week my great guard
was to avoid even the least offence against *Temperance,*

leaving the other virtues to their ordinary chance, only marking every evening the faults of the day. Thus if in the first week I could keep my first line, marked T, clear of spots, I suppos'd the habit of that virtue so much strengthen's and its opposite weakened, that I might venture extending my attention to include the next, and for the following week keep both lines clear of spots. Proceeding thus to the last, I could go thro' a course complete in thirteen weeks, and four courses in a year. And like him who, having a garden to weed, does not attempt to eradicate all the bad herbs at once, which would exceed his reach and his strength, but works on one of the beds at a time, and having accomplishe'd the first, proceeds to the second; so I should have, (I hoped) the encouraging pleasure of seeing on my pages the progress I made in virtue, by clearing successively my lines of their spots, till in the end, by a number of courses, I should be happy in viewing a clean book after a thirteen weeks' daily examination.

Franklin was aware that the key to self-mastery is not to be found in appeals to such inner resources as willpower, but rather in the knowledge of how to use various stimuli to increase or decrease certain responses. It is the person who learns how to manipulate his own sources of stimuli by arranging his environment (internal as well as external) who achieves self-control. Some of the knowledge necessary for self-mastery is presented in this chapter.

There is a sequence in developing self-control. The person begins by observing some specific behavior, recording and analyzing the frequency and conditions with which it occurs, developing a plan to change specific things, and deciding if the desired change has occurred. The four steps in self-control include:

1. Defining the problem in terms of specific behavior in specific situations.
2. Collecting data on how often the specified behavior occurs, the antecedents that precede it, and the consequences that follow it.
3. Developing a plan for modifying the behavior.
4. Maintaining and adjusting the plan for producing behavioral change.

Defining the Problem Behavior

The very first step in self-modification is the identification of the problem behavior. In some cases this task is very easy. The problem might be that of stopping or reducing the smoking of cigarettes, wanting to lose weight, or trying to save more money. In these cases specific goals can be established. During the first week after the program has been initiated the goal might be to reduce the number of cigarettes per day to no more than a dozen, or to lose two pounds, or to save at least five dollars.

Other problem behaviors such as aggression or shyness are not so easily defined. The statement "I am overly aggressive" tells us nothing about what is meant by "aggressive" nor about the circumstances surrounding aggressive behavior. In this situation one of the best things to do is to identify some specific examples in real life when aggressive behavior has been a problem. Write down these examples including a description of the events that led up to the behavior in question and the consequences. Then look for some common element in these situations. It might be that one recognizes that he or she is too aggressive in trying to impress members of the opposite sex. Or it might be concluded that aggressive behavior is a problem in situations where there is competition between people for the attainment of some goal. If these generalizations can be made it becomes much easier to define specifically what is meant by "being too aggressive." In cases where no common elements among examples of the behavior in question are apparent it is necessary to treat each example as a separate problem.

Determining the Frequency of the Problem Behavior

The second step is that of determining with what frequency and under what circumstances the problem behavior occurs. This involves record-keeping or what is often referred to as the collection of baseline data. The purpose of establishing a baseline showing the frequency of the target

Figure 3.1. Chart for Recording Time of Day Target Behavior Occurs.

Hour	Date AM	PM	Date AM	PM	Date AM	PM	Date AM	PM	Date AM	PM	Date AM	PM	Date AM	PM
12														
1														
2														
3														
4														
5														
6														
7														
8														
9														
10														
11														

behavior is to provide a standard of comparison. It is difficult to determine whether you are smoking less or losing weight unless you know how much you previously smoked or weighed.

There are numerous ways in which the frequency of target behavior can be counted and recorded. One of the most popular self-observing devices is the wrist counter which was developed originally for use by golfers. This counter has been adopted by Lindsley (1968) for use as a counter at home, in school, or at work. Each time the target behavior occurs a button is pressed on the counter and a running total of the responses is available at all times. The counter can be reset at any time it is desired. Other self-observation techniques include various kinds of tally sheets and charts of which the following are representative.

Figure 3.2. Chart for Recording Circumstances in Which Target Behavior Occurs.

Date	Significant antecedents and/or consequences

The frequency of occurrence of the behavior can be recorded on the first form and relevant information surrounding the occurrence of the behavior on the second form. Information recorded on the second form will prove especially helpful when we come to the third step, that of developing a program for changing the target behaviors.

Following is a chart which can be used for recording weight losses or gains.

Figure 3.3.   Chart for Recording Weight on a Weekly Basis.

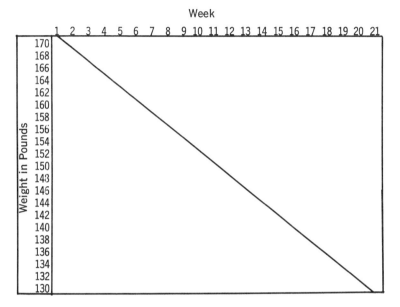

In making a chart for personal use one should start with present weight and proceed downward to the desired weight. Dates are recorded across the top of the chart. The diagonal line should represent the goal. Actual weight is recorded each week, and colored lines can be drawn between the various points on the chart—reflecting progress toward the goal. Daily records of weight can be recorded if preferred. If the weight for a given period of time is above the diagonal line this means that the goal is not being achieved; if the recorded weight falls below the diagonal line more progress than expected has been realized. It is a good idea to use a red pencil when graphing the weight line above the diagonal and green for connecting the lines below the diagonal. Following is a hypothetical chart after completion.

Figure 3.4. Chart for Recording Weight on a Weekly Basis.

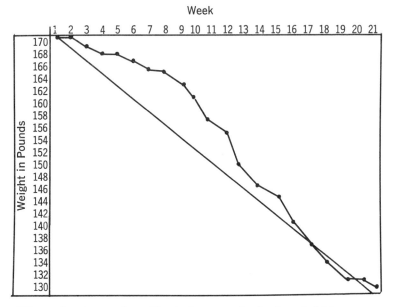

These charts can be adjusted to any desired weight loss over any time period.

The target behavior must be recorded on the spot when it occurs. It can later be calculated or transferred to stationary charts and graphs. A major argument in favor of the wrist counter is its convenience for recording purposes. Watson and Tharp (1972) report a case in which a girl who wanted to increase the number of times she performed a particular behavior carried toothpicks in her purse and moved one into a special pocket of the purse after each occurrence. A boy carried pennies in his left pocket and moved one of the pennies to the right pocket every time he engaged in his undesirable behavior. A cigarette smoker could begin the day with a given number of cigarettes and determine the number smoked per day by counting how many he had left at the end of the day.

One cannot be too strict in counting the target behavior; all occurrences of the behavior should be recorded. Accurate counting and recording actually serves two purposes: (1) it forces us to pay close attention to the target behavior, and (2) it provides an accurate standard of comparison once the intervention program is begun.

From the data recorded in Figure 3.1 a graph can be drawn. Usually time is recorded on the horizontal axis and behavior frequencies on the vertical axis. To record daily cigarette smoking, the graph might look like this.

Figure 3.5.   Baseline for Average Daily Cigarette Consumption.

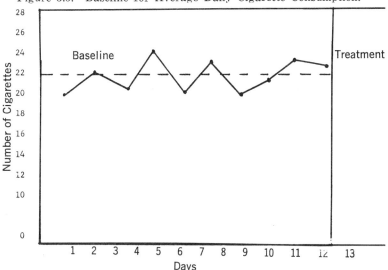

The recording period lasted for ten days during which time a range of from nineteen to twenty-four cigarettes were smoked each day with the average being approximately twenty-two. The intervention program could be begun on the eleventh day from which time record-keeping is continued in the same manner.

How long should the data be gathered before the intervention program is begun? Of course there is no absolute answer, but the minimum for behavior that occurs daily should be one week. Sometimes a week is not enough, especially when there is a large daily variation in the frequency of the target behavior. Figure 3.6 is a hypothetical graph showing wide variations in the amount of time spent in study each day ranging from four hours on Wednesday to no study at all on Sunday.

Figure 3.6.   Daily Hours of Study.

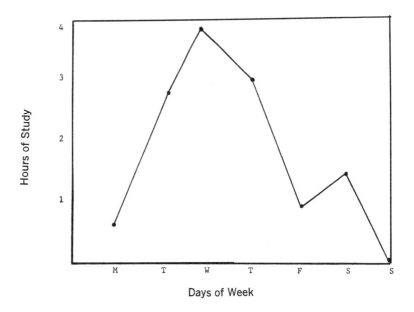

Days of Week

For behavior with this striking variation of frequency, the period of recording should extend for at least two weeks. A good rule to follow would be to continue to record until you understand the patterns of your behavior frequencies. If after two or three weeks of collecting data there are still wide variations in daily frequency of the behavior, an average may be figured. You should also make an effort to record behavior frequencies during a normal period rather than during some atypical time such as during final exams.

Built into the intervention program should be some kind of reinforcement for accurate record-keeping. One simple way of doing this is to require yourself to record the target behavior before permitting yourself to engage in it. If you are trying to lose weight you might permit yourself to eat food only after you have recorded the amount of the food to be consumed and also relevant circumstances such as time, place, and so on. Another possibility is that you permit yourself an extra dollar of spending money for every day of accurate record-keeping. In establishing these kinds of contingencies you are limited only by your imagination or ingenuity.

In commenting on the necessity of accurate record-keeping Watson and Tharp (1972) phrase the need this way:

> Self-modification of behavior is itself a behavior and follows the same rules. It can be influenced in its frequency by its consequences. You want to be positively reinforced for each attempt at self-modification, for that will increase the chances that you will attempt self-modification again when it would be desirable. The best way to ensure success is to have every aspect of the system working well. If you are failing to produce the necessary behavior at any state—if you are not gathering the baseline, if you are not reinforcing yourself—*you should view your failure as a result of the nonperformance of a necessary behavior and work out a system to increase that particular behavior by positively reinforcing it.*

Developing an Intervention Plan

Once the frequency of the target behavior is established the intervention program can be initiated. This program is likely to incorporate the learning principles with which you are now familiar. Some combination of two basic strategies, stimulus control and behavior programming, are likely to be employed. Stimulus control involves the association of undesired behavior with stimuli that are gradually reduced in frequency, and desired behavior with stimuli whose frequency are systematically increased. Behavior programming is a technique of behavior control based on altering the consequences of behavior rather than manipulating stimuli that precede it.

The use of stimulus control as a method of self-regulation was first suggested by Ferster, Nurnberger, and Levitt (1962), who described its feasibility in the management of weight control. They pointed out that eating behavior is frequently associated with many environmental cues such as watching television, studying, the sight of an "easy" chair, a restaurant, or vending machine which may gain control over eating behaviors. These researchers recommended that weight watchers restrict their eating to a relatively few situations, thereby decreasing the number of environmental cues, like those listed above that are associated in some minds with eating. They also stressed the importance of developing behaviors incompatible with eating such as pauses between bites, drinking water before and during meals, doing exercises, etc.

Several investigators including Stuart (1967), Harris (1969), and Stuart (1971) have successfully applied stimulus-control techniques, sometimes in conjunction with other techniques, to the problem of obesity. These studies will be discussed in more detail in the chapter devoted specifically to weight control.

Stimulus-Control Techniques

Fox (1962) described a plan for the improvement of study skills through the implementation of stimulus control. The underlying strategy was to establish a situation conducive to studying and to establish associations between specific cues and study behavior. For example, a student might limit his study to a specific chair in a particular room. Studying—and only studying—should take place in that room; when the student finds himself engaging in any behaviors incompatible with study (daydreaming, drowsiness), he should immediately leave the room. This action would prevent undesired associations between inappropriate behaviors and the study environment. Fox also recommends the use of small, but gradually increasing study assignments (shaping), reinforcement for study behavior, and the SQ4R technique, a structural procedure for study consisting of six ordered steps: (1) Survey; (2) Question; (3) Read; (4) Recite; (5) Rite; (6) Review.

Stimulus control has been successfully applied to smoking behavior. Nolan (1968) restricted the smoking behavior of his patient to a "smoking chair" which was placed in some out-of-the-way and nonentertaining location such as the garage. Before smoking, this person was to go to the garage, sit in the "smoking chair," smoke the cigarette alone, and return to the house. Other researchers (Levinson, Shapiro, Schwartz, and Tursky, 1971; Shapiro, Tursky, Schwartz, and Shnidman, 1971) were able to reduce smoking behavior by having smokers carry small portable parking-meter timers and to permit themselves to enjoy a cigarette only when given an audible cue from their timer. Each timer was initially set to go off at intervals closely approximating the smoker's normal period between cigarettes. This procedure was helpful in breaking the associations between smoking and the usual cues such as the end of a meal or a cup of coffee and also establishing new stimuli (under the smoker's control) that became the only cues for smoking. Smokers were requested to gradually increase the timer intervals so that the time between cigarettes was increased and the frequency of smoking behavior was reduced.

Another form of stimulus control, commonly called contingency contracting, involves an agreement with respect to the requirement for reward or punishment. Boudin (1972), through the use of legally binding contracts, was reportedly successful in the treatment of excessive amphetamine use. One black female client agreed to donate $50 to the Ku Klux Klan for every violation (use of amphetamines) of her contract and found this contingency invaluable in the elimination of her drug problem. Contracts were used by Mann (1971) in the treatment of obesity. Overweight participants deposited valuables with an experimenter, who either returned or kept them, depending on the progress of the subject.

Behavioral Programming

Behavioral programming involves the modification of behavior through self-determined consequences which follow rather than precede the behavior to be controlled. This procedure usually involves one or more of the following: (1) self-reinforcement following desired behavior, (2) the removal of reinforcers following undesirable behavior, (3) self-punishment following undesired behavior. The literature on this subject abounds with studies supporting the effectiveness of these techniques. Summaries of illustrative investigations are presented below.

Rehm and Marston (1968) used a combination of self-desensitization and self-reinforcement in treating male college students who experienced anxiety in heterosexual relations. The boys were asked to construct hierarchies of hypothetical situations involving various degrees of interaction with girls. Items in the hierarchy were arranged so that each aroused greater anxiety than the preceding one. The boys were then asked to designate a point on the hierarchy at which they felt their anxiety would become so serious as to cause them to avoid these situations. The hierarchy for one boy began with the following items in the order presented here: (1) taking a seat next to a girl in a class, (2) being introduced to a girl while with a group of friends, (3) calling a girl to ask her for a date, and (4) dancing with a girl on a date. The progression went on until it reached the most intensive sexual item—kissing.

The participants in the study were instructed to imagine each of the situations until they felt no anxiety and to record their progress. They were also told to reward themselves with points (0 for avoidance, 1 for minimum performance, 2 for moderate performance, and 3 for maximum performance), and to engage in self-praise upon the achievement of a goal, i.e., having performed a given act in the hierarchy. At weekly meetings individual progress of participants was discussed and verbal praise was given by the experimenter for success in anxiety reduction. These boys showed greater improvement in their own reports of both anxiety levels and actual overt behavior than did control groups; their performance in a standardized test situation was also superior to the other groups. These improvements still persisted at a follow-up seven to nine months after the termination of the study.

Jackson and VanZoost (1972) demonstrated the effectiveness of self-reinforcement in the improvement of the study habits of college students. Students registered for the program by depositing $10 and signing a contract stating that the money would be regained by attendance at six weekly one-hour meetings and completion of assigned exercises. During these weekly sessions they received some instruction on the improvement of study skills. These students were assigned to one of three experimental conditions: (1) no reinforcement (deposit was earned by regular attendance and completion of questions at the end of study); (2) external reinforcement (money was given by group leader for the completion of exercises, the quality of work and amount of money being determined by the leader); and (3) self-administered reinforcement (participants evaluated their performance following feedback from leader and determined their own earnings within prescribed limits). Both reinforcement groups showed significant gains in study habits that were maintained over a four-month follow-up period while the no-reinforcement group showed no such improvement.

Mahoney, Maura, and Wade (1973) investigated the effects of self-reward, self-punishment, and self-monitoring (merely observing behavior and collecting data) on weight reduction. Several groups received instruction in the use of stimulus-control procedures. Subjects in the self-reinforcement group gave themselves money for the purchase of desired items and entertainment for weight loss while those in self-punishment group imposed fines (loss of money) on themselves for lack of weight-loss progress. The self-reward procedures were found to be more effective than self-monitoring, self-punishment, or stimulus-control procedures with self-reinforcement.

In a later study Mahoney (1974) randomly assigned obese individuals to one of four groups, three experimental and one control. Subjects in the experimental groups kept records of their eating habits and body weight throughout the treatment period. Following a two-week baseline period, experimental subjects practiced different forms of self-control for a period of six weeks. One group (self-monitoring) set weekly goals for weight loss and improvement of eating habits. In addition to self-monitoring and goal-setting, a second group (self-reward-weight) awarded themselves money or gift certificates whenever they a-chieved a predetermined weight loss, while a third group (self-reward-habit) made their awards of money or gift certificates contingent on the improvement of eating habits rather than weight reduction. A fourth group (control) received no treatment for the six-week period but, after the study was completed, they also pursued a self-control program in which self-reward was made contingent on both habit improvement and weight reduction. On a follow-up assessment four months later, self-reward was found to be more effective than self-monitoring. The self-administered reinforcers were also found to be more effective in producing weight reduction when the rewards were made contingent on the improvement of eating habits than when made contingent on weight reduction. The control group also experienced success once the self-reward contingencies were begun.

The previous studies have demonstrated the efficiency of self-reinforcement in the development of behavioral self-control. Attempts at negative self-reward are less numerous, but there is some indication that, at least in some cases, this method can produce desirable outcomes. Penick, Filion, Fox, and Stunkard (1971) had obese participants store pieces of pork fat in a prominent place in their refrigerators and remove pieces of it in relation to the amount of weight loss. These bags of fat represented each person's excess flesh. It is reported that participants readily accepted the idea, and those who used it in conjunction with stimulus-control techniques were very successful.

Some studies (McGuire and Vallance, 1964; Mees, 1966) have investigated the effects of *negative punishment,* usually a self-administered shock. This technique has been used with problems such as stuttering but its value is presently undetermined and, for this reason, none of that research will be reviewed.

Self-Contracting

A control feature of any self-change program that distinguishes it from common-sense attempts such as the New Year's resolution lies in systematic planning, i.e., a detailed specification of its implementation and evaluation. One method of behavioral programming is through the use of contracts. Contracts are agreements between two or more parties which specify the responsibilities of all parties concerned when the agreed-upon action *is* or *is not* carried out. A self-contract is one in which the person involved agrees to make predetermined consequences contingent upon the occurrence or nonoccurrence of the behavior in question. The self-contract is a form of stimulus control since it involves the setting of stimulus cues and consequences to modify a behavior.

According to Mahoney and Thorenson (1974) a self-contract should indicate clearly what action the person will take relative to the target behavior. Since a decision reflected in a self-contract is subject to change, it should specify a review date when one may reconsider the behaviors to be performed and the consequences provided. Either or both may need to be altered. In any contract the reward should immediately follow the desired behavior. The reward should be individually tailored to the person's situation and should be provided in small amounts on a frequent basis.

Coverant-Control Procedures

Our thoughts exert a certain amount of control over behavior. Homme (1965) argues that thoughts, or coverants as they are called in this case, may be thought of as internal behavior subject to the same principles of learning applicable to overt behavior. He has described the use of coverant control of smoking behavior. The smoker makes a list of thoughts relating to smoking which he or she personally finds aversive and which might include consequences such as lung cancer, coronary disease, bad breath, discolored teeth, and shortness of breath. When he next feels the urge to light a cigarette he engages in a coverant such as "Smoking may cause me to die of lung cancer" or "Smoking makes it hard to breathe." Reinforcers such as

Figure 3.7. Sample Self-Contract

Self-Contract

Date: _____
Name: _____

Goal: **To reduce food intake**

Agreement

I agree to eat only three meals per day (no snacks) and to eat only in the dining room. I further agree to eat no [list forbidden foods here] and to consume no more than 2,000 calories per day.

Consequences

For each week (ending at 6:00 P.M. on Saturday) I stick to this agreement I will reward myself with a movie [or reasonable activity or gift, except food].

If contract is broken: For each week that I fail to keep this agreement I will see no movie. In addition I will [do my laundry on Saturday evening, make myself forego a date, fine myself $10, or something considered appropriate for failure to live up to the agreement].

Signed: _____
Witness: _____

_____
Review Date

favorite activities should be made contingent upon the successful use of the coverants. The thought "I'll die of lung cancer if I smoke" might be followed by a cup of coffee, a rest, a pause, a kiss from wife or girl friend, or even another thought of the positive effect of not smoking such as "My food will taste so much better now" or "How fresh and cool it feels when I inhale."

One of the first applications of a technique which Cautela (1966) later called covert sensitization was by Miller (1959), who hypnotized an alcoholic patient and asked him to vividly re-experience his worst hangover, including the nausea, vomiting, and pain that accompanied it. The patient was conditioned to associate the smell and taste of alcoholic beverages with these aversive consequences and was reported to have shown considerable improvement.

Finding Effective Reinforcers

Anyone attempting to develop self-control through contingency management can construct his own list of reinforcers. This list could include activities such as going shopping, attending a party, free time, making love, smoking a cigar, engaging in sports, reading a book or magazine, going for a drive, taking a bath, or relaxing on the couch or in a favorite chair. Although this list could be continued indefinitely its length is not of crucial importance. Of much greater significance is whether the activities listed are really reinforcing to the person involved. If so, they can serve as powerful reinforcers. Remember that what others find reinforcing may not be for you; determining reinforcers is an individual matter. Watson and Tharp (1972) suggest three things to consider in choosing reinforcers: (1) the consequence has to be a reinforcer for you. You need to select consequences that are tailored to your particular situation and needs. (2) The consequences you select must be available and accessible to you. They must be under your control. (3) They should be relatively strong reinforcers. The more powerful the reinforcer the more likely it is to be effective in helping you change your behavior. Watson and Tharp recommend that in evaluating the strength of a potential reinforcer we ask ourselves this question: "Do I really think that I will stop performing the undesirable behavior—or start performing the desirable behavior—just because I will gain X (the reinforcer)?"

Developing a Program for Self-Control

Once the target behavior has been clearly identified and sufficient data indicating the frequency and duration of the behavior and the conditions under which it occurs have been gathered, you are now ready to develop a specific program for producing behavior change. Here are some guidelines for program development.

1. Identify specific cues which seem to trigger the behavior. Make a list of the situations in which this behavior occurs.
2. Identify the consequences that seem to maintain the behavior. What does this problem (target) behavior seem to produce or remove? Make a list of the consequences which seem to maintain the behavior.
3. Reduce the number of cues (situations) associated with the undesirable behavior. Make an attempt to avoid these situations or engage in an incompatible behavior when these cues are present. If you are tempted to eat while talking to friends reduce the time you spend with the friends, do something incompatible with eating (jogging, tennis, etc.) while in their presence.
4. Determine what kind of behavior is to replace the undesirable behavior.
5. Make the consequences that formerly reinforced the undesirable behavior contingent upon desirable behavior and make sure that these consequences no longer follow the undesirable behavior.

Maintaining the Program

The development of a self-control program may be insufficient for producing long-term results. Many people, for example, go on a weight-control program, lose the desired amount, forget the program, and return to their former weight. Some people lose hundreds of pounds in these cycles over a period of years. For lasting results the program must be maintained indefinitely. Of course, it can be modified to suit one's goals; it should be altered so that the goal is shifted from further weight reduction to the prevention of any weight increase. Once you have developed a program and found it to be effective you should have little difficulty modifying it for long-term effects. You use the same guidelines suggested previously for program development.

Summary

With this background we will now turn our attention to specific kinds of troublesome behaviors. Each of the following chapters will be devoted to a particular kind of problem and a plan will be presented which should be effective in helping you cope with that particular behavior. Should you try one of these programs, feel free to tailor it to your individual needs and desires. You may not choose the entire list of recommendations. Some may be much more practical and effective in your particular case than others. You may also want to try only a few steps at a time and gradually build up to a complete program. The primary concern is that you get results. Do not scrap the plans if you fail to reach your goal; it may be necessary to revise the program several times before the most effective procedure is found. Anytime the program needs to be altered just follow the steps with which you are now familiar.

1. State the specific problem.
2. Collect data.

3. Identify antecedent conditions or events.
4. Identify consequences that maintain the behavior.
5. Reduce antecedents and/or develop incompatible behavior in their presence.
6. Make positive consequences contingent upon desirable rather than the undesirable behavior.

Part 2
Application of Self-Management Techniques to Specific Problem Areas

4/Overeating and Obesity:
I feel like a cow in a herd of antelopes

Most Americans eat too much. Anyone can substantiate the fact by sitting for a few minutes on a park bench or in a modern shopping mall and observing the frequency with which broad butts and bloated bellies go waddling by. We as people have become accustomed to consuming too much of many commodities including food, which, like other current sources of energy, may become increasingly scarce in the future. In the long run there is little doubt that we will be forced to learn to consume less.

There are also many immediate reasons for a reduction of food intake and these are of a physiological and social nature. That obesity is associated with such infirmities as hypertension, cardiac disorders, and reduced physical endurance is an accepted fact. Ball (1974) lists some of the hazards of obesity from a medical standpoint. They include: (1) increased incidence of heart disease (severely obese persons of a given age can anticipate a 30 percent greater risk of dying than those of an ideal weight; (2) increased incidence of hypertension (when obese people lose weight, blood pressure is lowered and mortality rate is decreased); (3) increased incidence of complications following surgery (postoperative mortality following surgery, for example, is about 2.5 times greater for the obese than for the non-obese); (4) increased incidence of pulmonary difficulties; (5) increased incidence of insulin antagonism in diabetes; (6) increased incidence of irregular menstrual cycles in women (obese women also frequently have difficulty becoming pregnant); and (7) increased incidence of toxemia (obese women have an increased risk of hypertension, toxemia, and large babies; they should lose weight before becoming pregnant).

We live in a society that places great value on a youthful appearance which includes plenty of hair and a slender profile. One's physique can determine the ease and degree to which he or she is able to establish and maintain social relationships and to gain social acceptance. The person who is able to accept his or her physique and be proud of it probably has more confidence and a better state of mental health than one who cannot. These are some of the powerful motives for weight reduction.

Why do some people eat too much? We do so as a result of habit. Certain cues such as the sight or smell of food, contractions of the stomach, or a given time or place during the day become associated with eating behavior. Instead of learning to be hungry when one needs nourishment, many people learn to be hungry at eating time or at the sight or thought of food. This seems to be especially true for obese people. Schachter, as a result of his 1971 research, has concluded that eating by the obese is unrelated to any internal visceral state but is determined by external food-related cues such as the sight, smell, and taste of food. For people with normal weight Schachter found that external cues did clearly interact with the internal or visceral state. He has made an attempt to identify some of the cues that trigger the eating response in obese people. He cites a study by Nisbett (1968) in which the effects of the sight of food on eating behavior were examined. Before implementing his research, Nisbett reasoned that if the sight of food is a potent cue, the obese person, having greater sensitivity to food than the nonobese, should eat as long as food is in sight, but when he has consumed all available food he should make no further attempt to eat. In contrast, he hypothesized that the amount eaten by normal subjects should have greater dependence on physiological needs than on the quantity of food in sight.

To test this hypotheses, Nisbett made available to subjects who had skipped a meal either one or three roast beef sandwiches. Subjects were instructed to help themselves and as Nisbett was leaving the room he pointed to a refrigerator and said, "There are dozens more sandwiches in the refrigerator. Have as many as you want." Obese subjects ate significantly more than normals when presented with three sandwiches, but ate less when presented with only one sandwich. Apparently the sight of food is an important cue to the obese person.

Decke (1971) examined the effects of taste, another external cue, on eating. If the effects of taste of food are the same as those of sight, then good taste should stimulate the obese to eat more than normals and bad taste should have the reverse effect. Normal and obese subjects were given either a regular vanilla milk shake or a vanilla shake plus quinine.

Obese subjects consumed more of good-tasting food but less of the bad-tasting food than did those of normal weight. Taste is another external food-related cue to which the obese person is very sensitive.

Schachter (1971) with the help of an assistant designed a study to examine the effects on eating behavior of effort required to get food. Subjects were to sit at a desk and fill out a number of personality tests and questionnaires. In addition to the usual clutter on the desk there was also a bag of almonds. The experimenter ate a nut and invited the subject to do the same and then left the room leaving the subject alone with the questionnaires for fifteen minutes. In one condition the nuts had shells on them and in the other condition the nuts were without shells. Results are shown in Table 4.1.

Whether or not the nuts had shells had little effect on normal subjects, but a very pronounced effect on fat subjects. Nineteen of twenty fat subjects ate nuts that were

Table 4.1. Effect of Effort in Procuring on the Eating Behavior
of Normal and Fat Subjects[1]

Nuts have	Number who	
	Eat	Don't Eat
Normal Subjects		
Shells	10	10
No shells	11	9
Fat Subjects		
Shells	1	19
No shells	19	1

shelled but only one of twenty fat subjects ate nuts that had
to be shelled. Effort does seem to be a relevant cue to the
obese person. When food is easy to get, more is eaten than
normal; when food is hard to get at, significantly less is
eaten.

These findings indicate that the obese person seems to be
stimulus-bound, being under external rather than internal
control. In other words, physiological state has little relationship to the amount of food consumed. External situational factors are more important. When a food-relevant cue
is present, the obese are more likely to eat and to eat a great
deal more than do normals. When such a cue is absent, the
obese are less likely to eat or to complain about hunger.
Keeping this information in mind, let us now turn to the
problem of establishing a baseline of eating behavior.

Establishing a Baseline

Before attempting to revise or modify eating habits, it is
imperative that we know when food is being consumed, how
much is consumed, and under what conditions it is being
consumed. This recording period should be at least two

---

1. Schachter, S. Some extraordinary facts about humans and rats.
American Psychologist, 1971 *26*: 129-144. Copyright © 1971 by the
American Psychological Association. Reprinted by permission.

weeks in duration. Accurate recording of the quantity and circumstances of eating behavior is extremely important, for only through accurate recording can you hope to establish the relationship between your behavior and your weight. You should not take this point lightly. If you fail to record everything you eat, you might mistakenly convince yourself that your weight problem is not due to your behavior.

Precisely what is it that you are to record? Several records may be helpful in controlling eating behavior. They may include (1) a record of everything you eat, (2) a record of conditions of your eating (time, place, mood, mode of food preparation, and so on), and (3) a record of your weight. You may also find it helpful to keep records of caloric intake. Recording the conditions of your eating behavior should provide important clues as to how to change that behavior. A chart similar to Figure 4.1 can be used for recording all the information in one place. By placing your graph in a conspicuous spot (on the kitchen cabinet or refrigerator door, for example), you will find that it serves not only to reinforce appropriate behavior but also to remind you of when, what, and how much to eat.

After a period of two weeks data can be analyzed to see how much is being eaten, the time of day this is likely to occur, and the conditions which accompany eating behavior. As you learned in the previous chapter the data should be carefully studied in an attempt to identify the situation which seems to elicit eating behavior and the consequences which seem to reinforce eating behavior. You may discover that you have a tendency to snack while reading, watching TV, talking with friends, studying, or when near a vending machine. A list of the situations associated with eating should be made. Consequences that encourage eating include not only the obvious—the taste of the food—but also the mere activity of putting food in the mouth, chewing and swallowing, the reduction of hunger. Other reinforcers might include a pleasant atmosphere such as friendship, entertainment, relaxation, or conversation. The process of recording the amount of food consumed can be a traumatic

Figure 4.1. Baseline Eating Monitoring Form.

Food Eaten		Time	Social		Where Eaten	Mood When Eaten
Quantity	Type of Food	Give time if food was part of meal	Alone?	With Whom?	Home, Work, Restaurant Recreation	A—Anxious B—Bored C—Tired D—Depressed E—Angry

Reprinted with permission from Richard B. Stuart and Barbara Davis, **Slim Chance in a Fat World: Behavior Control of Obesity.** Champaign, Ill.: Research Press. 1972.

experience. We are frequently astounded at how often we eat and the number of calories we consume. For some, record-keeping is a difficult process; it is easier to deny that a problem exists. When this happens you need to develop a program that will strengthen record-keeeping behavior.

In addition to keeping records of food consumption, a weight baseline must be established. Because weight fluctuates during the day it should be checked at the same time each day. A weight chart is very easy to maintain. Time or dates are recorded on the horizontal axis and weight on the vertical axis. Weight range on the vertical axis can start at slightly above current weight and go down to the desired weight level. Dates can extend indefinitely. A diagonal line across your chart can be used to indicate the amount of average weight loss required to reach a given weight level in a specified period of time.

From the figure you can see that the weight during the ten-day period ranged from 168 to 170 pounds. During intervention period do not expect immediate weight reduction. As previously indicated one or two pounds per week would be reasonable. If you find it frustrating to weigh yourself so often with so little reduction, you might try weighing only once a week at the same time. With this procedure you should experience a weight loss at each weigh-in. The primary disadvantage of weighing only once a week is that it is not possible to detect trends in weight during the week. By weighing each day an acquaintance of mine soon discovered that his weight was constant during the week but increased by about two pounds each weekend. He concentrated on reducing food intake on weekends, the time in which he had previously consumed large quantities.

Intervention Program

As you know by now behavior can be controlled either by changing the antecedent conditions or the consequences or both. You are also aware of the fact that immediate consequences are more effective than are delayed consequences.

Figure 4.2.   Chart for Recording Weight on a Weekly Basis

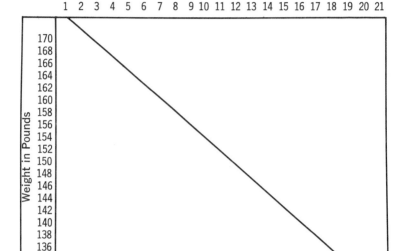

This last principle is extremely important in the control of obesity. The positive effects of eating (good taste, and so on) are experienced immediately while the positive effects of not eating (weight reduction and praise from friends) come only after days or weeks of sustained effort. Another complicating factor is the fact that eating is not all-or-none as is the case with smoking or nail biting for example. We can completely stop smoking but no one can stop eating. It is a matter of how much we can reduce the eating habit by being reinforced for not eating and maintaining good health. This balance will require sustained effort at behavioral self-control.

The most immediate goal of weight reduction is a reasonable weekly weight loss, probably between one and two pounds per week. An attempt to lose at a more rapid rate than this has a greater probability of failure for two reasons: (1) it is much more unpleasant and (2) one is less likely to reach the goal. Either of these reasons is likely to decrease the duration of the program and cause the participant to surrender in self-defeat. For these reasons any goal must be modest enough to make it likely that one can meet it. Having achieved a goal is a powerful source of reinforcement.

The next goal is that of determining the total weight to be lost. The advice of a physician could be helpful in determining this goal. Not only should a physician indicate how much weight can be safely lost but he should also be consulted about a diet which you should use in conjunction with the intervention program.

The minimal requirement of a weight-reduction routine is that it enable a person to lose weight and keep it off for a long period of time without causing serious disruption in daily life or health. The ultimate goal of the routine would be the production of permanent weight loss with minimal expense of time or money and with the new eating pattern becoming both habitual and satisfying so that the individual is not constantly troubled by desires to eat.

A basic step of any intervention program is to create an *awareness* of what one is eating, especially the caloric content and food value. Without this awareness it is virtually impossible to reduce the quantity of food consumed. Charts used in the establishment of a baseline should facilitate this kind of awareness.

Specific Recommendations for Control of Eating Behavior

Following is a list of suggestions based upon data presented earlier in this chapter and on learning principles which should aid in self-control of eating. It is recommended that persons following these suggestions use only those that they feel will be best suited to their individual situation, making only small changes which they are sure they can maintain, and which are in the direction of the permanent eating pattern they desire to establish.

Remember that research has indicated that obese people are particularly sensitive to food-relevant cues such as the sight, taste, or smell of food; food for which little effort is required to get, and perhaps to other cues such as a particular location, friend, or television program associated with eating. With this in mind the following guidelines are recommended.

Stimulus-Control Techniques

1. *Remove easily available or readily prepared foods from the house.* Foods such as cookies, cakes, pies, potato chips, candy, and so on, should be removed from the house thereby reducing the sometimes otherwise uncontrollable urge to eat. Many other foods requiring no preparation such as bread, cheese, and instant cereals should be eliminated. Even leftover items should be frozen so that much effort is required before this food is edible. The more difficult and the greater the effort required to prepare the food, the less likely one is to be an impulsive eater. When preparing a food that needs to be cooked, prepare enough for only one serving. Clear leftover food directly into the garbage so that it will not serve to trigger more eating behavior. Any reasonable measure to make the accessibility of food more difficult should be considered.

2. *Establish a specific location where eating is to take place.* The enjoyment that an individual thinks he gets out of eating is often supplied by satisfaction other than food: good company, a television program, a book, music, or even pleasant memories and associations that have developed over the years. A major goal is to separate the food satisfactions themselves from satisfactions derived from other activities, i.e., to make eating as pure an experience as you can. Once you have identified the situations that encourage eating, make sure that you do not eat in those situations. Food should be allowed in no room except the kitchen or dining room and you should permit yourself to engage in no other activity while eating.

Obviously you are not always going to isolate yourself in

a corner, eating by yourself in total silence, although there may be times when extreme measures are necessary. But, while eating, you can turn off the radio or television set, put the book aside, and eat only in a specific chair at the dining table. You can also discuss your goals with those you are eating with. The more support you have from others in changing your behaviors, the easier it will be to meet your goal. The best way to make eating as pure an experience as possible is to eat slowly and think about your new goals. In fact, a discussion centering on your behavior modification program with those persons you normally share meals with might be the perfect way to kick off your campaign. The idea behind eating in a specific location is to establish strong eating patterns, i.e., if you're sitting in a certain spot, you think of eating; if you're not, you don't think about eating.

3. *When you have finished eating, leave the table, even if others are still eating.* Many people, having finished their own meal, continue to nibble away at food while waiting for others to finish. So if you can't resist temptation after you've finished, excuse yourself and leave the table.

4. *Serve your meals on a salad plate rather than a larger one.* This makes a smaller amount of food seem larger.

5. *Always leave some food on your plate every time you eat, even if you don't feel quite full.* Most of us have been taught to clean up our plates and, in an attempt to do the "proper" thing, eat too much. You can start by leaving only a small amount of food on the plate and gradually progress to larger amounts, or, serve yourself smaller portions.

6. *Make eating a slower more deliberate process.* Think about the fact that you're eating. Have soup with a teaspoon rather than a soup spoon and make sure it is served piping hot so it takes longer to consume it. Use your eating utensils for everything including sandwiches. It's much more difficult and time-consuming to cut a sandwich rather than just pick it up and devour it. Try the "one-bite-at-a-time" method. Pick up your knife and fork. Cut one piece of meat. Put it in your mouth. Place the knife and fork down. Begin chew-

ing. Don't touch your utensils until you've finished that bite. Repeat this procedure.

You might also have several pauses of three to five minutes during a meal. This helps you learn to be in the presence of food without constantly eating it. Make a conscious effort to increase the amount of time you use for eating. This allows your system to begin digesting your food while you are still eating, helping you become satiated, or full, with less food. Satiation can also be increased by drinking water with your meals and by beginning your meals with bulky items like lettuce, celery, and other raw vegetables which go a long way toward curbing your appetite without making you eat more than you actually need or want.

7. *Do grocery shopping only from a list made out in advance and eat only foods prepared from this list.* Go shopping after a meal rather than before eating. These precautions reduce the temptation for impulsive eating and purchasing behavior.

8. *You might want to establish an additional contingency by depositing some money or other valued possession with a friend or family member with an understanding that each time a weight reduction goal is reached a certain portion of the money or merchandise can be re-earned.* In other words, the other person becomes a caretaker and refunds the money according to progress. If no progress is achieved the money is forfeited. Another possibility is that of establishing a contingency whereby you have to give up something of value each time you do not reach a goal. For instance, you might decide to donate a certain amount of money to some organization or group for which you have contempt each time you fail to reach a goal.

Controlling Response Consequences

1. *Keep stimuli that inhibit eating such as food and weight charts in full view while eating.* You might want to eat before a mirror. This increases awareness of the amount of food being consumed. If success is being realized the reduction in calories and pounds indicated by your records

will be immediate reinforcement for eating less rather than eating more. If you are too embarrassed to gorge yourself with food when other people are around, force yourself to eat in their presence. Hang photographs taken or garments of clothing worn before the weight reduction program was undertaken on walls or in some conspicuous place. These kinds of stimuli should produce unpleasant associations with eating and thereby reduce the eating behavior.

2. *Reward yourself when a subgoal is achieved.* This can be accomplished by permitting yourself to engage in some desirable activity only when a goal has been reached (Premack Principle). For example, if during the week you attained your goal of two pounds weight reduction, go to a movie, ball game, or bowling. Perhaps you can purchase a new article of clothing. This is an excellent reinforcement for weight loss. DO NOT GO TO A RESTAURANT FOR A FEAST! You should never reward success in weight reduction with food.

3. *Enlist members of the family or friends to provide social reinforcement in the nature of praise or compliments for goal attainment.* Social approval is a powerful reinforcer.

4. *Activities formerly associated with eating can be made contingent upon the formation and practice of good eating habits.* Instead of eating while watching TV, reading, or being with friends, you can permit yourself to engage in these activities only when a reasonable amount of the proper foods have been consumed.

5. *Covert sensitization may also be used in combination with the procedures described above.* As you recall, this is a mental process involving the use of imagery in order to associate aversive consequences with the problem behavior. For example, the dieters may, at the sight of food, imagine themselves bulging out of the bathing suits they wish to purchase for the summer. Others may picture themselves in social situations where everyone else is slender and attractive and they are fat and ugly. Homme (1965) reports the case of a nurse imagining a scene she had witnessed in

the operating room in which a very obese person was being operated upon. She imagined herself with the rolls and layers of the ugly fat she saw on the patient. Any imaginary scene can be effective for the dieter so long as it is repulsive enough to help him resist eating more food.

It would be wise to use covert sensitization only with certain designated foods or only after a predetermined amount of food has been consumed. With indiscriminate use of this technique one could develop an aversion to all foods 'and probably create more problems than he solves. This technique could well be used in conjunction with a diet. When you are consuming the proper amount of food on the diet you could imagine your slender physique fitting nicely into that desired bathing suit, admiring glances from sunbathers on the beach, more fun in bed with a sex partner, and so on. At the sight of foods not on the diet or that you should not eat, you should imagine an aversive situation such as those above. One person, who lost over a hundred pounds within a period of a year, imagined that forbidden foods contained quinine or some toxic ingredient such as arsenic which would make him deathly ill or kill him. He developed an aversion to these foods and was able to successfully refrain from consuming them.

The key to the success of covert sensitization is that you discriminate between recommended foods and those not recommended for the dieter. Pleasant images or associations should be paired with recommended foods and aversive thoughts should be paired with the sight and consumption of fattening foods. Keep searching until you find a scene that is aversive to you. What would be nauseating to one person might have little effect on another. If you imagine yourself becoming ill or extremely obese and unsightly when near forbidden food, you should imagine that you are feeling much better and more attractive when you move away from the forbidden food. Be sure to make positive associations with desirable behavior and aversive associations with the undesirable or inappropriate behavior.

Should coverant sensitization fail to be sufficiently aversive to prohibit the intake of certain undesirable foods, create a situation in which aversive consequences actually do occur. This procedure might be called "overt" sensitization. If you find it impossible to curb your desire for a certain off limits delicacy, you might pour castor oil or some other foul-tasting substance over it before eating. Then force yourself to eat a full serving. This action should produce an unpleasant association with that particular food. From that point on at the sight of this food, you need merely to remind yourself, through covert sensitization, of the consequences of eating that item.

A form of noxious stimulation for some nonsmokers is the inhalation of cigarette smoke. Morganstern (1974) used this technique with a patient who was a compulsive eater. In addition to eating three meals a day, this patient reported that she ate candy and "junk" all day long. An analysis of her eating habits revealed an enormous consumption of five principal types of food: candy, cookies, doughnuts, ice cream, and pizza. Baseline data revealed a weekly intake of close to two-hundred pieces of candy and dozens of cookies and doughnuts. In addition, she indulged in pizza and ice cream at least once per day and often as many as three times a day.

When several techniques had been tried without success the patient, called Miss C, reported that a few experiences with smoking had produced extremely unpleasant sensations for her that included nausea and dizziness. It was decided that she should light a cigarette and hold it in her hand as she took a a bite of forbidden food (candy was used first since it showed the highest rate of consumption during the baseline period) and chewed it for a few seconds. Before swallowing the candy she took a long "drag" on the cigarette and immediately spit out the food, exclaiming at the same time, "Eating this junk makes me sick." This procedure was repeated for ten times at each session and she practiced it for three sessions daily. After several weeks of this procedure candy consumption was completely eliminated. When the technique was later applied to the consumption of cookies and doughnuts, the rate of consumption for those items per week also dropped to zero.

When the treatment was terminated after eighteen weeks, Miss C was satisfactorily maintaining a low-calorie diet and because of its success, had terminated the self-aversion procedure. During this period of time her weight dropped from 180 to 139 pounds. During the six weeks following the termination of the aversion procedure, Miss C lost an additional 12 pounds bringing her total weight reduction to 53 pounds.

Morganstern (1974) feels that it is unlikely that non-smokers would acquire the smoking habit in this manner. The effective use of this technique would obviously be limited to those people who do not smoke. As an alternative to smoking, for those who already smoke and for those who do not want to risk developing the tobacco habit, the inhalation of other noxious stimuli could be tried.

Acquiring Responses Incompatible with Eating

It is not uncommon for people, when analyzing the conditions associated with eating behavior, to discover that emotions such as anger, frustration, and depression seem to trigger the eating response. Penick, Filion, Fox, and Stunkard (1971) report the case of a thirty-year-old housewife who, in her analysis of her eating habits and for the first time in her life, recognized that anger stimulated her eating. Following that discovery, whenever she became angry she left the kitchen and wrote down how she felt, thereby decreasing her anger and aborting her eating. Exercise routines are an excellent outlet for anger and frustration that is highly incompatible with eating. Should you find that you are tempted to eat more when exercising, you could do push-ups, sit-ups, walk, or jog around the block, or ride a bicycle about the neighborhood when you find yourself tempted by food. These activities can lower the intensity of the emotions and also burn up calories. Exercise programs are most compatible with (and can be made a part of) dieting programs. A plan for developing and maintaining exercise programs will be presented in a later chapter.

The chaining principle can be effectively used in the modification of eating behavior. As you recall from an earlier discussion of this technique, chaining consists of breaking one simple activity into all of its components. Eating consists of a number of sequential movements before you reach the moment when you actually put the food in your mouth. You do such things as prepare the food, place it on the table, come to the table, sit down, pick up a utensil, cut the meat, and so on. Every meal, including snacks, can be broken down into many links which form the chain. If you know that walking into a coffee shop with friends starts a chain that ends with eating doughnuts or a hamburger, do not walk into the coffee shop. Walk on by to some other place and do something else. When this is done you have substituted a response that is incompatible with eating behavior.

You can also discourage eating by lengthening the chain of behaviors that precede it. If you stop buying foods that require no preparation (potato chips, cheese, peanut butter, luncheon meats) you lengthen the chain by requiring either a trip to the grocery store or time-consuming food preparation—both of which lengthen the chain. The number of links in the chain can be increased by preparing only one unit of food at a time (boil one hot dog instead of a pot of them). This forces you to go through the entire chain of preparation if you want a second item. It also increases eating time so that you feel satisfied with food more quickly.

Increasing Motivation to Lose Weight

Many people could easily lose weight if they desired but, as we have previously indicated, the problem is that the desire to lose weight is outweighed by the reinforcing powers of food—whether it be the taste of food, the actual act of eating, or the appearance. Thus, a major step in any weight-reduction program is that of raising the motivational level of the person to get those extra pounds off. The following are some suggestions for raising the motivational level of the possible weight loser:

1. Use mental imagery and picture yourself as a slender person. Picture yourself in several different situations as a "new" person, such as walking into a party and catching the eyes of other attractive persons. Think about the new you and all of the new situations and opportunities you could have as a slender person.

2. Buy one piece of special clothing that you will be able to fit into only after you have reached your weight goal.

3. Go through a magazine and find photographs of attractive slender persons and paste these on the refrigerator and other parts of the kitchen as rewarding cues for being slender. (Be alert to the fact that you may become immune to these cues, so periodically change these pictures.)

4. Go to various department stores and look at all the new clothes. Try on a bikini or other type of clothing which all of your slender friends are wearing now but which you cannot because of your weight. (It appears that clothes play a major part in a person's opinion of himself or herself. More times than one when obese people lose weight they begin to buy the new styles of clothing, therefore, it is assumed that clothing would play a major part in the desire of a person to lose weight.)

Guidelines for Self-Modification of Eating Behavior

1. *Set a realistic goal for weight loss.* A realistic goal would be between one and two pounds per week. You can reach these goals without upsetting your entire life-style or routine, and you also feel a sense of accomplishment when the goal is reached. These conditions increase the probability that you will continue the intervention program.

2. *Be sure to establish an accurate baseline for eating behavior and weight before the intervention program is initiated.* Baselines provide a reliable standard of comparison for changes in eating behavior and weight.

3. *Consult a physician to determine an appropriate diet and to help you set reasonable goals for weight loss.*

4. *Initiate the intervention or weight control program in a step-by-step manner.* You may try only one or two of the aforementioned suggestions in the initial stages of the self-control program and incorporate others as practical and appropriate. It is important that you not try too much too soon. Start in modest degrees and progress from there.

5. *Keep accurate and regular data as you proceed with the program.* If progress is being made in decreasing food intake and weight, the recording and graphing of these results can be a most gratifying experience and ensures continued participation.

6. *Be willing to modify your program.* If, after a reasonable time, you are not getting the desired results, try to identify problem areas and make adjustments accordingly. For example, if you find that your program works at home but not at a restaurant or at a neighbor's house, develop programs for those situations. If you are still unsuccessful it may be necessary to avoid eating in those places. Or you may find yourself becoming negligent about recording the necessary data. If this happens you must develop a program to correct this. You might, for example, permit yourself to eat appropriate foods only after you have all charts up-to-date.

Inevitably some problems such as those described above will be encountered and the key to success is not to scrap the programs but to identify problem areas and develop appropriate reinforcement contingencies. When this process is continued progress toward accomplishment of the goal is very likely to be realized.

5/Eliminate Smoking
Behavior: My heart tells me to

Smoking, like overeating, is a habit that millions of people would like to break and, again like overeating, it is a behavior in which the reinforcement for engaging in it (pleasure derived from smoking) is immediate while the harmful effects (coronary disease, cancer, emphysema) may be long delayed.

It is now accepted as common knowledge that cigarette smoking is a major health hazard, being causally related to lung cancer, emphysema, coronary problems, and a generally reduced state of physical fitness and well-being. The life span of heavy smokers is not only shorter than that of nonsmokers but also of poorer quality. Heavy smokers suffer more chronic illnesses and miss more days of work than do nonsmokers. According to Haddock (1973), the smoker's chances of dying from *cancer* are 110 percent greater, from *lung cancer* 700 percent greater, than for those who have never smoked on a regular basis. The risk of dying from lung cancer for men between the ages of thirty-five and eighty-four who smoke less than one pack of cigarettes per day is *six* times greater, and for those who smoke two or more packs a day *sixteen* times greater than for nonsmokers. Cancer of the larynx is six times as frequent and cancer of the esophagus is four times as frequent in cigarette smokers as opposed to nonsmokers.

If one stops smoking before cancer has actually started, lung tissue tends to repair itself. Beginning one year after smoking is stopped, the risk of lung cancer decreases progressively until after a few years it is only slightly higher than for those who have never been regular smokers.

Another disease closely associated with smoking is heart disease. It is the most frequent cause of death in the United States. Coronary disease occurs when a coronary artery or vein or one of their branches becomes clogged or obstructed. This is usually due to the formation of thrombi within the blood vessel. Autopsies show that the hearts and coronary arteries of smokers have considerably more thrombi than nonsmokers. The death rate from coronary disease of men and women who smoke a pack or more a day is 70 percent higher than for nonsmokers.

There are many more diseases that have a high correlation to cigarette smoking. Chronic bronchitis and emphysema are among the leading causes of severe disability. Chronic bronchitis is a persistent or recurrent inflammation of the bronchial tubes. This causes an excessive amount of mucus, which requires a chronic cough to expel it. Emphysema is a disease in which the lungs lose their elasticity and cannot expand and contract normally. The result is a slow crippling disease which seriously reduces the ability of the lungs to get rid of carbon dioxide. The death rate from these two diseases is 500 percent higher for cigarette smokers than for nonsmokers. Peptic ulcers, sinusitis, high blood pressure, speeding up of the pulse rate, gastric and duodenal ulcers, and cirrhosis of the liver are just a few more of the diseases highly correlated with cigarette smoking.

In addition to having the desire to stop smoking for reasons of health, many people want to quit because of the effect it has on children. Children see their parents and other adults smoking and, although they know it is harmful to their health, they start. Surveys show that the majority of smokers in high school and college had parents who smoked.

Smoking in some places interferes with the rights of those who do not smoke. Sometimes, there is no way the nonsmoker can avoid smoke inhalation and he may be allergic to it, or it may make him sick. This is another reason why some people may want to quit or reduce their smoking behavior.

Although facts and statistics such as those given here may be convincing, they will not kick the smoking habit. The desire to stop smoking is not enough. What is needed is a program based on the results of scientific investigations which includes specific recommendations that anyone with a desire to stop smoking can follow. The aim of this chapter is to make a list of those recommendations.

When you make a definite decision to stop or reduce your smoking you proceed in exactly the same manner and use the same steps as employed in the previous chapter to the problem of obesity. The procedure for the treatment of all problem behaviors discussed in this book is as follows:

1. Defining the specific behavior to be modified.
2. Gathering and analyzing baseline data.
3. Establishing an intervention program based on:
   a. utilizing stimulus-control techniques
   b. altering response consequences
   c. developing responses incompatible to the target behavior.
4. Evaluating, altering, and maintaining the program.

Once the problem (in this case the reduction or elimination of smoking behavior) has been defined, you proceed with observing and collecting data regarding frequency and circumstances of smoking. The number of cigarettes smoked per day can be kept with a wrist counter, tallies on a small card, switching toothpicks or pennies from one pocket to another, or any number of different ways. The important thing is that the system must be portable and convenient so that it is on your person at all times. You also need a pencil and paper to describe the situations in which you smoked. Each evening this information can be recorded on charts and graphs kept at home. The chart for total cigarettes per day might look like this:

Figure 5.1. Chart for Recording Daily Cigarette Consumption

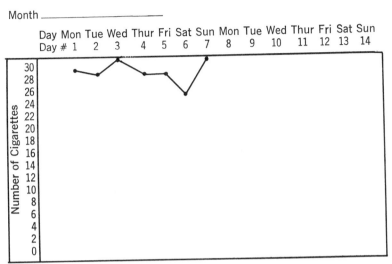

This chart shows that for the first seven days one hypothetical smoker consumed between twenty-five and thirty
cigarettes per day. A chart like this should be maintained
for about two weeks before any attempt is made to change
smoking behavior. It should be carefully inspected to determine if approximately the same number of cigarettes is being consumed each day. You may find that on some days of
the week, such as Saturday or Sunday, you smoke considerably more or less than on other days. If this is the case you
should make a careful analysis to determine what specific
cues or consequences on those days alter your smoking
behavior.

A more detailed chart showing the time of day each cigarette is consumed along with the situation should be especially helpful to you. (See Figure 5.2.)

An analysis of records such as these should help you to
identify the times and situations which seem to trigger the
smoking response. You may find that there are times when

Figure 5.2. Chart to Record When and under What
Circumstances Smoking Occurred.

Date _____

Time of Cigarette	Situation in which smoking occurred
7:00 A.M.	Had cigarette when I got up
7:45 A.M.	Smoked while driving to work
9:30 A.M.	Cigarette after coffee break
12:30 P.M.	Cigarette after lunch
1:30 P.M.	Argued with boss; smoked two cigarettes

you really *need* a cigarette (getting up in the morning, for example) and other times when you smoke as a result of habit (like after a meal). Your smoking may increase when you read the newspaper, study, prepare reports, socialize with friends, become nervous, or irritated, or angry. Knowing what triggers the smoking will be beneficial in the designing of stimulus-control techniques to remove those cues which tempt you to light a cigarette.

You should also try to identify the consequences of each cigarette you have. Does it relieve tension, give you something to do with your hands, make you feel more important or independent, help you gain the approval of others, or what?

To the extent that you can find answers to these questions, you can establish different kinds of contingencies which will decrease the reinforcement for smoking and increase the reinforcement for not smoking. Remember that behavior has no perpetual motion; it is maintained by its consequences. If smoking produces desirable results it has served its purpose and is likely to be continued. When it ceases to produce satisfaction for you, you will now find it more profitable to stop smoking. We will shortly explore some possibilities for helping you reap greater benefits from *not smoking* than from smoking.

Incidentally, you should continue to keep records of smoking frequency, number of cigarettes smoked per day, and the situation in which smoking occurs. This is necessary for two reasons: (1) to determine the success of your program,

Figure 5.3. Chart for Recording Number of Cigarettes per Day during Baseline and Intervention Periods.

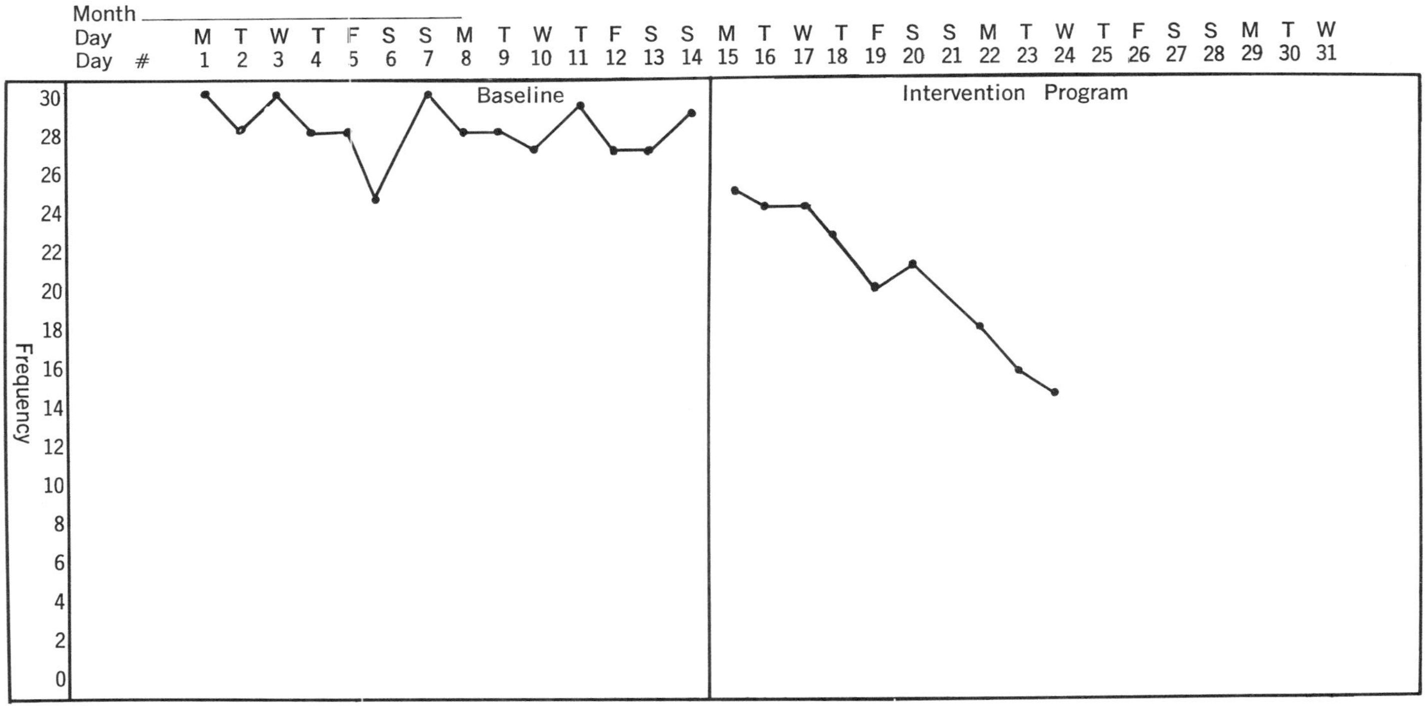

81

and (2) to provide help in case you need to make alterations in the program as originally designed. You keep modifying until you find something that produces the desired results. Figure 5.1 might be expanded to include both *baseline* and treatment data. Figure 5.3 shows how a hypothetical chart reflecting success in the reduction of cigarettes might appear. Figure 5.3 reflects that rapid progress in cigarette reduction is being made during the first week following initiation of the intervention program. This chart should be continued indefinitely until you have either quit smoking completely or reduced smoking to a tolerable level for a prolonged period of time.

Some Experimental Programs

Before listing specific techniques for managing smoking behavior, let us review some of the experimental programs in which this habit has been successfully reduced or eliminated. In a previous chapter we learned that smoking could be greatly reduced by restricting it to a particular place (Nolan, 1968). Nolan used his wife as the subject. He told her to smoke as much as she wanted, but while doing it she was not to engage in any other activity and was to sit in a particular chair—the smoking chair. This smoking chair was placed in such a way that she could not watch television or conveniently carry on a conversation with other members of the household. No one spoke to her while she was in this chair and no reading materials were readily available. She kept a record of her daily cigarette consumption and of the amount of time spent in the smoking chair.

When this plan was instituted the number of cigarettes consumed daily dropped from thirty to an average of twelve per day and remained at this level for over a week. When it appeared that this level would be maintained indefinitely, Nolan hypothesized that if the chair were made less readily accessible, smoking behavior might be further weakened. Hence, the chair was moved to the cellar of the house and her cigarette consumption dropped to five per day. After about three weeks at this level Mrs. Nolan became disgusted with her inability to quit smoking and decided to quit completely. The smoking chair was eventually returned to the living area of the house and six months later (at the writing of Nolan's article) his wife had not smoked another cigarette. Roberts (1969), using himself as the subject, replicated Nolan's findings.

Some researchers have used electric shock to reduce smoking. Powell and Azrin (1968) devised a special cigarette case that automatically delivered painful electric shock whenever the individual opened it. Berecz (1972) concluded that a self-administered shock following *imagined* smoking behavior reduced smoking just as much as did a shock administered after actually taking a long drag on a cigarette.

A form of aversive conditioning is to make cigarettes distasteful by coating the filters with an obnoxious tasting substance. For this one could use the products that parents use to stop children from sucking their thumbs—it is bitter and leaves a lingering after-taste.

Homme (1965) recommends a thought control process in which the smoker makes a list of thoughts (self-verbalizations) relating to smoking that he personally finds aversive. These thoughts might include the dangers of smoking such as lung cancer, heart disease, bad breath, and poor physical condition. The smoker then selects something (money, food, a preferred activity, a pleasant thought) that he finds rewarding. When the urge to smoke is experienced, rather than engaging in the usual coverant, "I really want a cigarette," the smoker activates an antismoking coverant or thought such as "I'll die of lung cancer if I smoke" or "I'll have bad breath and feel terrible if I smoke."

Presumably, if a prosmoking coverant leads to overt smoking, then an antismoking coverant should have the opposite effect. Since there is nothing inherently reinforcing about engaging in the antismoking coverant it is necessary that this response be immediately reinforced. Every time you associate a negative thought with the urge to smoke you could allow yourself some extra spending money, eat an apple or some enjoyable piece of food, or simply follow the antismoking thought with a pleasant thought such as, "If I don't smoke my food will taste better," or "I'll feel much better now," or simply "Smoking will kill you; I do not smoke."

Covert sensitization has been applied to the problem of smoking. Cautela (1966) recommends that after the smoker learns deep muscle relaxation techniques (described in Chapter 9) he imagines a scene associated with smoking which is extremely repulsive to him. You must remember that what is repulsive or aversive to one person might not be to another so you keep searching until you are able to imagine a scene that literally "makes you sick" when you think of smoking. For many people a scene such as the following would be sufficiently aversive:

> You are taking a break in the lounge at work and start to reach for a cigarette. You find that you are getting a nauseous feeling in your stomach. You feel as if you are going to vomit. You take a cigarette in your hand and feel sick. You have intense stomach cramps and particles of food mixed with hot, bitter liquid come into your throat. As you start to put the cigarette into your mouth, you puke all over the pack of cigarettes. The cigarette in your hand is covered with slimy green vomit. The stink coming from the vomit makes you even sicker and you start to puke again. Your clothes are covered with puke. So is the pack of cigarettes. The cigarette in your hand is soft and limp from being soaked with the slimy green puke. You turn away from the cigarettes and this mess and begin to feel better. You go take a shower and feel great being away from the mess and the cigarettes.

Elliott and Tighe (1968) operate on the assumption that many "stop-smoking programs" fail because the smokers are not sufficiently sensitive to the real dangers of smoking. In seeking an alternative to such sensitivity, they searched for a smoking-connected hazard that they hoped would generalize to everyday life when the smoker was no longer participating in the treatment program and decided to make the loss of money a punishment for smoking. Each participant in their program was required to deposit approximately $65 with the understanding that the money was to be returned only if he or she refrained from smoking. The longer the abstention, the more money returned. Total abstinence was required; the participants were not allowed to substitute pipes, cigars, and so on. If the participant smoked at any time during the treatment program (which lasted three or four months), he lost all his money.

The contract which each participant was required to sign contained the following stipulations:

1. No tobacco consumption of any nature for sixteen weeks.
2. Sixty-five dollars would be given by each person in denominations of $10, $10, $10, $15, and $20. No checks or promises to pay were accepted since these could have been nullified at will by the participant.
3. A graduate system of refunds was to be made to each participant for periods of abstinence as follows:

First two days	$10
First two weeks	$10
Five weeks	$10
Ten weeks	$15
Sixteen weeks	$20
	$65

4. A single incidence of tobacco consumption would incur forfeiting all money not yet refunded, to be divided equally among those who lasted sixteen weeks.
5. Each person agreed to read some antismoking literature supplied by the instructors.
6. Each person agreed to assume responsibility for reporting his or her smoking if and when it occurred.

The program was highly successful while it was in effect, with twenty-one of twenty-five participants abstaining for the full sixteen weeks. Winett (1973) also found the use of contingency contracts to be effective in the reduction of smoking.

Some investigators (Shapiro, Tursky, Schwartz, and Shnidman, 1971) have tried to help smokers associate smoking with a novel environmental stimulus rather than cues that elicit smoking behavior. Smokers were asked to record the times throughout the day when they smoked. They carried a portable parking-meter timer and set it to go off at periods equal to the smoker's average interval between cigarettes. No cigarettes were smoked until the timer sounded. This meant that persons began breaking previous associations with smoking such as the end of a meal, reading the newspaper, cup of coffee, and so on. The sound of the timer became the sole cue for smoking. Subjects were instructed to gradually increase the timer intervals so that the periods between cigarettes were lengthened. In this manner, the daily smoking frequencies *were reduced.*

Developing Your Self-Control Program

Stimulus-Control Techniques

1. A stimulus-control program can be established whereby you gradually reduce the cues associated with smoking. The approach suggested here is similar to that of Nolan (1968) and Roberts (1969). You might begin the first phase by ceasing all social smoking. Smoke anywhere you desire but always do it alone. Never smoke with anyone else.

When you have learned to smoke alone and to refuse offers from others to smoke (two weeks should be sufficient), restrict smoking to your home or residence. Make it a point never to smoke outside your house. Smoke anywhere in your house you choose. Next, choose a particular place in your home to smoke. Restrict your smoking to a particular place in a particular room. Do not allow yourself to watch TV, talk with other family members, read the newspaper, or engage in any other activity while smoking.

During the final phase you should move your smoking chair to some isolated and inconvenient place such as the cellar, bathroom, or garage. Continue to engage in no other activity while smoking.

During the entire process continue to keep a record of the number of cigarettes smoked per day. You should find a decrease with each new phase of the program. When your chair is in an out-of-the-way place you should be enjoying your smoking less and wondering if it is worth the effort. When the effort becomes too great, you should be able to completely quit.

2. You could use an approach similar to that of Shapiro, et al. (1971) if you prefer it. This method, as you probably recall from our previous discussion, is designed to help you learn to associate smoking with a novel cue rather than the previous cues such as the end of a meal, or cup of coffee. In order for this program to be effective you would need to follow these steps:

a. Record when, where, and how much you smoke each day. (The charts suggested previously should be adequate.)

b. Select a timing device with a buzzer which can be set to go off at various intervals of time.

c. For one week prior to the initiation of your intervention program sound the timer before lighting any cigarette. The purpose of this procedure is to strengthen the association between the buzzer and smoking, i.e., a new smoking cue is being strengthened.

d. Although you may continue smoking at the same frequency as previously, do not smoke at the same time. Vary your schedule by at least five minutes. If you have been lighting a cigarette immediately following a meal, for example, set your timer to go off five or ten minutes after the meal. Continue your normal cigarette consumption for two or three weeks, but smoke only at the sound of the buzzer or alarm and make sure that you smoke after every signal.

e. No later than the beginning of the fourth week begin reducing the number of cigarettes smoked per day. If your timer has been cueing you to smoke twenty-five times per day reduce it to twenty per day for a week. The following week reduce your smoking to something like fifteen cigarettes per day but continue to smoke only on cue (the sound of the buzzer). You gradually reduce your smoking frequency each week until you have either stopped or reached a tolerable level. As your smoking consumption approaches zero cigarettes per day you may not want to continue to reduce consumption each week at the rate of five per day; you may prefer a weekly reduction in consumption by two or three cigarettes per day.

f. At any time that stress, internal or external, makes further reduction difficult, maintain for a week or two the level of consumption which you have reached. Do not try to make further reductions until the stress has subsided. Never forget to maintain your cue, however, even in stress-provoking situations.

3. A third approach could be based on the degree of need for a cigarette. Most smokers find that there are a few times during the day (such as after a meal) when the urge to smoke seems almost irresistible. At other times you may find that you unconsciously light a cigarette while talking with friends, reading the paper, or taking a break. From the charts which you have made of your smoking behavior make a list of all the situations in which you smoke, starting with the least necessary (habit) cigarettes and progressing through the most needed (need) cigarettes. Try to eliminate the habit cigarettes first. You might begin by not permitting yourself to smoke while watching TV, reading the paper, or on break at work. When you have learned to control your smoking in one situation begin working on the next situation on your list until you have at least eliminated the habit cigarettes. Then you try to stop the need cigarettes, i.e., those for which the urge seems to be the greatest.

This procedure can be combined with other techniques listed under the headings "Altering Response Consequences" and "Acquiring Incompatible Responses" which follow.

NOTE: *Do not attempt to mix the latter three programs we have given as Stimulus-Control Techniques. While*

any should be effective when used alone, confusion
would result from an attempt to use two or more
of them simultaneously. Stick with the one that
seems best suited to your situation.

Altering Behavior Consequences

There are numerous kinds of satisfaction that can be derived from smoking. What is more, the satisfaction and enjoyment derived from smoking are immediate while the threat of aversive consequences (lung cancer, heart disease) is remote. It is important that you identify the reinforcers that maintain the smoking habit so that these established contingencies can be altered.

Most people begin smoking for at least one of two reasons: (1) to demonstrate independence and maturity and (2) to gain peer approval and acceptance. Although these aims, often unconscious, offer sufficient incentive for one to start smoking, other kinds of pleasures soon become associated with smoking behavior. A student of mine, after some self-examination, listed several reasons why he smoked. His list follows:

1. They serve as a crutch. In times of boredom they give me something to do with my hands.
2. They provide me with a prop, emphasizing my moods, depending on the way I move my arms with cigarette in hand. Depending on when and how I smoke, they can make me appear anywhere from nonchalant and noncommital to earnest and aggressive.
3. They help me to relax. When I am tired or nervous I find comfort in a cigarette.
4. They provide an excellent complement to social gatherings. When smoking I am doing something rather than just sitting and looking awkward. Cigarettes give me something to handle.
5. I derive pleasure from blowing smoke and watching it swirl through the air.

Other reasons for smoking could well include *stimulation*

(just getting started in the morning), *addiction to nicotine and oral gratification* (need to have something in the mouth), and *force of habit* (a behavior pattern that is followed unconsciously). You might think of other reasons why you smoke.

Analyzing your reasons for smoking should help you to realize that some of these reasons are difficult for you to logically defend. You may also discover that there are numerous other ways of obtaining the same results. If you smoke because "it gives me something to do with my hands," for example, you should be able to think of dozens of other activities such as squeezing a rubber ball, playing cards, carrying a swagger stick, and so on, which would give you something to do with your hands. We will have more to say about these possibilities in the section following the next, "Acquiring Incompatible Responses." The primary advantage of any kind of record-keeping and analysis is that it increases *awareness* of smoking which, like any other habit, can become so well ingrained that we are not usually cognizant that we are engaging in the behavior.

Suggestions for Altering Behavior Through Its Consequences

1. Use some form of coverant control or covert sensitization so that you have thoughts of unpleasant consequences when you smoke. This procedure can take several forms. You might imagine a scene similar to the one presented earlier in the chapter in which you become extremely nauseated when you start to smoke. You might prefer to repeat some simple statement over and over when you start to light a cigarette such as "Cigarettes cause cancer," "Smoking will kill me," "I'll have a heart attack if I don't stop," and so on. Keep searching until you find some thought to which you are very sensitive. By doing this you create an incongruence between your overt behavior and your inner thoughts. This incongruence is called cognitive dissonance, i.e., inconsistence in your private thoughts. It just doesn't make sense to smoke if you think smoking is

harmful to your health. This conflict produces tension and discomfort which can be relieved by reduction in the cognitive dissonance. Assuming that you do desire to continue to live and have good health, you cannot enjoy smoking while at the same time thinking, "Smoking will kill me." You are now associating unpleasant consequences with the act of smoking. The logical way to reduce this dissonance and to relieve the tension is to stop smoking. If you pick up a cigarette, each time make yourself think of the aversive consequences; when you put it away without lighting it, or have the urge but do not reach for a cigarette, each time think such thoughts as "I feel so much better now," "Now I can breathe again," "Refusing that cigarette will add several minutes to my life," "I'll feel healthy and strong," and so on. You must think of some pleasant consequence for not smoking that is especially meaningful to you. Continue over a long period of time to associate the unpleasant thoughts or imagined consequences with smoking and pleasant thoughts with not smoking.

2. Start an exercise or physical fitness program in which smoking will interfere with your new goals. Smoking then produces a consequence that blocks you from achieving some worthy objective. You can also now think "If I smoke I'll never be able to jog," or "When I don't smoke how much better I can breathe and further I can run!"

3. Some people get a great deal of support from a friend or acquaintance who is also trying to quit smoking. If the two of you try it at the same time you can lend mutual support to each other when the going is difficult. Human beings can tolerate and cope with greater discomfort when in the presence of another person. You can also share the enjoyment of success when you are making progress toward the reduction or elimination of smoking.

4. Enter into a contract with someone whereby you deposit money or other valuables with them and earn them back by reducing your smoking behavior. Another kind of agreement is one in which you establish a contingency whereby for each time you smoke you donate money to some

cause, group, or organization which you do not ordinarily support or believe in. Or you might prefer a contingency in which each time you do not smoke you deposit some money into a "shopping fund" which you can spend on yourself.

In any contract of this sort you must make the consequences significant enough to have an effect on your behavior. If you are opposed to the Ku Klux Klan, for example, and have agreed to donate $10 to that organization for each cigarette you smoke, you will have second thoughts about smoking. Do not enter into a contract, even if it is with yourself, that is not binding. You must follow through if the agreement is to be effective.

5. Think of something you really enjoy, and permit yourself to engage in this activity only when you have reached a goal in smoking reduction. You could combine contingencies where you deposit some money each day for every cigarette you can eliminate and at the end of the week or so permit yourself to go shopping and buy yourself a gift. When you do not make progress, do not permit yourself to engage in the desired activity. In other words "pay the price" for smoking and "reap the reward" when you do not smoke.

Acquiring Incompatible Responses

Your analysis of baseline data should have helped you to identify the time of day and situation in which you are most likely to smoke. It may also have helped you to identify some of the various kinds of satisfaction desired from smoking. In developing responses incompatible with the target behavior, you are really attempting to substitute another habit (we hope it is helpful rather than harmful) which becomes associated with either the cues or the consequences previously attached to smoking behavior. Here are some examples of things you might want to try:

1. Let's assume that the ritualistic act of reaching for a cigarette, taking it out of the pack, and lighting and puffing it is reinforcing. In this case you might substitute some-

thing in place of the cigarette such as a "dummy" cigarette, a piece of gum, or a toothpick. This permits you to go through virtually the same response chain without experiencing the harmful effects of smoking.

2. Each time you get the urge to smoke while studying, working at your desk, or reading the newspaper you might try walking five times around the room, doing ten push-ups, jogging in place for five minutes, or anything that seems most reasonable in your particular case. The idea is that you engage in some behavior other than smoking in those situations that once elicited smoking behaviors. It is helpful to take up some relatively simple activity, game, or skill in which you really want to become adept and practice it instead of smoking.

3. If you are tempted to smoke after a meal, simply excuse yourself and go for a walk or engage in some hobby or wash the dishes.

4. When you experience the urge to smoke and seem obsessed with these thoughts you might simply say to yourself or aloud, if you prefer, "To hell with this! I am not a slave to anybody or anything including a cigarette. I am a free person. *I do not smoke.*" Then shift your thoughts and your actions to something else. This should give you a feeling of strength and power to control your behavior in order to achieve self-control.

Comment: It should be emphasized that you are not expected to use all the suggestions presented in this chapter. An attempt to incorporate them all would be overwhelming and self-defeating. Remember the purpose of this book is to help you to develop greater self-control and that includes making your own decisions. When you decide to stop smoking, you should find some of these procedures and techniques helpful to you. Feel free to combine and/or modify them so that they are tailored to your particular situation. You should be able to simultaneously employ some of the stimulus-control, behavior consequence, and incompatible response techniques. Of course, as has been previously called to your attention, you could not use all of the stimu-lus-control techniques listed in this chapter at the same time. These specific suggestions are presented with the hope that you can find something that will be applicable to your situation, but do not hesitate to alter them to suit you.

6/Learning Efficient Study Techniques: These cheat notes take so much time to prepare

It probably comes as no great surprise to you that many people are unsuccessful in school or fail to reach their vocational objectives not because of the lack of intellectual ability but because they never developed efficient techniques of study. They may spend as much time reading a textbook and reviewing their notes as more successful students without getting the same results. Lack of academic success may promote anxiety, guilt feelings, and a general sense of inadequacy and ineptitude. Students who learn how to study not only avoid these undesirable emotional penalties but also find themselves more able to reach their objectives and to feel that they do have the power to control their own destiny.

Research on Increasing Efficiency of Study

Beneke and Harris (1972) attempted to help college students develop self-control programs for study. Their investigation was based on extensive research (Goldiamond, 1965; Kanfer, 1971; Marston & Feldman, 1970; Zimmerman, 1970) emphasizing the importance of self-control procedures in changing behavior. Marston and Feldman (1970) suggested that the success of a self-control program depends on two variables: the strength of the commitment (or covert decision to change one's behavior) and the effectiveness of the self-controlling responses (the particular techniques used by the individual to change his own be-havior). Beneke and Harris attempted to affect both vari-ables by first increasing the students' awareness of their reasons for wanting to change their study behavior and then instructing them in methods which could be used to facilitate such changes.

During the first week the students were asked to develop an awareness of their current study habits. They were in-structed to continue their usual pattern of study but to keep records of their study time. Each student made lists of rea-sons for studying and for improving his or her study behav-ior. This was done in order to increase the strength of the commitment to study since studying is another one of those behaviors from which the rewards are delayed while the re-wards for behavior incompatible with study (dating, talk-ing to friends) are more immediate.

Each student was informed of the principle of stimulus control and its application to everyday situations and was instructed to establish not more than two places (and preferably one only) as a stimulus to study. The stu-dents were to choose a place that was well lighted, free of distracting stimuli and not associated with behavior incom-patible with studying. Explicit instructions were given to do all their studying at these places and to absolutely avoid doing other things there.

The entire program for study improvement was pre-sented in eleven lessons, one of which was devoted to the concept of positive reinforcement and the importance of using powerful, immediate, and contingent reinforcers. Sug-gested reinforcers included high probability behavior, food, money, and so on. Students made lists of reinforcing activi-ties and stimuli that would strengthen study behavior. They were also taught to graph their study behavior (hours studied per day as a function of days) so that an increase in their study time would be obvious and might provide extra reinforcement.

The students were given several lessons on the SQ3R

study method (Robinson, 1970). An adaptation of this method will be discussed in some detail later in the chapter. They were also encouraged to set up additional reinforcers for longer-term goals such as reading three chapters in history in one week. The requirements of each student's goals were that they be: (a) explicit, (b) met in a week or less, and (c) written down and put in a prominent place at the study area. Instructions were given for them to reward themselves generously when they attained a longer-term goal.

The use of punishment as an option for dealing with behavior incompatible with studying was discussed. Suggested types of punishment for engaging in incompatible behavior included fines, denying oneself a pleasant activity, and asking a friend or spouse for criticism.

Instructions regarding more effective note-taking techniques were presented, with students being encouraged to outline lectures by listing the major points, minor points, and a few examples in outline form. Hints were given for identifying key points in a speech. Revising notes by reorganizing and clarifying details, preferably on the same day, was stressed, and the importance of frequent review was emphasized.

These lessons were found to produce a gain in grade-point averages that lasted for two semesters following the lessons. Furthermore, this effect appeared to be independent of whether the students worked individually on the lessons or attended group meetings. The effectiveness of this program was not primarily due to the increase in study time but to the development of more efficient study techniques. Beneke and Harris concluded that while some minimal study time appeared necessary for increasing grade-point averages, the gains resulting from this project appeared to be due to increases in the quality rather than the quantity of study. These results suggest at least two possibilities: (1) students can acquire more efficient study habits on their own by reading a book such as you are now doing, and (2) they do not have to greatly increase the time spent studying to get better results. With better study habits one can accomplish more in the same or less time.

Jackson and VanZoost (1972) had college students register for a study program by depositing $10 and signing a contract stating that they could regain this money by attending sessions, completing exercises, and answering questionnaires and tests. They met for an hour per week for six weeks.

The students were then placed in one of three experimental conditions, each varying in the manner of earning back the $10 deposit: (1) *no reinforcement* in which the money was returned for attending the meetings and completing questionnaires, (2) *external reinforcement* in which a group leader evaluated the students' answers to the exercises and paid them according to prearranged monetary values, and (3) *self-administered reinforcement* in which the students evaluated their own performance on the exercises following feedback regarding acceptable answers and paid themselves whatever they judged their answers merited. At the beginning of each session the group leader would determine the maximum amount that the student could earn during that session.

The results showed that both of the reinforcement groups developed better study habits that were maintained over a four-month follow-up while the "no reinforcement" group did not. Follow-up groups continued to improve their study habits more than the external reinforcement group.

In a later study Jackson and VanZoost (1974) continued to investigate the effects of self-reinforcement during study-skill sessions on study behavior. This time they added the condition that students teach the content of the study program to peers and then self-evaluate and self-reward their teaching performance. A control group was exposed to the identical study-skills program and self-reinforcement procedures, but they were not asked to teach the content. The students that were required to teach what they had learned to other students performed better than did the control group that did no teaching.

Stimulus Control of Study Behavior

One of the first steps in developing good study habits is to put study behavior under the control of environmental cues. Many students attempt to study under conditions that affect their ability to concentrate on the subject at hand. They attempt to study in places where too many distracting stimuli are present. A pretty girl sitting at another table in the library might divert a young man's attention from his physics book, for example. Noise, other people, and daydreaming are some of the more common forms of distracting stimuli. Some students are so distracted by other activities that they never get around to even setting a time for study.

Goldiamond (1965) reports the case of a young lady who complained of feeling sleepy when she studied. She was instructed to use a brighter lamp at her desk and to turn the desk away from the bed. Since her desk was to control study behavior only, writing letters was to be done in the dining room, comic books were read in the kitchen, daydreaming was done in another room, and at her desk she was to engage in her school work and *only* her school work. She learned to associate the desk with study and nothing else.

Suggestions for Improved Study

As a result of the previous review of research and our experience in this area, these recommendations are made:

1. *Make a list of your goals and your reasons for developing better study habits*. This should increase your commitment to improve your study behavior.

2. *Bring your study behavior under stimulus control by limiting your studying to a particular location*. Find a desk and chair that are free of other distractions and do all your

studying in this place. Do not do anything but study in this location. If you want to read the newspaper, draw pictures, talk on the phone, relax or sleep, make yourself go to another room or location within the room to engage in these activities. If you find yourself daydreaming or thinking about something else while studying leave the desk immediately and return only when you are able to concentrate on study.

3. *Set specific goals to be accomplished at each study session and reward yourself when a goal is reached.* You may establish contingencies by permitting yourself to have a date, to go see a movie, and so on, only when you have completed the required amount of study. Students frequently complain of various kinds of distractions while studying, such as talking to other people, especially when they study in the library. One boy said that he always tried to study in the library near a stairway but could not concentrate because of the girls going up and down the stairs. He solved this problem by studying only in his room at his desk and then permitting himself to go to the library and watch girls climb the stairs only when his studying was completed. In this way girl-watching did not interfere with his studies and neither did his school work distract him from his girl-watching. As the saying goes, There is a time and place for everything.

4. *Use a master schedule to help you budget all of your time.* For those of you who find other activities so distracting that you do not find the time to study, make a chart of all your activities for a week at a time. The chart should start with the time you get up in the morning and continue until bedtime. The time periods should be clocked according to your particular class schedule. Figure 6.1 shows the way a master planning chart might look.

The chart shows a hypothetical two-day schedule. It could be extended for a week. You first list all the activities that are predetermined and must be completed. This leaves vacant periods throughout the day. This chart shows a Monday schedule with unallotted time between 9 and 11 A.M., 7 and

Figure 6.1.   Master Planning Schedule

Day

Hour	M	T	W	T	F	S	S
7:00	Rise, dress Break-fast	Rise, dress Break-fast					
8:00	Class						
9:00							
10:00		Class					
11:00	Class						
12:00	Lunch	Lunch					
1:00	Class	Class					
2:00		Class					
3:00							
4:00		Meet-ing					
5:00							
6:00	Din-ner	Din-ner					
7:00							
8:00	Meet-ing						
9:00							
10:00							
11:00							

(AM: 7:00–11:00; PM: 12:00–11:00)

8 P.M., and from 9 to 11 P.M. Each morning you should inspect the chart to determine the unallotted time for that day. Make a list of work to be accomplished and allocate various time periods to specific tasks.

Another helpful procedure is that of breaking complex tasks down into a series of simple tasks. If you are assigned a paper to write you might set a deadline for selecting a topic, one for the review of literature, one for the rough draft, and a deadline for the final product. Reaching a subgoal on time should provide additional incentive for beginning work toward the next one. You can make some reward contingent upon reaching a subgoal thereby increasing the frequency of reinforcement. Each attainment of a goal strengthens the desire for further action. It is essential that you be continually alert to the need for setting new goals as fast as earlier ones are attained. The achievement of each immediate goal may be considered a step in the right direction but it usually takes several steps before that ultimate goal is reached. Each morning you should determine the goals to be pursued that day and study the master planning schedule to determine the time that can be devoted to each task. A daily schedule can be derived from the master schedule.

5. *Develop a specific plan or technique for study.* Remember that Beneke and Harris found that the quality of study was more important than the quantity of study. Several plans have been developed, two of which will now be described.

6. *Learn to take lecture notes efficiently and effectively.* Most students at the high school and college level attempt to take some kind of notes from teacher-instruction. Many note-takers simply write down some material with little attention to structure and organization or to integrating it with what they already know. Consequently, reviewing such limited "notes" is seldom very profitable; something always seems to be missing. The notes have gotten "cold."

A systematic note-taking procedure, called "The 7 C's of Note-Taking," has been formulated by Bowman (1975). He recommends that the student first block off his note-taking paper so that it resembles Figure 6.2.

In order to "sail the 7 C's of note-taking" Bowman recommends that you follow the steps listed below:

(A) COPY   Record in the 5½-inch column as many significant ideas as you can as they are presented by the lecturer.

(B) CONDENSE   Soon after the lecture's completion, summarize the notes you have taken. Write this condensed version of key words and statements in the 3″ column.

(C) CONVERT   Covering the 5½-inch column and using only what you have written in the 3-inch column as a prompt, try to recite the lecture's most important

Figure 6.2. Diagram for a Note Page

(This space is for key words and summaries of your original notes.)	(Write the original notes in this space.)

(Synthesis of new material in this lecture and prior knowledge of the subject is written here.)

Note: For 8½" by 11" paper, use the following dimensions: 5½" column for original notes; 3" column for key words from lecture notes and summaries; and a 2" by 8½" block for synthesis of content of the lecture and previous knowledge.

points. Do not rely on note memory for this: instead convert ideas to your own words.

(D) CONFIRM   Now, uncovering your original notes, confirm what you have just said. This "putting yourself to the test" is the most sensible study technique there is.

(E) CONSIDER   Consider what you have gained thus far by comparing the newness of the lecture's content with what you already know about the subject. This will help you establish relationships among details.

(F) CONSOLIDATE   Try to write the results of your thinking from (E) above. Use the 2" x 8½" block for this synthesis.

(G) COMMEMORATE   Honor your notes by reviewing them periodically. If pressed for time, refer to the condensed version of your notes on the left and the synthesis you recorded at the bottom of your page. This procedure should help you to remember much of what you have been exposed to in the lecture.

7. *Study in the same manner as you will be expected to reproduce the material.* Objective tests may require more memorization whereas essay tests require some knowledge of broad ideas which may be presented in outline form. Specific instructions for taking essay and multiple-choice exams will be presented later in the chapter.

8. *Study the teacher as well as the subject matter.* Different teachers have different biases, backgrounds, and preferences. Be alert to what topics the teachers emphasize, their philosophical or theoretical orientations, and the kinds of tests they usually give. These observations should help you to improve your test performance.

9. *Develop some system for marking, underlining, and making notes in the textbook.* This makes review much easier by adding structure and memory aids to the material.

10. *Break complex assignments down into subgoals and reward yourself when each part of the assignment is completed.* This reduces procrastination and makes possible

more frequent reinforcement. It should also reduce the anxiety generated by the assignment of a difficult task.

11. *Teach the material to another student.* You may never realize how much or how little you really know about a subject until you try to teach it to someone else. Help the other person study. Ask each other questions. Try to anticipate questions that might be on an examination.

12. *Try to relate the material in one course to something learned in another course or to some other experience you have had.* The greater the number of associations you can make with new learning the more meaningful it becomes. Try to think of examples and applications of principles that you are learning.

PQRST Study Plan

Spache and Berg (1966) recommend what they call the PQRST plan for reading academic materials. It is summarized as follows:

P—*Preview* the material by reading the title, headings, introductory and summary paragraphs.

Q—*Question* the content during the preview by making a list of questions. Turn the headings into questions and try to anticipate the possible answers the writer has to offer.

R—*Read* trying to find answers to the questions written down during the P and Q steps.

S—*Summarize* during your reading by making some notes based on the answers to your questions. Most of your questions should be answered by identifying the main idea of each paragraph. In addition to reading to answer your questions, also read to determine the author's central idea for each paragraph and state it in your own words. When you have accomplished this you will have outlined the material.

T—*Test* your understanding of the material. Try to anticipate some questions the instructor may ask and answer them orally or to yourself.

As you look at this outline you will see that several paragraphs can be brought together to form a more inclusive idea. These clusters can then be grouped together into the central theme of the material. As you learn to group units of ideas, summarize them, and combine them into a general, main idea you will find that your comprehension becomes more rapid and accurate. Although you may not continue to make a paragraph-by-paragraph written summary each time, make sure that you go through the same mental process.

Perhaps the best known strategy for improving reading study skills is Robinson's (1970) SQ3R method: survey, question, read, recite, and review. The staff of the Reading Laboratory and Clinic at East Tennessee State University has added an extra step to Robinson's technique and named it the SQ4R method of study. The six steps included in this method are presented in order.

SURVEY   Glance over the title, introductory paragraph(s), major headings, graphic aids, summary or conclusions, and questions stated at the beginning or end of the text. Such skimming will help you to obtain quickly a general idea of the text. You will have found the core ideas around which the study will be developed. Robinson suggests that students need to look at merely the headings at first and then guess what the lesson is about. Otherwise too much reading is likely to be done before learning how to survey.

QUESTION   If you have formulated a question in your mind, you will probably develop curiosity, purposeful direction, and increased comprehension in the material to be read. Therefore, you should convert the first major heading into a question. (If the text contains no major headings, use those found at the beginning or end of the chapter, or formulate your own by lifting one question based on the main idea from each paragraph.) All questions should relate to the title and to your present bank of knowledge.

READ   Read for the specific purpose of answering the question. Think how the answer will appear; look for clues. In the active search for the answer, concentrate on the question. Try to relate all information to your present knowledge of the subject. People who read fiction often find it difficult to read textbooks. Different techniques are required for different kinds of materials. Fiction is read for fun; reading textbooks is work. To read a text efficiently you must know what you are looking for, look for it, and then organize your thinking on the topic you have been reading about.

RECITE   Answer the question in your own words, not the author's. There are several ways of testing yourself: marginal notes, outlining, note-taking on paper, responding aloud, and others. Perhaps the least profitable method of recitation is underlining entire sentences in the text. Some students might find it sufficient to mentally review answers to questions but it is probably better to write the answers or to say them aloud to yourself or to someone else. The greater the number of senses used in study, the more effective it is. When you write notes you are provided with visual and kinesthetic cues as well as the verbal imagery from thinking about it. Orally reciting answers helps you test your ability to verbalize what you have learned in a way that you do not get from recitation to yourself.

    According to Robinson these written notes should be brief rather than the lengthy note-taking in which all details are copied from the book. You should follow three rules in writing notes: (1) write no notes until a section under a specific heading is read, (2) jot down notes from memory and not from the book, and (3) notes should be in your own words and should be very brief—no more than a word or phrase.

REPEAT   Repeat the foregoing steps Q, R, and R for each section of the text. This is done by converting each major heading into a question, reading to answer that question, and reciting the answer.

REVIEW   Go over the major items which were highlighted in the recitation and try to integrate newly acquired ideas into your present knowledge. Try to recall each major point and all its subpoints. Both immediate (following the assignment) and delayed (preparing for an exam) review is recommended.

Either of these techniques should help you improve your study skills. They should help you to develop a plan for study so that you can accomplish more in less time.

Taking an Essay Examination

Essay questions emphasize the ability to understand, organize, and recall information. They may require you to compare, summarize, generalize, evaluate, and draw conclusions. You have great latitude in which to discuss and qualify your responses. Essay examinations provide an opportunity for you to show the depth and breadth of your knowledge and also to demonstrate your ability to communicate in written form your ideas to other people. As we have previously indicated, while studying you should make a list of possible test questions and answer them.

Other suggestions for essay exams are:

1. *Survey the examination before you begin writing and estimate the time you can devote to each question.* This can keep you from losing track of time if it is a timed test.

2. *Answer the questions that you know best first.* This not only enhances your self-confidence but may also help you think of answers to the more difficult questions.

3. *When you start to answer a question, jot down the point which you want to include in your response.* This can be done on scrap paper or on the margins of your test paper. Jotting down important points keeps you from omitting them and also helps you to organize your discussion around these points.

4. *Write neatly and legibly.* Also outline answers, indent,

and number important points. Although most teachers are fair and impartial, they are also human. This means that they prefer to grade a neat paper rather than a messy or illegible one. Essay examinations have a tendency to be competitive and to be compared, either intentionally or unintentionally, with others in the class.

Taking Multiple-Choice Exams

Make sure that you understand the instructions. You should be clear as to how to indicate the correct answer and whether more than one alternative may be correct. You should also inquire whether or not you will be penalized for guessing when you are not sure of an answer. Specific suggestions for multiple-choice tests include the following.

1. *Go through the test and answer all the items to which you feel you know the correct answer.* This keeps you from spending too much time on difficult items. It may also build your confidence by responding to easier items first.

2. *Go through the test a second time and answer any items that now seem obvious.* You may have answered another question that gives you a clue to this one.

3. *Study the items you do not know and see what alternatives can be eliminated.* Alternatives that do not fit grammatically with the stem are not usually correct. Ridiculous alternatives can be eliminated. On a four-choice item you can increase your chances of getting it right by chance from 25 percent to 33 percent simply by eliminating one alternative. If you can narrow the answer to one of two alternatives you have a fifty-fifty chance of being correct.

4. *Having eliminated as many alternatives as possible, choose what you consider to be the best remaining answer.* This procedure is more systematic and productive than simply guessing.

5. *If you do not know the correct answer and cannot eliminate a single alternative take the second or third alternative.* They are slightly more likely to be correct than the first or last.

6. *If you are penalized for guessing, leave the item blank*

unless you can limit your response to one of two alternatives. Your adjusted score will probably be higher when you omit the items that you do not know than when you guess at the answer.

7. *When finished check your paper carefully.* Make sure you haven't inadvertently omitted any items, or failed to make erasures when you have changed responses.

Learning from Exam Mistakes

Evaluating exam mistakes can be a useful study guide. Typically, mistakes come in two forms—fact errors and concept errors (Elliot, 1966). Fact errors usually result from faulty recall or from overlooking material during study. Concept errors are more complex but generally stem from a lack of understanding of the material, and in this case, one is likely to confuse facts in a test situation.

To benefit from your test errors, evaluate the mistakes. Are they primarily factual or conceptual? If they are factual, pay closer attention to the material and cover it more thoroughly. On the other hand, if your mistakes are conceptual, you probably did not understand the material to begin with. While studying, explain the material in your own words. Ask yourself hypothetical questions and answer the questions without referring to the text or notes. For a more complete understanding, relate the concepts to daily happenings or give examples which apply to the concept. Learning from one's mistakes is one of the oldest methods for increasing one's understanding. Unfortunately, it is often overlooked. When taken into consideration, it provides insight into the weaknesses in one's study habits.

Those who are successful in their school work are often those who achieve greater success in later life than those who are not successful in school. To begin working toward being a more effective student, recognize the three goals of a college student. The short range goal is the test; the intermediate goal is the course; and the long range goal is to graduate (Moor, 1970). Take one goal at a time, for simplicity's sake and a greater degree of success than otherwise.

If you follow the suggestions contained in this chapter, there is little doubt that your academic performance will greatly improve. Your performance in other areas (dating, athletics, and so on) may also improve because of your ability to budget your time and use it wisely; the reduced anxiety about academics gives you increased energy for other activities.

7/Control of Drinking Behavior: It makes me sick to think about it

Drinking behavior, including alcohol abuse, is learned behavior and, therefore, subject to modification through principles and procedures discussed throughout this book. The material contained in this chapter is designed not for the skid-row resident but for the person who feels that alcohol consumption is becoming a problem and desires to exert greater control over his or her drinking behavior.

What are some of the consequences that seem to strengthen drinking behavior? Sobell and Sobell (1973) feel that the degree of excessive consumption of alcohol is a function of stress reduction. They list three potential reinforcers for drinking under stress: (1) alcohol is a sedative—the physiological component of stress can be reduced by drinking, (2) excessive drinking can lead to physical debilitation and subsequent removal from an unpleasant situation, and (3) intoxication can provide one with an excuse for otherwise unacceptable behavior. Flirtations and aggressive or sexual behavior may be excused on the grounds of intoxication. The reinforcement value of these behaviors plus reduced chastisement serve to strengthen drinking behaviors. Other reasons for drinking include peer pressures and lowered inhibitions. Many reinforcers are available to strengthen behavior that is highly detrimental to one's best interests.

Drinking behavior can be modified through stimulus control and through altering the consequences of this behavior. Before developing a program with specific recommendations, let us now review some of the work that has been and is continuing to be done in the treatment of alcoholism.

Therapeutic Approaches Based on Aversive Conditioning

Aversive conditioning is based on the classical conditioning paradigm as developed by Pavlov. Early attempts at treatment of alcoholism involved the use of electric shock as the unconditioned stimulus and the presence of liquor as the conditioned stimulus. Later nausea-inducing agents such as emetine and apomorphine were substituted for electric shock as the unconditioned stimulus. Voegtlin and Lemere (1942) were somewhat successful in using a variation of this procedure. Their procedure was as follows: The patient is placed in a soundproof room in which the lighting is subdued except for the array of liquors, spotlighted so as to attract the patient's maximum attention. To the patient's arm chair is attached a large vomiting bowl. After being made comfortable, he is given an injection containing a mixture of emetine hydrochloride (to induce nausea and vomiting), ephedrine (to combat any possible fall in blood pressure), and pilocarpine (to produce sweating and salivation). He then drinks emetine dissolved in saline water followed shortly by alcohol. Under the circumstances the patient is on the verge of nausea and vomiting before he takes the alcohol. The additional gastric irritation of even a small drink produces nausea within less than a minute and vomiting usually follows. The idea is to have the patient associate consumption of alcohol with nausea.

Miller, Dvorak, and Turner (1960) used a modification of the Voegtlin procedure in groups of four with two physician participants. Each patient completed a series of ten daily sessions. In each group was a previously conditioned patient who performed dual roles: (1) to help instruct the novices in matters of routine and (2) by virtue of his low tolerance for the sight, taste, or smell of alcohol, to initiate and facilitate a kind of chain reaction of gagging, retching, and even vomiting among new members of the group. Each patient was encouraged to drink large amounts of tepid water to potentiate vomiting and obviate "dry heaves." They were instructed to sniff frequently at the beverage of their choice but only drink when gagging began. Of the twenty patients who underwent this technique none failed to acquire an excellent conditioned aversion to all forms of alcohol that were presented to them.

Raymond (1964) used apomorphine in an aversive conditioning paradigm skillfully constructed to ensure the maximum amount of conditioning together with the minimum rate of extinction. He first discussed with his patient the treatment and its rationale.

During the first few sessions careful determination was made of the "nausea time" and the minimum dosage of subcutaneous apomorphine required to induce the desired effect. It was then possible to time matters so that the patient begins to drink just before the first sign of nausea. Only small amounts of alcohol are given.

Raymond avoids the use of spotlights and jocularity and the atmosphere is one of quiet encouragement. Once nausea has passed, the patient is not permitted to drink. The small variety of alcoholic beverages employed includes the patient's favorite drink and—at least in the early stage—one to which he is ordinarily averse. During the postnausea stage, when the patient is usually drowsy, the hazards of alcohol are discussed with him and he is repeatedly told that it will henceforth be possible for him to live without alcohol.

This procedure is repeated for about ten days until there are indications that the patient is beginning to develop an effective aversion to alcohol. At this point, without any warning or explanations, the routine is changed. The patient is given his usual injection—but of saline solution instead of apomorphine. And, upon arrival in the treatment room, he finds various soft drinks among the alcoholic ones. When told to drink whatever he wishes, he invariably chooses a non-alcoholic one. At this point the atmosphere is immediately relaxed, conversation is encouraged and he is assured that he will in no way feel ill.

According to Raymond, the average length of treatment is about three weeks. The patient is then provided with antabuse and advised to take it regularly to guard against the possibility of the first drink. Antabuse is a drug which, when taken, causes one to become extremely nauseated after drinking alcohol. Its action is carefully explained to both the patient and any cooperating relative.

Cautela (1966) has developed a method whereby the subject is asked to *visualize* in detail both the pleasurable stimulation of the alcohol and the process of vomiting with all its unpleasant accoutrements. This method is called covert sensitization. The patient is first taught to relax and the principles and aims of the covert sensitization explained to him. Care is taken to ensure that the visualized vomiting occurs just before the patient "reaches" for the alcoholic drink but *after* he has seen it and has the desire to drink. The subject is also told to practice this procedure at home on a daily basis.

As Franks (1966) points out, this method offers several advantages over the more conventional aversive procedures: (1) the hazards of either electric shock or drugs are avoided, (2) no apparatus is necessary, (3) the technique is unpleasant for neither therapist nor attendants, and (4) it is easy for the patient to carry out self-treatment at home.

Covert Sensitization

Cautela (1967) treated an individual with a compulsion to overdrink using a covert conditioned stimulus (CS) and a covert unconditioned stimulus. Although an aversion therapy, it is applied without the use of instruments or machines, or any other kind of external aversive stimulus, and it utilizes certain subjective attributes most individuals possess innately, i.e., the abilities to relax and to visualize actions.

The procedure consists of a systematic progression through a series of steps in the following order:

1. The patient is told to lie down on a couch or sit in a chair, close his eyes and to relax, then indicate by raising his index finger when he has achieved complete relaxation without tension. Several sessions with the therapist may be needed before the patient learns to achieve deep muscle relaxation.
2. The patient is told he has not been able to stop drinking because drinking is a strong learned habit which he enjoys very much.
3. He is told to think of drinking as being associated with an unpleasant stimulus, such as vomit, because it will help him eliminate his drinking habit.
4. He is asked to visualize in sharp detail the drink he likes best. He raises his index finger to indicate he has the vision in mind.
5. He visualizes himself looking at the glass with his drink in it.
6. He visualizes holding the glass.
7. He visualizes moving the glass to his lips.
8. He is instructed to visualize that the glass is about to touch his lips and at the same time to think that his stomach is upset.
9. He visualizes that he starts to vomit. It rises into his throat, gags him; it goes into his mouth and nasal cavity. He is forced to let it pour out. He visualizes himself vomiting all over the floor. He is both sick and repulsive.
10. The therapist goes through the sequence with him again.
11. The patient visualizes the sequence several times by himself without prompting.
12. The patient is told to visualize the scene to the point of becoming nauseous. He again indicates with his index finger when he feels nauseous.
13. He is instructed to visualize that he is about to take a drink; his nausea increases.
14. He promptly puts the glass on the table. His nausea diminishes and he becomes calm and relaxed.

When the patient signals that he is responding to the

therapist's directions, the therapist asks him to visualize vomiting and feeling sick five more times, and five more visualizations of *not* taking the drink which is associated with feelings of calm and relaxation. Cautela alternated vomiting and calm trials. The patient is advised to practice the procedure once or more a day at home and to coincide the vision of vomiting or feeling of sickness with the moment he is about to drink or when he first tastes the liquor.

Cautela developed the process of covert sensitization in treating a twenty-nine-year-old nurse who suffered severely from pervasive anxiety complicated by alcoholism. Trembling made enjoyment in social situations difficult. About eight years prior to her therapy with Cautela, she started drinking in order to calm the tremor and to enjoy herself more in social situations. She claimed it helped her. As time went on she discovered that the liquor was losing its potency and that she had to drink more to obtain any benefit.

A desensitization technique was tried prior to her therapy with Cautela, but she could not transfer what she was taught to her real life situation. She was able to reduce her alcohol intake but she felt compelled to drink if she felt unsure of herself. Her anxiety was only reduced.

During initial sessions with the patient, Cautela discovered that she was anxious because she drank so much and also anxious when she did not drink. Apparently the acute anxiety (drive) experienced in social situations was reduced by the intake of alcohol which acted as a primary reinforcer. Her drinking habit had become so strong it had become difficult to overcome. He treated her successfully by the method of covert sensitization described above.

Covert sensitization is a specific treatment in the sense that should the person want to drink red wine but not white wine then he can take the treatment and have himself sensitized against white wine. His dislike for white wine does not generalize to other drinks nor to foods. Once a person is sensitized to one object then it is easier to sensitize him to other objects, however.

This procedure is called "covert" because it refers to the

fact that the undesirable stimulus (alcohol) and the aversive stimulus (vomit) are present only in the imagination of the patient. In sensitization the therapist develops in the patient an avoidance response to alcohol by causing it to be associated with sickness and vomit. As a brief history of the patient's case is taken, attention is paid to the characteristics of the drinking behavior. Cautela attempts to determine the following:

1. history of the drinking problem.
2. frequency of drinking.
3. place patient does his drinking.
4. what the patient drinks.
5. the conditions and cues that prevail prior to drinking.

If, for example, the patient prefers whiskey-drinking in a barroom then the therapist has the patient go through the sequence of visualizations in which he does his drinking in a bar.

Habit strength makes it advisable to consider whether the particular patient should visualize his commonly practiced drinking routine or whether he should visualize a drinking situation that occurs least often where habit strength would be weaker.

Cautela describes a stepwise procedure in administering covert sensitization: The patient visualizes himself walking into a bar. He decides to have a glass of whiskey. He walks toward the bar. As he comes nearer the bar a strange feeling starts in his stomach. He feels nauseous. Sour liquid regurgitates into his throat. He tries to swallow it but instead food begins to come up also. He reaches the bar and orders a glass of whiskey. As the drink is poured, stomach content rises into his mouth. He tries to swallow it. He reaches for the whiskey to wash the stuff back into his stomach. The patient visualizes touching the glass and as he does he vomits. He sees his vomit go all over his hand, into the whiskey, onto his suit, onto the bartender, onto the table, onto his friends, and it slops out onto the floor. He looks around and sees other customers watching. He sees himself vomiting more. He turns away from the whiskey and immediately starts to feel better. He runs out of the bar and feels even better. He feels wonderful as he gets out into the fresh air. Finally he visualizes himself happily going home and cleaning up.

The patient's practice at home accomplishes three important behavioral effects: (1) the patient gets additional reinforcement to that provided by the therapist; (2) he has a procedure under his control. He can apply the procedure whenever tempted to drink; and (3) his overall anxiety level is reduced.

Avant (1967) uses a technique similar to Cautela's covert sensitization. Like covert sensitization, it begins with a state of relaxation. Several therapeutic sessions are required to carry out the process. They are listed as follows:

1. The patient relaxes.
2. The patient is asked to tell about his drinking; when it began; how long he has imbibed; how he began; the drink he prefers; where he usually drinks; and whether he prefers to drink alone or not.
3. He then is told to breathe deeply and to imagine that he is breathing in fresh air and to have refreshing thoughts; and each time he exhales to imagine that disturbing thoughts and ideas are leaving him.
4. He is asked to imagine drinking scenes specifically prepared by the therapist. The patient imagines himself drinking whiskey and beer alternately in his basement, then in his living room, in a beer parlor, at a party, and lastly at a friend's house. In these imaginary scenes he has a bottle of liquor from which he takes one or two drinks. The drinks invariably lead to change in taste, stomachache, sickness, and vomiting.

After the taste of liquor has become aversive to the subject, he imagines that the mere smell of the liquor which he is about to drink makes him sick. Finally he imagines himself becoming sick by the mere desire to drink.

During the final session the therapist teaches him to differentiate between beverages containing alcohol and soft drinks. The patient is asked to imagine he starts feeling ill whenever he wants to have a drink of liquor, but as soon as he thinks of soft drinks instead, he feels fine.

Avant's investigation consisted of twenty-six subjects who completed the procedure. Their age range was from nineteen years to fifty-five, with the majority in their thirties. The one female included was on drugs as well as being an alcoholic. The therapist treated eleven individually, and fifteen were treated in four groups. At the time he prepared his report, the former patients had abstained for periods ranging from eight to fifteen months. Suggestion, negative conditioning, and raising the patient's self-confidence were the factors Avant felt contributed most to the cure.

Ashem and Donner (1968) investigated the use of covert sensitization in the treatment of twenty-three volunteer male alcoholics hospitalized at the New Jersey Neuro-Psychiatric Institute, Princeton. All had seen psychiatrists and/or participated in Alcoholics Anonymous with no success.

The subjects were forty-five years old or under, of average intelligence, and free of any sign of gross psychological disturbance. They were available for a six-month follow-up study. Treatment for alcoholism was for six-weeks duration. During this period the patients took part in group psychotherapy and other activities of the treatment unit.

Ashem and Donner's procedure was to place the patients into three groups of nine people each matched in IQ, age, and drinking experience. In the first group the mean age was thirty-five, mean IQ 103, and the mean for years of drinking was eighteen. For the second group, mean age was thirty-nine, mean IQ 103, and mean for years of drinking was twenty. The mean age of the control group was thirty-six, the mean IQ was 101, and the mean for years of drinking was eighteen. A screening battery of tests and a questionnaire were administered. There was a control group who were not treated and not seen again. During treatment, one patient left the FCC group and two left the BCC group.

The control group lost one member. In the first session the therapist interviewed the test patients for fifteen minutes partly to find out the situations in which they drank and to briefly describe the treatment to them. They were told that the treatment was a learning experience in which their bad habit of drinking would be stopped. The patients were also told that a new technique had been developed that was successful in treating alcoholics; that they would be taught deep muscle relaxation which would be a help to them later whenever alcohol tempted them; and that the treatment would make drinking an extremely unpleasant experience.

During the second session, relaxation procedures were initiated. The patient relaxed for ten minutes. When the patient was relaxed on a cot the therapist presented him with a series of scenes, one at a time, and told him to imagine that each was happening at that moment. The patient imagines himself arriving home from work. He is sitting in his easy chair in his living room. He watches the news report on TV. He imagines seeing a can of beer on a table near him. He reaches for it. He imagines it in his hand. He opens it. He has a strong desire to drink it. He sees himself raising it to his mouth and as he raises it he imagines he tastes it. The can touches his lips. He imagines drinking some of the beer.

Just as soon as the patient signals that he is tasting the alcohol in his imagination the therapist presents the aversive stimulus. The patient is told that he feels very uncomfortable. He imagines the beer is warm and that his stomach feels nauseous. His throat feels uncomfortable. He imagines that he feels very sick and that the food from his last meal is beginning to turn over in his stomach. His beer begins to rise in his throat. He uncontrollably gags. He imagines he is very sick. Undigested food rises into his throat. It goes into his mouth and begins to force its way out. He vomits into his beer, all over his shirt. He feels disgusted. He imagines he can't stop. The sequence ends there. The patient is instructed to stop imagining and to clear his mind. During this session he repeats the scene three times.

During the third session, the patient gets five minutes of relaxation training and twenty minutes of aversive conditioning in which he repeats the above scene seven times. A similar procedure was repeated through a total of nine sessions. During the remaining sessions, the patient imagines for five minutes that he pushes away alcohol and relaxes. He also imagines a feeling of well-being and adequacy associated with sobriety.

Forty percent of the treated patients became nondrinkers. These findings lend additional support to the use of covert sensitization. Although covert sensitization alone would probably be inadequate to completely cure the confirmed alcoholic, the use of this procedure should be effective in helping anyone who is concerned with his or her drinking habits to reduce alcohol consumption. What's more, covert sensitization is another one of those techniques which you can learn to use yourself.

Recommendations

On the basis of the material presented in this chapter, the following suggestions should be helpful to you as you attempt to modify your pattern of drinking behavior.

1. Decide upon the particular kind of alcoholic beverage that you want to reduce or eliminate.
2. List the place or places (situations) in which drinking is most likely to occur.
3. Practice visualizing your having a drink in one of these places or situations. Make the image as vivid as possible by including the color, smell, and taste of the drink.
4. Learn to completely relax every muscle in your body. You may use the procedure described in Chapter 9.
5. While deeply relaxed, imagine yourself in a situation where you are about to imbibe. Let the image follow the sequence:
   a. You are looking at a glass or can with the drink in it.

b. You are picking up the glass.

c. You move the glass to your lips.

d. Your stomach feels upset.

e. You start to vomit. The puke blows from your mouth and nose.

f. Your glass and the surrounding area including your clothes are full of chunks of mucus, snot, and vomit.

g. You put the glass down, wash up, and feel much better.

6. Repeat this scene several times. Continue to practice it on a daily basis.

7. As you progress you may visualize this scene every time you even think about having a drink.

8. You can also imagine having a choice of an alcoholic or nonalcoholic beverage. You choose alcohol and feel nauseous; when you choose a nonalcoholic one you feel great.

9. Continue until you feel nauseous at the sight or thought of alcohol.

Please keep in mind that these procedures have been translated from the research of professional therapists interacting with subjects into this self-help book on behavior change. By all means seek professional assistance if these self-help procedures do not work for you.

8/Learn to Manage Your Time More Effectively: I'd love to, if I only had the time

Since time is life, it is your most valuable possession. What happens in time is irreversible; lost time is irreplaceable. What you are able to accomplish in life depends on how you manage your time. Time, like many other commodities, can be bought and sold; like money, it can be earned, saved, spent, wasted, and carefully managed. Since time, like life and money, is so precious it behooves each of us to use it as wisely as we can. This chapter is designed to help you learn to manage your time more effectively.

Time management involves careful planning, i.e., bringing the future into the present so that you can do something about it now. It involves making decisions about what is really important to you. Lakein (1973) recommends that a self-control program for managing time should begin with a statement of your lifetime goals. All of us have goals, of course, but unwritten goals may remain vague. There are differences between dreams and specific goals. Writing goals down on a piece of paper not only helps to make them more concrete and specific, but it should help you gain new perspective on what you really want out of life. A written list of goals should also increase your commitment to them and your determination to see that they are attained.

Establish Goals and Set Priorities

Lakein (1973) also suggests that you ask yourself questions such as: *"How would I like to spend the next three years?"* and *"If I had only six months to live, how would I spend that time?"* These kinds of questions should help you state shorter-range objectives and to discover if there are things that are important to you that you are not doing now.

The next step that Lakein recommends is to take the lifetime goals statement and select your top three goals labeling them A-1, A-2, and A-3. Do the same for your three-years list and your six-months list. From the nine goals that you have now screened from the list (three from each list) you now select the three most important goals from this list of nine. This constitutes your "Life Goals Statement." This statement is not static: it should be reviewed periodically, possibly at the beginning of the calendar year or on your birthday. The degree to which you grow and change over the years can be reflected in your statement of goals.

Once the A-goals have been identified you are now ready to make a list of those activities that will help you reach your goal. What things must you do in order to achieve the goals you have set? Then set priorities for these activities so that you can begin on the most important one immediately. This involves organizing and scheduling the activities necessary for goal attainment. Once again, Lakein suggests the ABC Priority System whereby an "A" is assigned to those activities having highest value, a "B" for medium value, and a "C" for low value. The activities given a value of "A" should take precedence over activities of lower value and importance. In setting up a time schedule for A-activities, they can be broken down into A-1, A-2, A-3, and so on. The value of these activities can change over time. What is today an A-activity may later be assigned a value of B or C. It depends on the immediacy of the goal and its relationship to other goals.

Let's see how this priority system might work in a given instance. Assume that one of the top goals of a married couple is improving their relationship and that this requires that they spend more time together. A-activities designed to provide more time together might include a trip or vacation, eating breakfast and dinner together, developing new hobbies, interests or other leisure-time activities, and so on. A value of A-1 might be assigned to eating meals together, A-2 to planning a vacation, and A-3 to developing new hobbies and interests. Priority is given to eating meals together and scheduling activities which will permit this. Once this pattern is established, eating together may drop to a lower priority. Obviously, planning for a vacation would be dropped from the hierarchy of activities when it is completed. The long-range goal of improving relations might remain important but different activities would be appropriate to the goal at different times. Some of life's goals and certainly the activities which increase the probability of their attainment need frequent revision.

It is also helpful to arrange daily schedules into a system of ABC priorities. Many highly efficient people plan their daily schedule and list activities to be completed on the preceding evening. Lakein believes it is a good idea to list more activities than you may get completed so long as you complete all of the A-items on the list. In planning a daily schedule of activities a Master Planning Schedule should be helpful. (See Figure 8.1.)

The planning schedule has the normal working day broken into blocks of one hour each. You may prefer blocks of time that are more suited to your particular schedule or routine. It is a good idea to go through each day of the schedule blocking out the time periods in which you have a continuing or constant schedule such as getting up, dressing, and eating breakfast. If you are a student you should cross out the time periods when you have scheduled classes, meetings, and so on. Housewives may have a set time for doing the laundry, cooking, or shopping. If so, these allotted time periods should be crossed off. Figure 8.2 shows the hypothetical schedule of a student for a particular day.

You will note that a student with the schedule for Wednesday has a free hour between 10:00 and 11:00 A.M., an unscheduled block from 2:00 to 6:00 P.M. and more time after

Figure 8.1. Master Planning Schedule for One Week

Time	Sun.	Mon.	Tue.	Wed.	Thur.	Fri.	Sat.
AM 7:00							
8:00							
9:00							
10:00							
11:00							
12:00							
PM 1:00							
2:00							
3:00							
4:00							
5:00							
6:00							
7:00							
8:00							
9:00							
10:00							
11:00							

9:00 P.M. This planning schedule shows a total of seven hours during the day that are flexible and open to a choice of activities.

By using a planning schedule similar to these it is possible each evening to make a list of the activities and tasks to be completed the following day, to arrange them in terms of their priority by assigning values of A, B, and C. The activities to be completed can then be matched with the schedule for that day. This schedule will really reveal how much unscheduled time is available. High priority activities can then be scheduled at the most appropriate times during the day. Some people try to carry their daily schedule and list of tasks to be accomplished around in their heads. Why waste your energy and clutter your mind with things that can be written down? When you write it down, you are freeing your mind for more creative pursuits.

Do not fill up every moment of your free time with scheduled activities. Too much rigidity and following demanding

Figure 8.2. Daily Schedule Derived from Master Planning Schedule

Daily Schedule
Wednesday

	Time	
	7:00	Get up, dress, eat, prepare for class
	8:00	History Class
AM	9:00	Physical Education
	10:00	
	11:00	Algebra
	12:00	Lunch
	1:00	Psychology
	2:00	
	3:00	
	4:00	
	5:00	
PM	6:00	Dinner
	7:00	Fraternity Meeting
	8:00	
	9:00	
	10:00	
	11:00	

schedules without any variation may create a feeling of regimentation which can be very unpleasant. If you have no free time you are bound to become nervous, frustrated, and tense. Lakein suggests that one reserve at least one hour per day of uncommitted time. There are always unexpected phone calls, people dropping by, and other unexpected events which can never be scheduled in advance. You should try to complete tasks of highest priority early in the day so that you will be less annoyed by unexpected interruptions and distractions which inevitably occur. A proper balance of scheduled and unscheduled time can prevent you from wasting time or using it unwisely; it will also help prevent the feeling that your life is under the control of the clock and that you really have no time to use as you choose. Later in the chapter we will see how free time may be used as a reinforcer for the completion of scheduled activities.

Some persons may be so overwhelmed with the things that need to be done that they feel helplessly inadequate to the task. Lakein suggests that you not worry about completing all the activities on your list each day. "It's not completing the list that counts," he says, "but making the best use of your time." Perhaps it is necessary to leave unfinished some of your C-activities. For many this failure to complete the list, regardless of the amount of work accomplished, is still uncomfortable. If you are one of those, Lakein recommends the 80/20 rule which states, "If all items are arranged in order of value, 80 percent of the value would come from only 20 percent of the items, while the remaining 20 percent of the value would come from 80 percent of the items" (p. 84). According to this rule, if you have a list of ten items, the completion of the two most important ones will yield about 80 percent of the value of having them all done. This idea suggests that the percent of the total value of having your scheduled tasks completed is much more important than the total number of tasks completed. Some people may spend their time on C-activities and realize very little value from their day's efforts.

There are many C-activities that you may get by without doing. They include such things as getting the car washed or watering the lawn just before a rain, mopping the floor just before the children come in from the mud, or straightening up your desk when you have a lot of paper work to do. C's that can be indefinitely deferred without harm are what Lakein calls CZ's. Some C's should deliberately be deferred to determine if they will become CZ's, i.e., activities that do not even need to be completed. Lakein makes notes on 3 x 5 inch index cards and puts them in a file folder labeled "Possible CZ's." Each month he looks through the folder, throws most of the cards in the trash, and congratulates himself on all the things he did not have to do.

This technique should prove especially helpful to all of us who have difficulty keeping up with paperwork. Many people pile all their current mail including bills, announcements of sales, magazine subscription notices, and letters from friends in the same drawer or container. When they go to pay a bill or answer a letter they find that other bills are past due, magazine subscriptions have lapsed, and the big sales are over. It is much better to use a file box with separate compartments or folders with such labels as bills, recipes, letters, coming events, and so on. This simple procedure not only saves time but also prevents you from neglecting some high-priority and very necessary activities.

The Special Problem of Procrastination: A Case Report

All of us have postponed tasks that were unpleasant or that we felt somewhat inadequate to perform, i.e., we are prone to procrastinate. Procrastination is usually at the root of poor time management. Following is a detailed report of the problems a graduate student (Janice) had with writing term papers. She chose to develop a plan for helping her overcome her special kind of procrastination. Here is her account of how she dealt with her problems.

"The first term-paper assignment encountered by me occurred in the first quarter of graduate school. I procrastinated, as was my usual pattern with short papers, but this time I completed the paper only after much anxiety and last-minute rush; I also turned it in two days late. During the spring quarter, I took three courses, each of which required a major writing project. As a result of poor time-management and more anxiety than I was able to work under, only one of these assignments was completed. I presently have two incompletes for not finishing the other papers. The satisfaction which came from completing the very large paper was marred by my feelings of disappointment, guilt, and depression over not having completed the assignments for the other two courses. Thus many negative associations accompany my thoughts of having to write a paper.

"My first step was to review the research regarding procrastination in an attempt to get ideas for setting up a program to combat my tendency for procrastination. From my review I learned that a well-trained, accurate observer is a must in the recording of any kind of behavior. A very useful and accurate way of recording thinking behavior is for the observer-subject to recognize that his or her thoughts are self-verbalization. Ellis (1973), in the development of his rational-emotive therapy (RET), says that the basis of humankind's emotional disturbances and the resulting ineffective behavior is illogical thinking or the failure to use the ability to think and reason logically. Man determines his emotional condition by the way he intervenes between the environmental input and his emotions. Ellis believes that man is biologically and sociologically prone to an illogical thinking process. This illogical thought occurs in the form of self-verbalization. A person begins learning these illogical self-verbalizations from his experiences; once these illogical thoughts are learned, they tend to be self-maintaining because of their association with the recurring life events from which they first originated; also they tend to generalize easily to new situations. Ellis defines a response repertoire consisting of illogical responses to the whole range of stimuli or life events. Any illogical self-verbalization a person makes will be basically identical to one of these eleven illogical thoughts. These responses have been learned early in life in the socialization process. The person learns to make unrealistic demands upon himself or unrealistic evaluations of his behavior because he has developed an internally verbalized set of assumptions about life. Ellis points out that a person feels and acts according to how he is thinking. His statement of illogical assumptions is paraphrased as follows:

1. Everyone with whom I come in contact must like me and approve what I do.

2. If I do not excel in everything I try to do I am not a worthy person.
3. Some people are bad, wicked, or villainous and should be blamed and/or punished for their actions.
4. It is terrible when things are not as I want them to be.
5. Unhappiness is caused by external circumstances and I have no control over it.
6. Dangerous or fearsome things are causes for great concern and I must continually be aware of their possibility.
7. It is easier to avoid than face certain difficulties and responsibilities.
8. I should be dependent on others and need someone stronger than myself to rely on.
9. My present behavior is caused by past experiences and events and there is nothing I can do to change it.
10. There is always a right or perfect solution to every problem, and it must be found or the results will be catastrophic.

"Homme (1965) also makes a similar observation that covert operants closely approximate overt behavior. The problem then is to break this self-maintaining pattern of negative self-verbalization. Ellis believes this can be accomplished by learning to make new responses to replace the old irrational responses. One learns to use his potential for being rational and thus learn new verbalizations which are substituted for the old irrational ones. Thus a new association is formed, resulting in behavior which is not subject to illogical evaluation and which in turn produces a happier individual. Ellis's principle of replacing an old self-verbalization with a new one makes for reinforcement of the new because the new response is pain-reducing; it is not self-accusing and self-degrading like the old illogical verbalizations.

"Although using one's capacity for rational thought can be reinforcing in that it reduces the pain which accompanied the old illogical self-verbalization, there remains the problem of a life-long habit which must be unlearned. It would seem feasible to aid the process of unlearning the old habit and learning the new by reinforcing the new behavior covertly as well as overtly. Homme suggests the application of Premack's principle here. Using Homme's terminology, the principle is that a highly preferred behavior will reinforce a less preferred behavior when the opportunity to engage in the preferred activity is made contingent upon the occurrence of the less preferred behavior. It is essential that the less preferred behavior occur first.

"In using coverants—or thoughts that will guide our behavior—we ourselves must be at the controls. In planning this program of self-control, then, it is necessary to first decide what the consequences will be for self-management. Care must be taken to maintain the controlling response in such a way that the desired behavior will continue to increase in frequency. It is very easy for extinction of the new response to occur if it is not reinforced frequently either covertly or overtly. In writing a paper it would be important to reinforce the accomplishment of small portions of the writing at frequent intervals. At times when writing seems to be at a standstill, one could apply Homme's suggestion of thinking of the aversive consequences of not writing or not finishing the paper, then think of the positive consequences of writing and finishing the paper. It would seem, in the case of one who panics easily and tends to readily generate negative thoughts, that the positive coverant would be most appropriate.

"Homme points out that positive thinking is a special case of coverant control. He suggests an exercise by which one can become aware of his own drastic mood swings by simply making a list of negative thoughts and dwelling on these for a specified period of time. To contrast the resultant mood, he then suggests the same exercise using a positive approach.

"Johnson (1971) points out that desirable behavior may be increased rapidly using the procedure, but there is the tendency in some to retain negative coverants (as Ellis also points out) and eventually allow these to disrupt the desired behavior. This can happen when one is writing a paper and is suddenly beset with the panic that time is running out, or that the paper is not good; the result may be immobilization and inability to engage in the target behavior of writing. When this happens, Johnson suggests the use of index cards, each printed with a positive verbalization which one is to rehearse before engaging in some designated highly preferred behavior. In place of the depressive thoughts then, the positive verbalizations are substituted, and the subject learns how not to fall prey to a state of depressed immobility.

"The purpose of the present program, then, is to immediately implement a plan which will change the build-up of negative emotions and failure to write into a drive to complete all assignments due this quarter while maintaining a healthy mental attitude. (In light of the amount of work to be done and the short amount of time, the two—mental attitude and work—cannot actually be separated; one is dependent upon the other.) This plan involved the substitute of positive self-verbalizations, the identification of barriers to writing, and the use of reinforcers in the form of preferred activities to strengthen the writing responses and to affirm overtly the newly learned covert reinforcing responses.

"The plan of attack was (1) to identify preferred activities and reinforcers in order to apply the Premack principle with covert as well as overt behaviors; (2) to become more aware of negative emotional states by recognizing that these emotional states are a form of verbalizing to self, and to identify and list the actual negative verbalizations directed toward self; (3) to list positive self-verbalizations which are the opposite of the negative self-verbalizations so that these new verbalizations become responses to the cues that originally elicited the negative responses; (4) to recognize success as it occurs in small increments and to reward covertly and overtly these small steps toward the larger goal; (5) read Ellis's list of illogical assumptions, restate them logically and apply to my thought-response patterns."

Identify Highly Preferred Activities

"I observed a number of high probability behaviors which

occur during study and writing periods. They are:
Go to kitchen
  raid refrigerator
  eat cookies
  get something to drink
Straighten up study area
Clean house
  vacuum
  mop
  dust
  (these are HPB's only when I'm supposed to be study-
  ing or writing)
Take a bath
Wash clothes
Talk on phone
Play with dogs
Play the piano
Take a nap

When I am studying and working on assignments which require reading, however, it is observed that these highly preferred activities occur *after* periods of concentrated and intense study. Thus these activities are being used to reinforce the desired study behavior. This sequence was not consciously planned by me, but it is noted that this habit probably originated early in the formation of good study habits. Good study habits are being maintained through intrinsic enjoyment of the task as well as through overt reinforcement provided by these highly preferred activities (HPA). These HPAs seem to be an outward confirmation of the internal feeling of satisfaction and self-verbalization: 'You've worked hard and done a good job; you deserve to take a break for a few minutes. Just look at all you have accomplished, and so on.'

"Completing reading assignments has not been a problem during my time in graduate school. There are two possible reasons: (1) enjoyment of reading was learned as a child; (2) frequent tests maintain the incentive to keep up with reading assignments. The opposite effects are operating in writing assignments, however; and it is interesting to observe that here the HPAs serve a very different function and conform to a very different sequence pattern from that of the reading.

"In observing baseline behavior associated with a writing assignment it is noticed that the same HPAs, which served a reinforcing function to the reading are now being used as avoidance tactics. The HPAs are occurring *before* the writing occurred, thus reinforcing the nonwriting behavior. Homme points out that in the application of the Premack principle the HPAs must *follow* the behavior which is to be strengthened. Avoidance HPAs must be delayed until *after* writing; then they will serve to reinforce writing."

Change Negative Emotional States to Positive

"I recorded a sequence of negative self-verbalizations which occurred when writing seemed to be blocked. This negative thinking not only kept writing from taking place but also interrupted the thinking and mental organization that are prerequisites to writing. The list of negative self-verbalizations indicate covert processes associated with not getting down to the job of writing. These verbalizations may begin with specific task-related statements and accusations; but, if allowed to continue, they generalize to a much broader area and tend to create a negative outlook on everything. The mood shift which accompanies these verbalizations reaches the point of rendering me physically and psychologically depleted.

"I made a list of these negative self-verbalizations and substituted a positive statement for each negative statement. They are as follows:

Negative self-verbalizations

1. You've wasted three hours.
2. You're tired.
3. You can't possibly get it all done now.
4. You're getting depressed.
5. You might as well give up and go to sleep.

6. You guess you'll just have to take another incomplete.
7. You're so slow.
8. Your ideas are stupid.
9. You're getting mad at your husband.
10. Just think of all you have to do before Sunday.
11. You have seven tests next week.
12. You have four final exams next week. When are you going to have time to study?
13. You have an oral presentation for next Thursday.
14. You have company coming for Sunday and Monday; won't be able to study while they are here.
15. You are probably going to blow your 4.0 grade-point average and that would be the worst thing in the world, because then you probably won't get accepted into the doctoral program at U.T. and then your whole life will be ruined.
16. You're probably too stupid to be in graduate school anyhow.
17. If you have this much trouble writing papers, you shouldn't think about going into a doctoral program.

Positive self-verbalizations—New Response to Old (anxiety producing) Stimuli

1. You've worked hard all day. You deserve a few hours off.
2. You will feel better after taking a break.
3. You've scheduled your time well. You'll get it done.
4. Stay happy.
5. You're making progress.
6. You will have all your assignments finished this time because of good self-management.
7. You're moving right along.
8. You're coming up with some pretty good ideas.
9. You're feeling good about yourself and everybody.
10. Just look at all you've accomplished during the past five days.
11, 12, 13. You've kept up with your work. With some

good time management, you'll have time to study for tests and give your oral report.

14. You have company coming. That will be a good break from studying and writing.
15. I have good grades so far. I'll have good grades this quarter. It wouldn't be the worst thing in the world if I made a B.
16. You're doing well in graduate school.
17. You've made great strides toward overcoming your writing problem this quarter.

The positive verbalization was rehearsed until the negative feelings were diminished."

Recognize Success—Reward Small Steps

"I have previously stated that I did not acknowledge anything but completion of the paper as success. With a large project, such as a term paper, I found this to be unrealistic. Completion of a small section or writing for a given short time interval should be rewarded by positive self-verbalizations, allowing me to experience a feeling of achievement in moving toward the ultimate goal. In terms of this task I recognized that the feeling of accomplishment is the most effective reinforcer. My overt reinforcers were as follows:

Kitchen: Lay in a store of concrete reinforcers
    diet colas
    peaches
    apples
    iced tea
Change of location
    move from living room to kitchen to write
Change of activity (brief intermission after a period of writing)
    Get a drink of water
    Snack
    Wash face
    Eat lunch
    Pet dogs

Rest—sit on patio five minutes
Do small household chore—make bed, put in load of wash
Water plants
Play piano
Make telephone call
Shift from writing to studying or reading in another subject area."

A Rational Look at Life in General

"Perfectionism is at the root of most evils. I realized that I was trying to come up with perfect wording before writing anything down. It was often at this point (searching for right words) that the urge to procrastinate was overwhelming. I observed that many of the negative self-verbalizations contain illogical expectations and assumptions and imply an irrational attitude toward self. To prevent this I attached a copy of Ellis's illogical assumptions to the dashboard of the car so that I could rehearse and reverbalize these while driving to and from school. These were memorized and available for application in any frustrating experience."

Result

"Formulating a plan to take positive action against a problem was in itself an incentive to attitude change. I am amazed at the difference it makes to arrange work into small segments and to reward the completion of each part. The outline I made was more detailed than usual, and this was helpful. After completing the outline for the paper, I next started on the review of the literature on my topic, because I dreaded this part the most. After this was finished the rest was easy. Also during the time this paper was in process I have also written two smaller papers, given two major oral reports, and taken five tests, one of which was a final exam. The recording of the completion of each task or subtask on the calendar was probably the most reinforcing and encouraging feature. The calendar is readily visible in the kitchen and serves as a reminder that progress is being made; the feeling of satisfaction associated with this is a crucial factor in maintaining my movement toward the ultimate goal of being completely finished with all work by Friday, August 8. The ultimate reward is leaving on vacation Friday evening. As I wind up this paper, perhaps the best feeling I have is that my self-management program (the first I have tried, other than brute willpower) has been successful. When I leave on vacation Friday I can leave with a sense of completeness which was so strikingly absent at the end of spring quarter. The next self-management program will be initiated as soon as I return from vacation; the new program will involve finishing the two papers from spring quarter and removing the incompletes. Most important to me is that I feel that I can use what I have learned here in my future graduate work. This has broken what I feel may have been the beginning of a pattern of not getting work finished by the end of the quarter; thus I consider it a most valuable learning experience."

Guidelines for Managing Time More Effectively

Based on material presented in this chapter, the following guidelines should help you to manage your time more effectively:

1. Make a list of the most important goals in your life.
2. Make a list of the activities necessary to help you reach these goals.
3. Arrange this list of activities in a hierarchy of A, B, and C, with A, activities being most important.
4. Complete your A, activities before the B, and C, activities.
5. Make a master plan similar to the one previously described which will indicate periods of unscheduled time each day.
6. Make a list of activities to be completed each day.
7. Schedule these activities in the unscheduled time periods on your planning schedule.

8. In scheduling your activities allow for interruptions and have a tentative alternate schedule which you can fall back on if original plans do not materialize.
9. Leave at least one hour of each day free so that you do not get the feeling that your life is completely under the control of the clock.
10. Do not be upset if you do not complete all of your C-activities. Time may show that some of them can go undone with no negative residual effect.
11. Break large tasks down into smaller steps.
12. Make rewards contingent upon the completion of a step toward the goal.
13. Develop an awareness of the negative self-talk that is occurring when you are having difficulty getting tasks accomplished.
14. Make a list of the negative statements and a list of positive statements which are appropriate for the same situations or conditions.
15. Substitute positive self-verbalizations for the negative statements.
16. Review Ellis's list of illogical assumptions; check those that apply to you; and substitute more logical and rational assumptions. Doing this should also help you decide what goals are really important to you and which activities should be completed first.

9/Coping with Anxiety and Tension: Hanging loose in an uptight world

Although the times we live in have sometimes been referred to as the "age of anxiety," people in all ages have probably had their share of emotional turmoil. Anxiety, fear, worry, and depression seem to be permanent emotions in human history. Anxiety has been defined as the "apprehension which an individual experiences when his personality is threatened" (Carrol, 1969). The man on the street has his own terms for anxiety, including fear, worry, nervousness, nervous tension, having the jitters, and being shaken up.

Anxiety may be objective or nonobjective depending on whether it seems commensurate with the threat imposed by a situation. Objective anxiety implies that the source of danger is actually known and that the arousal is proportional to the explicit threat. This kind of arousal is frequently referred to as "normal" anxiety or fear. If you have not studied for an important examination or the doctor tells you that you need major surgery, you have reason to be anxious about the outcome. All of us experience anxiety at one time or another and some anxiety is constructive in that it stimulates us to give our best effort or to find new ways of dealing with a threat or challenge.

Anxiety is considered nonobjective if it is not commensurate with the threat involved or if its source is vague or unknown. Many people are apprehensive about high places, flying in an airplane, driving on mountain roads, and so on, and are driven to avoid these situations at all costs. There are many other situations which involve little danger at all and which for no clearly discernable reason produce feelings of anxiety. These situations can include speaking before an audience, riding in an elevator, or seeing a mouse run across a floor. Nonobjective anxiety is sometimes referred to as neurotic or phobic.

Another way of classifying anxiety is situational or general. Situational anxiety occurs only under particular circumstances which many people learn to recognize and avoid. Some of us, for example, find contact with the opposite sex upsetting and tend to avoid dating, dancing, and so on. General anxiety on the other hand, rather than being associated with a particular situation, is experienced in many different sets of circumstances. Some people never seem to be able to relax at all. Their anxiety is unattached to specific circumstances but seems to be a permanent part of their personality makeup. This kind of anxiety is often called "free-floating" anxiety because it cannot be attached to specific cues.

Regardless of how we classify anxiety, it appears to be both an emotional and a behavioral reaction subject to reduction or elimination via systematic application of learning principles. You should be able to control your anxiety level just as surely as you can learn to reduce your eating or smoking.

Learning to Relax

Muscle tension is commonly associated with anxiety. Many symptoms of anxiety such as headaches, perspiration, butterflies in the stomach, shortness of breath, and rapid heartbeat seem to be preceded or accompanied by muscle tension. On the premise that muscle tension is related to anxiety and that one will experience anxiety reduction if the muscles can be made to relax, the goal of anxiety management is to learn to associate relaxation with the cues that were once anxiety-provoking. One method for effecting such a state of muscle relaxation involves the successive tensing and relaxation of voluntary muscles in an orderly sequence until all the main muscle groups of the body are relaxed. The procedure described below is similar to that recommended by Rimm and Masters (1974) but has been modified. You should be able to relax yourself by following these instructions:

Get as comfortable as possible making sure that all clothing is loosened. Your legs should not be crossed and all parts of your body should be supported by the chair. Assume a reclining position if desired. Take a deep breath and slowly let it out.

Now raise your arms and extend them in front of you and make a fist with both your hands, really hard, really hard. Do it really hard and notice the feeling of discomfort and tension which you are feeling in your hands and fingers. Hold your hands and fingers tense for about ten seconds. Now let your hands fall as if they were made of lead. Be sure that they fall into your lap rather than being placed in your lap. Now completely relax.

Repeat this procedure and notice how the tension and discomfort are draining from your hands. Notice how warm and pleasant your hands now feel in comparison to when you were tensing.

Be sure to tense only the muscles you are told to tense and not other muscle groups. For example, while tensing your hands do not tighten your stomach muscles or grit your teeth.

Extend your arms as before but this time bend your fingers backward, the opposite of making a fist. Notice the discomfort and the tension. Again be sure not to tighten other muscles in the body. Hold for ten seconds and then let your arms fall as before. Notice how relaxed your hands feel.

You are now ready to relax the rest of your body. Let's tense and relax other muscle groups by tensing for ten seconds, noticing the discomfort, and then completely relaxing and observing how loose you feel.

Tense the biceps. Relax. Tense the triceps. Relax.

With the shoulders straight, turn your head slowly to the right just as far as you can. Relax. With the shoulders straight, turn your head slowly to the left as far as you can. Relax.

Bring your head slowly forward until the chin digs into your chest. Relax. Open your mouth as wide as possible. Relax. Purse your lips in an exaggerated pout. Relax.

With your mouth open extend the tongue as far outward as you possibly can. Relax (allowing your tongue to return to a comfortable position in your mouth). Put your tongue back into the throat as far as possible. Relax.

Press your tongue against the roof of your mouth as hard as you can. Relax. Press the tongue into the floor of your mouth as hard as possible. Relax.

Open the eyes as wide as possible until your brow is visibly furrowed. Relax. Close your eyes as hard as you can. Relax by opening your eyes only slightly but not enough to see anything.

Take as deep a breath as you can, making several efforts to inhale even more deeply. Relax and resume normal, smooth, comfortable breathing. Exhale every drop of air out of your lungs and hold for about five seconds. Relax and resume normal, regular breathing.

Push your trunk forward and arch your entire back. Do this very slowly and stop if you feel pain. Relax.

Tense the muscles off your buttocks so that your midsection is slightly raised. Relax. Lower your midsection by digging your buttocks into the seat of the chair. Relax.

Extend your legs so that they are about six inches above the floor. Relax and let your legs fall to the floor. Now with legs extended dig your heels into the floor. Relax.

Suck in your stomach as if you are trying to make it touch the backbone. Relax until every muscle fiber in your stomach is free of tension. Extend the stomach as if you are preparing to receive a punch in the abdomen. Relax.

With legs extended on the floor bend your feet and toes toward you so that they point toward your head. Relax. Now bend feet in the opposite direction. Relax. (Should you experience cramps during this process, immediately relax and shake the muscles loose.)

With your legs supported and feet relaxed dig the toes into the bottom of your shoes. Relax. Now bend the toes in the opposite direction so that they touch the toe area of the top of your shoe. Relax.

Now completely relax your whole body so that you feel like a bowl of jello. Experience the warm, comfortable sensation that engulfs your entire body.

There will probably be occasions when you experience anxiety and it is not practical to go through the entire sequence outlined above (when in the company of strangers, speaking before a group, and so on). A shorter method of achieving relaxation is suggested by Bugg (1972)—a three-step technique for producing quick relaxation: (1) Take in a deep breath and quickly exhale. (2) Tell yourself to relax. (3) Think of something very pleasant and focus on it for a few seconds. You are now ready to redirect your attention to the task at hand. If anxiety continues, repeat the three steps. This technique is so simple that it can be used very frequently in either real or imagined situations.

Systematic Self-Desensitization

Although desensitization was developed for use as a clinical technique to be used by psychiatrists and clinical psychologists, there are indications that it can be used effectively as a self-modification procedure. Morris and Thomas (1973) had their patients use self-administered desensitization in their home environment. In three to ten weeks all patients reported successful completion of each hierarchy, and significant reduction in anxiety levels. There appears to be no harm in the use of this method even if it does not reduce anxiety. Watson and Tharp (1972) recommend that it be discontinued if anxiety reduction is not relatively smooth or if an increase in anxiety is noted.

The first step in systematic self-desensitization is to

identify the stimuli or situations that provoke anxiety. You might have a fear of enclosed places, high places, making a speech in public, crowds, or snakes. It is not usually difficult to identify situations that produce fear or anxiety.

The next step consists of building a hierarchy of situations that elicit the unpleasant emotion. These situations can be listed and described on 3″ by 5″ index cards which are then arranged in order so that the most disturbing situation is at the bottom of the stack and the least disturbing at the top. There should probably be somewhere between ten and twenty scenes in the hierarchy. A student who experiences test anxiety might use a hierarchy such as this:

1. Studying for a test which is two weeks away.
2. Studying for a test one week away.
3. Talking with a friend about the forthcoming test.
4. Studying for the test two days before test day.
5. Reviewing on the night before the exam.
6. Walking toward the classroom to take the test.
7. Entering the examination room.
8. Sitting in the examination room listening to other students talk about the upcoming test.
9. Sitting in the examination room when the instructor enters with the tests under his arm.
10. The instructor hands you a test booklet and answer sheet.
11. You open the test and begin reading the questions and writing responses.

The third step in self-desensitization is to achieve deep muscle relaxation by using one of the procedures described earlier in the chapter.

Once you have constructed your hierarchy and have achieved deep relaxation you are ready for the fourth step, i.e., the process of desensitization. The best place to achieve desensitization is at the place you have used for practicing deep relaxation. Paul (1966) recommends that one follow this procedure:

While in a state of deep relaxation look at the first card

in your hierarchy. Try to imagine the scene or situation which provokes anxiety in complete and minute detail including colors, odors, facial expressions, what other people say, how you react, and so on. You may need to focus on only one component of the situation at a time such as specific sounds, textures, colors, and odors. Then you may add facial expressions, exact conversation or dialogue, and your emotional responses.

It is crucial that you attain a vivid mental image of each situation. Practice should help you to achieve a clear mental picture. Paul recommends that you check the vividness of an item by comparing it with your imagination of some scene you know and can clearly visualize, such as what it looks, feels, smells, and sounds like to be lying on your bed listening to the stereo. First visualize this scene in your room and then compare it with the imagined scene from your hierarchy. If the two are comparable you have achieved a clear mental image of the scene that makes you anxious.

For self-desensitization to be successful, Watson and Tharp (1972) suggest that you should be able to do three things: (1) produce a vivid image, (2) start the image at will, and (3) stop the image at will. If you are not able to attain any one of the above, desensitization should be discontinued. If and when you are successful in doing these three things, you imagine a scene from the hierarchy until you feel very comfortably relaxed while imagining it. When this is accomplished, repeat that item once more before moving up to the next item in your hierarchy. Be sure not to leave an item until you are completely desensitized to it, i.e., without anxiety. It is rare that you will desensitize yourself to more than two or three scenes in a single session. Some items may require several sessions for each scene.

The Desensitization Session

Paul (1966) suggests that each session last from fifteen to thirty minutes. When you are completely relaxed begin with the first item from the hierarchy. During later sessions begin with an item to which you are already desensitized. You should allow yourself approximately ten seconds per item and when you can repeat an item three times while remaining relaxed, you are ready for a new one. Between items just concentrate on being completely relaxed. It is very important that you not proceed through the hierarchy too rapidly.

If, while imagining a situation, the image fades or will not come clear or if your anxiety begins to increase or your relaxation decrease, you should immediately halt the scene and concentrate on relaxing yourself.

A Case Report: Normal Anxiety

One of my students was successful in reducing anxiety associated with her estranged husband. She was a twenty-one-year-old college student who, in the course of a separation and divorce, developed intense anxiety about anything involving her husband. Symptoms included anxiety feelings, nausea, and a feeling of panic.

She first listed several instances which had caused her to be upset with her husband, ranging from mild embarrassment to extreme fear. These were arranged into a hierarchy and several gaps were filled with intermediate scenes. One scene which detailed a pleasant encounter with her husband was placed at the first of the list which gave a total of twelve hierarchy scenes. A relaxation scene was also chosen and detailed. Each scene was typed on an index card. Her hierarchy was as follows:

Relaxation Scene

I'm sitting on the screen porch about eight at night, looking at the back yard and neighborhood, just thinking how quiet and peaceful it is. I especially notice the high pine trees, planted when mother was a little girl. They sway in the breeze and birds are singing. The cool breeze blows through the porch.

Anxiety Scene 1

I'm sitting with Steve on the steps in the amphitheater. It's my first quarter in college. We're talking about ourselves and school. It's a sunny afternoon, and I'm wearing my long orange skirt.

Scene 2

We go to a Christmas party at the Smiths' and Steve has several drinks. I ask him to slack off. He keeps on drinking, his eyes get noticeably bloodshot, and he behaves in a drunken manner. All of my neighbors and my parents' friends are there and see him in this condition.

Scene 3

We go to New Jersey and the first afternoon Steve heads straight for the liquor cabinet. He wants to experiment with mixing drinks, and begins opening all of my parents' liquor.

Scene 4

I ask him for a twenty-dollar loan to pay my tuition and he says no, that I am to pay all of my school expenses.

Scene 5

I change my work schedule so I can be off on Fridays and Steve and I can spend some time together. The first Friday we're both off I plan a big dinner and buy tickets to the movies. I get home from school at 3 o'clock but he isn't there. I wait until 7:00 and call John's. David says that John and Steve aren't there, they're at the Carousel drinking.

Scene 6

We're at the Christmas party at the Red Pig and Steve's getting high. He says I'm not drinking enough and calls me a party-pooper. Then he picks up my drink and tries to pour it down me. I keep my mouth shut, so it spills all over my clothes.

Scene 7

Spot, our dog, runs off through the Harrises' hedge and Steve goes after her. I hear her squeal several times, and she comes running back. I see him behind her, beating her with his belt.

Scene 8

We're at a party at Mac's and I've brought Ginger with us. Steve gets stoned and when it's time to leave, I suggest that Mac or I drive. He insists he's OK. I ask him to please let someone else drive and he suddenly gets extremely angry. He starts yelling and suddenly raises his arm to throw his keys at me, trying to hit me in the head, but turns at the last minute and throws them at the house, putting a dent in the wood door frame.

Scene 9

Joe and Connie Tolas come over to see us just after we've moved into the church, and Joe and Steve leave to get a beer. Five hours later they return, very drunk and very stoned. They've been to a fraternity party, and neither of them is wearing their wedding bands. Steve sits down in the community room and begins to vomit. I try to get him into our apartment, because if it becomes known that he's drinking we could get thrown out, but he's too sick. He finally gets into the apartment and has the dry heaves all night.

Scene 10

I get sick at work and have to go home, so I leave and tell Steve who's at the Carousel. I get home at 8:30, but Steve doesn't come in until midnight. Spot gets frightened and wets on the bed, so Steve throws her at the wall and makes me change the sheets. The urine soaks back up through from the mattress so Steve takes all the blankets and goes to the couch, leaving me to sleep in the wet bed under my bathrobe.

Scene 11

Steve comes in at 12:30 from the Carousel, drunk. He pulls a girl's billfold from his pocket and claims he doesn't know where it came from. He goes to the bedroom to call her, and I look in and see him going through his own wallet for her number. He has her number, and those of several other girls.

Scene 12

I tell Steve that Becky's coming to stay with me until he moves out, and he becomes very upset. He goes into the study where he keeps his rifles. I'm on the couch with Spot. Suddenly he slams his fist into the door and screams "You can't do this!" I start to scream "I hate you!" Then I realize that he is standing behind me, holding a gun. I'm scared and I hold onto Spot because I'm afraid that if she runs, he'll shoot her.

By relaxing and following each scene in the hierarchy with a visualization of the very pleasant scene, this young woman reported that she was relatively free of the anxiety associated with thoughts of her husband in a few weeks. She felt that more rapid progress would have been realized had it not been for the fact that her divorce proceedings occurred during this time. The sight of her husband at the trial produced some anxiety which tended to slow her progress but she was very pleased with the decreased anxiety following self-desensitization.

A Case Report: Excessive Anxiety

Another student reported success in reducing anxiety over tests through self-desensitization after learning to relax. She compiled a hierarchy of anxiety-provoking scenes related to taking tests. Her hierarchy is shown below:
1. Walking in the classroom for the daily lecture.
2. The professor announcing the date of the exam.

3. Reading the material that I know I shall be tested on in the future.
4. Taking notes in class that I know I will be tested on in the future.
5. Organizing my notes to study two nights before the exam.
6. Studying for the exam the night before it is to be given.
7. Reviewing my notes one hour before the exam.
8. Talking with friends the hour before the test, about what they have studied.
9. Walking into the classroom the day the exam is to be given.
10. Waiting for the exam to be handed out.
11. Seeing the first question.
12. Listening to students around me turn the page of the test when I am still at the beginning of the first page.
13. Only fifteen minutes left in the test period.
14. Everyone handing in their tests when I still have items to answer.

The day before she began desensitization she visualized this scene:

> I am lying on the beach. I can feel the warm sun on my face.
> I can smell the salt air. I can feel the sand between my toes.
> I can feel the warm breeze blowing through my hair. I am
> surrounded by miles of sandy beach and vast ocean.

Her description of the desensitization process continues. "I began by putting myself in a deep state of relaxation. (It should be noted that when I feel the least bit anxious or tense I immediately turn my thoughts to the neutral scene. Upon regaining total relaxation, I continue with the items in the hierarchy.) Next, I imagine as vividly as possible that I am walking into the classroom for the daily lecture (ten seconds). I then imagine myself lying on the beach. I can feel the warm sun on my face. I can feel the breeze blowing through my hair. I continue relaxing, enjoying the calm, soothing feelings associated with relaxation (twenty seconds). Now I imagine myself back in the classroom and the professor is announcing the date of the exam (ten seconds). I then turn to the scene on the beach, the warm sun on my face, the smell of the salt air, and the breeze blowing through my hair . . . letting myself relax further and further (twenty seconds). Now I imagine myself sitting in the stuffed chair reading the material I know I will be tested on sometime in the future (ten seconds). Again, I turn my thoughts to the beach, the warm sun on my face, the smell of the salt air, and the breeze blowing through my hair . . . enjoying the deepness of the relaxation (twenty seconds). Now I turn my thoughts to the classroom; I am listening to the lecture—I know I will be tested over this material. This scene bothers me. I become anxious. I immediately turn my thoughts to the beach, the warmth of the sun and the smell of the salt air . . . letting myself sink into a deep pleasant state of relaxation . . . concentrating on breathing deeply and freely—deeply and more relaxed (thirty seconds). Now, completely relaxed, I imagine myself sitting in the stuffed chair reading the material I know I will be tested on sometime in the future (ten seconds). I now concentrate on the loose heavy feelings of deep relaxation as they spread throughout my entire body (twenty seconds). I then gradually open my eyes feeling quite relaxed and calm.

"I continued the procedure described above, exposing myself to two to three additional items each day with the exception of items 4, 6, 12, and 14. Due to the high level of anxiety associated with these situations, it was necessary for me to devote more than one session to each of them.

"Also, it should be noted that in my original hierarchy I had no step between step 12 (listening to the other students turn the page of the test when I am still at the beginning of the first page) and step 14 (everyone handing in their tests when I still have test items to answer). However, I found that due to the high-level anxiety provoked by step 14 a transition step was needed and I inserted the item "only fifteen minutes remaining in the test period." I also imagined the beach scene when I felt anxious while taking the test.

"This self-application of relaxation and systematic desensitization has produced the following results for me:

1. I can now put myself into a state of relaxation when confronted with anxiety-provoking situations.

2. Having been confronted with many tests since completing self-desensitization and not having experienced acute anxiety in these situations, I can state that this self-application of systematic desensitization has been successful."

Self-Implosion

Stampfl and Lewis (1967) recommend an approach to anxiety which they call implosion therapy. This procedure consists primarily of having the patient imagine a scene which is associated with high degrees of anxiety. It is based on the assumption that the fantasy serves as a conditioned stimulus which elicits the anxiety response. The basic premise is that anxiety is a learned response to sets of cues based on previous trauma in the person's life. If these cues elicit the anxiety response in the absence of primary reinforcement, the anxiety response should extinguish after repeated evocations. According to Stampfl and Lewis (1967) it is assumed that these cues (imagined scenes) essentially consist of avoided or repressed aspects of the personality, and that by envisioning the past dangerous situations and associations without primary reinforcement, extinction will occur. Consequently, it is essential that the patient select cues that are highly anxiety-provoking, i.e., those situations which he or she has previously sought to avoid.

Zimmerman (1975) assisted some students who were successful in reducing inner feelings such as jealousy, sulking, anxieties, and fears by using self-recording procedures and self-implosive therapy. Implosion therapy involves massive exposure to highly aversive stimuli via imagery. This technique is based on the assumption that aversive stimuli are related to the inner behavior problem and that massive presentation of these stimuli will lead to extinction of the aversive feelings.

One student was a twenty-two-year-old woman who had been separated from her husband for a year after two years of marriage. She frequently felt the pain of hurt feelings caused by significant people in her life, i.e., her parents, brother, roommate, ex-husband, and boyfriend. The hurt manifested itself in the form of a severe cramp or ache in one of her extremities. She purchased a wrist counter and kept a record of all hurt feelings over a sixteen-day period. In so doing she became aware of the situations which triggered the cramps and aches. Examples included (a) her mother questioning her decisions or behaviors, (b) her roommate asking her to leave the room for periods of time, (c) her ex-husband questioning her dating habits, and (d) her boyfriend flaunting to her acquaintances the fact that he also dated other girls.

Once this was established, the young woman began self-implosion. When she experienced a hurt feeling she went to a solitary place and fantasied the worst possible consequences of the situation which triggered the feeling. Upon learning that her boyfriend flaunted his dating others to acquaintances, for example, she found a place where she could be alone and fantasied marrying him, becoming dependent on him, and imagined that he failed to come home on many evenings. She imagined herself coming home one evening and finding him making love to another woman. After a fight, she asked him for a divorce, and found herself all alone. In each instance she continued this self-implosion until the hurt began to diminish. When the hurt began to ease she fantasized herself being in other hurtful situations usually in which she was rejected by people and having another divorce.

For the first six days of treatment she found that her fantasies left her more sensitive to criticism but, after twelve days of treatment, both the intensity and the duration of the hurts were decreasing. During a month of this procedure the number of hurt feelings was reduced to an average of less than one per day.

In a follow-up interview one and one-half years after completing this project she reported that she was happily married to a man whom she met after this treatment and that only rarely did she experience hurt feelings. Even then, their frequency, intensity, and duration were diminished.

Another student in one of Zimmerman's studies (1975), a twenty-one-year-old male, had been dating a girl of whom he was especially fond. His problem involved being beset with feelings of jealousy in her presence and distrustful thoughts in her absence. He attributed the origin of these feelings to his prior experiences with females. On two previous occasions girl friends had suddenly dropped him, one saying that she had been engaged all along and would not see him again and the other telling him that she had been using him and was now off to join her lover in California. He decided to develop a self-control program because he felt that his jealousy threatened the relationship with his present girl friend.

This young man purchased two golf counters and on one he counted jealous feelings experienced in the presence of Helen, his girl friend. To avoid a discussion of his self-control project, which he was not ready to reveal, he told her that he was counting "procrastinations." With the second counter he kept track of the distrustful thoughts after he left Helen each night until he fell asleep. During the baseline period he found himself having an average of more than one jealous thought per hour while in Helen's presence and an average of about six distrustful thoughts each evening after leaving her.

Stimuli that served to trigger these thoughts included any discussion of former boyfriends, male friends dropping by, and leaving notes, calling her, and so on. Parties were especially effective in producing jealous feelings.

Following a fourteen-day baseline, he decided to begin his

self-implosion program. During the last fifteen minutes of each day he fantasized about the day's events. He asked himself what happened that seemed threatening and then proceeded to imagine the worst possible consequences of the incident. On one occasion, for example, he imagined that Homer, a former boy friend of Helen who kept trying to resume their old relationship, met Helen after he had left her to go home. He fantasized them going out to eat, dance, and talk. In his fantasies he saw Homer's name scribbled on Helen's phone pad and finally Helen coldly telling him that she questioned her feelings for him and was interested in Homer again.

After several sessions of self-implosion, this person's number of jealous feelings dropped to less than one every two hours and his distrustful thoughts were almost completely gone. This student reported that following the self-control project he and Helen were more open, communication between them was improved, and his feelings of jealousy were rare and of short duration. In a six-month follow-up, it was discovered they were engaged to be married.

Zimmerman's (1975) data indicate that self-implosion, like self-desensitization, is an effective technique in the achievement of a greater degree of self-control. It appears to be particularly effective in modifying emotions and feelings which are sometimes labeled as "coverants" or "inners."

The Premack Principle and Anxiety Management

Johnson (1971) was successful in applying Homme's (1965) idea of coverant control to problems of depression, homosexual fantasies, lack of self-confidence, and so on. As you recall from a previous discussion, Homme makes use of the Premack principle, i.e., making high-probability behavior contingent upon low-probability behavior, in coverant control. Please keep in mind that coverants are thoughts or mental images as opposed to operants which are overt behaviors.

Johnson's treatment procedure combines the verbaliza-

tion of statements written on 3″ by 5″ index cards with behavioral rehearsal. The cards are carried by the client in a
convenient and conspicuous place such as the shirt pocket.
Only one statement relative to the problem is placed on each
card, and the client is then instructed to select a card and
read the statement on it before performing a high probability behavior.

One client, a college junior called John, complained of uncontrollable images of male genitals and the fear that he
might be disposed toward homosexuality. The images were
so frequent and threatening that he had transferred from
a prestigious all-male school which he had attended for two
years. He also complained of being uncomfortable and ill at
ease with most females. Particularly disturbing was the
fact that he was uncomfortable in the presence of a girl
whom he had dated for about a year.

Therapy was first directed toward increasing John's sexual arousal and responsiveness to females. *Playboy Therapy*
(Davidson, 1968) was recommended for him. This approach
consists of having a male practice masturbation while looking at erotic female photographs in magazines such as *Playboy*. Accompanying this procedure was a diminution of
homosexual images from approximately five to ten per day
to about one to three per week.

During the year John had dated his girl friend, no romantic relationship had developed. Physical contact was limited
to holding hands and an occasional kiss on the cheek and
there was almost no verbal expression of love or warmth.
John was able to increase his sexual feeling toward his girl
friend by incorporating images of her into his masturbatory
activities.

In an attempt to increase communication between the
couple a decision was made to use the index-card procedure.
These statements were placed on 3″ by 5″ index cards:
"We've been dating for approximately one year and we do
not know each other any better," or "We've been seeing
each other for some time now, and we don't seem to get anywhere." John first practiced saying these statements and

role-playing the possible responses of his girl friend, ranging from rejection to affection.

He put the cards in his shirt pocket and made the high-probability behaviors of eating and continuing to drive after stopping in traffic contingent upon reading the statements on the cards, and rehearsing the possible situations between him and his girl. The next step was to make one of the statements in the presence of his girl. John agreed that if he could not verbalize one of the statements while talking with her, then before leaving, he would actually remove one of the cards from his pocket and read directly from it.

When John met his girl on the next occasion the same trite discussion ensued. By occasionally coming into eye contact with the cards, however, he was able to verbalize one of the statements. This statement led to an involved discussion of their relationship and from that point on, it progressed in a much more desirable direction. The same procedure was later applied to some of John's other problem areas.

Another case was Don, a seventeen-year-old college freshman who was dependent, feared academic failure, and was frequently depressed. While depressed he would call his parents and it appeared that their attention and sympathetic statements were reinforcing his depression. It was decided that he should call his parents only when he was in a good mood and that, when depressed, he would engage in some enjoyable activity such as participation in athletic events, playing cards, walking around campus, talking with friends, and watching sports on TV.

After about two weeks, Don experienced severe depression again and contemplated suicide. His academic and social life was completely disrupted. At this point the index-card procedure was initiated. The statements used consisted of descriptions of good changes in his life such as dating, increased interaction with males, improved academic performance, and some general descriptions of the campus which were particularly appealing to him. Urination was made contingent on reading and reflecting upon these statements which represented more desirable behaviors. After two weeks Don reported no incidence of depression. He had also experienced several "spontaneous" positive thoughts about himself and the progress he had made in therapy.

Thoresen and Mahoney (1974) report the case of a depressed housewife who was instructed to write six positive thoughts about herself on cards trimmed to fit inside the cellophane wrapper of her cigarette pack. Whenever she was depressed, she was to read a positive thought from the card and then reward herself with a cigarette, a high-probability behavior. Using this principle she was able to greatly increase the frequency of positive thoughts and reduce feelings of depression and despair.

Recommendations for Anxiety Management

On the basis of material presented in this chapter, the following procedures should be helpful in lowering your inner conflicts to more manageable levels. Please keep in mind that these procedures have been translated from the research of professional therapists interacting with subjects into this self-help directory of behavior change. By all means seek professional assistance if these self-help procedures do not work for you.

1. Develop one or more techniques for achieving muscle relaxation. When in the privacy of your own home, you may want to use the detailed procedure for relaxing the various muscle groups that was presented at the beginning of this chapter. When in public you may prefer to develop deep breathing exercises or to imagine a very peaceful and pleasant scene.
2. Learn to associate cues that once triggered anxiety with relaxation so that they become signals for calm and serenity rather than tension and turmoil. One way of achieving this is through systematic self-desensitization. Let us briefly review the steps in the desensitization process.

  a. Learn to achieve a state of deep relaxation.
  b. Identify the stimuli that are anxiety provoking.
  c. Make a list of visual scenes that cause you to be anxious.
  d. Arrange these scenes into a hierarchy with the less stressful scenes at the beginning of the list.
  e. Place a verbal description of each scene on 3" x 5" index cards.
  f. While deeply relaxed imagine the scene on the first card.
  g. Repeat this visual image until you experience no anxiety.
  h. Proceed to the next scene and repeat the process. It is rare that you will desensitize yourself to more than two or three scenes in one session.
  i. When you start a new session repeat one or two of the scenes to which you have already desensitized yourself before trying new scenes.
  j. By completing from one to three scenes per session continue until you are able to visualize every scene in the hierarchy with no anxiety.
  k. Gradually place yourself into some of these actual situations (*in vivo* sensitization) and see if you continue to feel less anxious.
  l. During *in vivo* sensitization you may want to progress through a hierarchy in much the same manner as you did with the visual images.
3. You may desire to use self-implosion which involves massive exposure to anxiety-provoking stimuli through imagery. Massive presentation of these stimuli should lead to extinction of your aversive feelings.
4. For problems involving depression, lack of self-confidence, and so on, you should find it helpful to make high-frequency behaviors contingent on some positive thought about yourself. Write some positive statements on small cards and keep these in your possession. Before you engage in high-frequency behavior

such as eating, relaxing, or watching TV, require yourself to read and think about one of the positive statements. This procedure should increase the frequency of your positive thoughts and reduce feelings of depression and despair.

10/Anxiety Control Through Cognitive Procedures: I am in control and I know I can handle it

For the past decade Meichenbaum, et al. (1975) have been conducting research designed to bring together the cognitive analysis of behavior and the technology of behavior modification which includes procedures such as operant and aversive conditioning, desensitization, modeling, and behavioral and imagery rehearsal. On the basis of the research a cognitive theory of self-control has emerged in the form of a three-stage process: (1) self-observation, (2) incompatible thoughts and behaviors, and (3) cognitions concerning change.

The first step in the process of behavior change, according to Meichenbaum, is the person's becoming an observer of his own behavior. Through a heightened awareness and deliberate attention, one monitors, with increased sensitivity, his or her thoughts, feelings, and interpersonal behaviors.

Once the person has become an observer of his behavior and these self-observations have been reinforced by, and in turn reinforce, the conceptualization process, the second stage (thoughts and behavior incompatible with the non-desired behavior) occurs. The process of self-observation becomes the occasion or stimulus for the person to emit different cognitions and behaviors. For successful behavior change, what he now says to himself or imagines must initiate a new behavioral chain which is incompatible with the maladaptive behaviors.

The third stage of the change process (what the person says to himself about his newly acquired behaviors) determines whether the behavioral change will be maintained and will generalize to other situations and conditions. As we attempt to behave differently from before, we will often elicit various reactions from other persons that are important to us. What we say to ourselves about our behavior changes, and about the reactions of others will influence the effectiveness of our attempts at behavior change. Since the assumption is made that in order to bring about behavior change thoughts in the form of mental images or self-verbalizations generally precede or accompany overt behaviors, the key to the success of a self-instructional approach is learning appropriate and inappropriate "self-talk," i.e., task appropriate cognitive strategies. By learning different kinds of self-verbalization, one comes to perceive a situation consonant with the different manner, and behaves in a manner consistent with his perception and cognitions. If a college student, when taking an examination, engages in self-talk such as "I'll never be able to pass this test," "I wonder how they are doing," and so on, he is less likely to do well than if he learned to emit self-verbalizations such as these: "I have studied and I am prepared for this test," "I am going to concentrate on the test and nothing else," "I'm calm and in control, I'll concentrate on only one question at a time," "I know I can do it." In using positive self-verbalizations, you should be well prepared. You may get ideas from Table 10.1.

Stress Inoculation

From this cognitive analysis of behavior has emerged a behavior-management technique called stress inoculation. It is a cognitive-behavioral management technique in which people are provided with a set of skills cognitive and behavioral to enable them to deal with stressful situations effectively (Meichenbaum and Turk, 1975). In anxiety management the idea is to increase one's resistance to anxiety-arousing stimuli by exposure to a stimulus that is strong enough to arouse defenses without being powerful enough to destroy them.

Stress inoculation is a three-phase process with the first phase being educational in nature, i.e., designed to facilitate one's understanding of the nature of stressful reactions by providing a conceptual framework. The second phase consists of learning coping skills, behavioral and cognitive, which have been derived from the conceptual framework outlined in the initial phase. During the third stage the person is exposed to a variety of stressful situations in which he or she has an opportunity to practice newly acquired coping skills.

Meichenbaum and his colleagues have repeatedly demonstrated not only that one's self-statements mediate behavior change but also that explicit self-instructional training can facilitate desirable behavioral changes. The purpose of one of their investigations (Meichenbaum and Cameron, 1973) was twofold: (1) to determine the effectiveness of a self-instructionally based stress-inoculation technique in reducing multiphobic behavior, and (2) to determine the extent to which the effects of this procedure, as compared with systematic desensitization, might generalize to other problem areas. These investigators felt that since the visualization or imagery process involved in desensitization is a more concrete and specific representation of stimuli, there should be a minimum transfer or generalization of treatment effects to other phobic areas. On the other hand, self-instructional training which emphasizes coping self-statements, being more abstract representations of stimulus events, should result in greater transfer or generalization of the treatment effect to other areas.

This 1973 study consisted of five groups of subjects, including four treatment and one control. The groups were stress inoculation, systematic desensitization, a self-instructional rehearsal group, and an expanded anxiety-relief group. The last group received the same rehearsal training as the stress-inoculation clients, but did not receive any exposure to the stresses of unpredictable shock.

Subjects for this experiment were volunteers who responded to a newspaper advertisement offering treatment for multiple phobias for snakes and rats. These subjects included both sexes and ranged in age from seventeen to forty-five years. In nearly all cases their fears caused them to avoid activities such as camping, picnicking, and so on which involved the remote possibility of contact with snakes or rats.

Three dependent measures of behavior were used including a test consisting of a graded series of thirteen performance units involving increasingly threatening interaction with a five-foot corn snake and a white rat. The sequence units, presented by tape recording to ensure standardization, ranged from looking at the phobic animal from a distance of fifteen feet (step 1) to placing a hand against the cage (step 5), to touching the animal (step 9), to holding the animal barehandedly outside the cage for one minute (step 13). This test was administered to all subjects prior to treatment and again four to six weeks after treatment. Two self-report measures, designed to reflect the subjective level of anxiety associated with each sequence unit of the behavioral avoidance test, were also used. These behavioral measures were obtained both before and after the treatment procedures were administered.

Treatment Procedures for Each Group

Stress Inoculation

As previously mentioned, stress inoculation includes three phases. Training included six one-hour sessions over a four-week period. The educational phase began with a discussion of the nature of the client's fears and how he or she was currently coping with stressors in general and phobic fears in particular. The therapist pointed out that the fear reaction seemed to involve two major elements: (a) heightened arousal (increased heart rate, sweaty palms, rapid breathing) and (b) a set of anxiety-arousing avoidant thoughts and self-statements (disgust evoked by the snake or rat, a sense of helplessness, panic thoughts of being overwhelmed by anxiety, a desire to flee, and so on). The therapist then suggested that treatment would be directed toward helping the clients control their physiological arousal and substituting positive coping self-statements for the anxiety-arousing self-verbalizations previously used in stressful situations. The clients were told that they would be taught a set of physical relaxation exercises (the procedure for achieving deep muscle relaxation discussed in the previous chapter) designed to reduce physiological arousal. It was also pointed out that the use of these exercises in stress conditions involves doing something positive about discomfort and should tend to eliminate the negative self-statements.

Phase two involved practicing self-statements which could be used by the client in stress-provoking situations. Clients were taught to view the stress reaction as a series of phases rather than as one massive panic reaction. Table 10.1 shows the four phases and contains self-statements corresponding to each phase. These statements were practiced by the clients, first aloud and then to themselves.

According to Meichenbaum and Cameron (1973) these self-statements encouraged the client to: (a) assess the reality of the situation; (b) control negative self-defeating anxiety-engendering ideation; (c) acknowledge, use, and possibly relabel the anxiety they were experiencing; (d) "psych" themselves up to perform the task; (e) cope with the intense fear they may experience; and (f) reinforce themselves for having coped.

When the clients had mastered the relaxation exercises and the self-instructional technique they were exposed to an actual stressful situation which consisted of unpredictable electric shock (phase 3). They were given this introduction: "Sometime in the next two or three minutes, maybe in a few seconds, maybe after three minutes, maybe somewhere in

Table 10.1 Examples of Coping Self-Statements Which Stress
Inoculation and Rehearsal Groups of Subjects Practiced

Stage of Preparing for a Stressor

What is it I have to do?
I can develop a plan to deal with it.
Just think about what I can do about it. That's better than getting anxious.
No negative self-statements, just think rationally.
Don't worry. Worry won't help anything.
Maybe what I think is anxiety is eagerness to confront it.

Stage of Confronting and Handling a Stressor

Just "psych" myself up. I can meet this challenge.
One step at a time; I can handle the situation.
Don't think about fear, just about what I have to do. Make it relevant.
This anxiety is what the doctor said I would feel. It's a reminder to use my coping exercises.
This tenseness can be an ally, a cue to cope.
Relax; I'm in control. Take a slow deep breath. Ah, good.

Stage of Coping with the Feeling of Being Overwhelmed

When fear comes just pause.
Keep focus on the present; what is it I have to do?
Let me label my fear from 0 to 10 and watch it change.
I was supposed to expect my fear to rise.
Don't try to eliminate fear totally; just keep it manageable.
I can convince myself to do it. I can reason my fear away.
It will be over shortly.
It's not the worst thing that can happen.
Just think about something else.
Do something that will prevent me from thinking about fear.
Just describe what is around me. That way I won't think about worrying.

Finally, Reinforcing Self-Statements

It worked; I was able to do it.
Wait until I tell my therapist about this.
It wasn't as bad as I expected.
I made more out of the fear than it was worth.
My damn ideas, that's the problem. When I control them, I control my fears.
It's getting better each time I use the procedures.
I'm really pleased with the progress I'm making.
I did it.

---

between, you will receive a shock. Just exactly how intense and exactly when you receive the shock depend on a random, predetermined schedule. Try to cope with the anxiety and tenseness elicited by this situation by means of coping techniques you have learned [p. 13]." In each practice session they received ten one-second shocks ranging in intensity from .5 MA to 3 MA. Immediately preceding the shock trials, the therapist modeled how to use the coping skills and then the client rehearsed the coping strategy.

Self-instructional rehearsal group Clients in this group were treated in exactly the same manner as those in the stress-inoculation group, except they were given no opportunity to practice their skills under actual stress (shock) conditions. Instead, they received further practice in relaxation and self-instruction. This procedure permitted a comparison between these groups to determine the benefit derived from practicing the coping techniques in a stressful situation.

Systematic desensitization group Half of the clients in this group were desensitized only to rats and the other half were desensitized only to snakes. When a client feared one animal more than the other, he was desensitized to the one more strongly feared. The desensitization sessions were very similar to those described previously in this book, involving muscle relaxation and imagery in a fifteen-item hierarchy. Clients were led to believe that they were learning a general coping procedure which they could apply to other fears. They were also encouraged to apply what they had learned to all fearful situations, and especially in approaching the animal to which they were not desensitized.

Expanded anxiety-relief group This treatment consists of making aversive stimulation (shock) contingent on the client's verbalizing anxiety-engendering, avoidant self-statements, and shock termination is made contingent on the client's expressing positive, coping self-statements. The therapist would say either "rat" or "snake" which served as the cue for the client to verbalize negative self-statements such as "It's ugly; I won't look at it." Following the expression of these negative self-statements electric shock was administered in order to punish the negative "thoughts." By making positive self-statements ("Relax, I can touch it; one step at a time,") the client would terminate the shock. In other words negative thoughts were punished while positive thoughts were reinforced. Clients were encouraged to generate positive self-instructions indicating that they could look at, touch, and handle the feared animal, and that they were in control of how they felt.

Results An analysis of the behavior of each of the clients in approaching the feared animal indicated that the stress-inoculation training was the most effective treatment both in reducing avoidance behavior and in fostering fear reduction that could be generalized from one animal to the other. Systematic desensitization proved effective in reducing fear only to the desensitized object with minimal generalization effect. In contrast both the expanded anxiety-relief and the self-instructional rehearsal groups (self-instructionally based treatments) fostered generalization of fear reduction to other objects.

Self-instructional rehearsal training supplemented with the opportunity to use these statements in an actual stressful situation (unpredictable electric shock) resulted in greater fear reduction than did self-instructional training without the opportunity to confront a stressor. Although the group not exposed to the stressor verbally asserted that they were not anxious, this initial sense of calm dissipated when they were exposed to other stress-provoking tasks.

In summary, the stress-inoculation training procedure was most successful in eliminating phobic behaviors and in reducing fear arousal. Moreover, this treatment which emphasized the learning of coping self-statements was more effective in producing generalization of fear reduction to other situations than was the desensitization treatment.

Within the stress-inoculation framework the degree of treatment generalization is a function of a common set of self-verbalizations that are emitted in different situations. In other words, anxiety or fear reduction across situations depends on the likelihood that the same set of self-statements will be elicited. Meichenbaum, et al. are of the opinion that training clients to emit a set of self-instructional coping responses which are appropriate in different stress-inducing situations should enhance treatment generalization. Presumably the more varied and extensive the training, the greater the probability that the client will develop a general pattern of self-talk in order to cope with stress. "The possibility of explicitly teaching even nonclinical populations to cognitively cope by such diverse techniques as altering attributions and self-labels, imagery rehearsal, shifting attention, using distraction, self instruction, and relocation, etc., seems to hold much promise." (Meichenbaum and Cameron, 1973, p. 32.)

Self-Instruction and Test-Anxiety

Many students experience varying degrees of anxiety while taking examinations. Some of this anxiety is of the objective type, i.e., it is normal for students to feel anxious when they are not prepared for the test. One way to reduce anxiety is to study enough so that you feel that you know the material.

Other students seem to be test-anxious to the point where the anxiety they experience is detrimental to good test performance. Wine (1971) suggests that the difference in the performance of high- and low-test-anxious students is due largely to a difference in the focus of attention during task performance. The low-test-anxious student is able to concentrate on or attend to task-relevant variables while taking the examination. The high-test-anxious student, on the other hand, may be focusing on internal feelings of helplessness, inadequacy, and fear of failure. Since difficult tasks require full attention for best performance, divided attention between internal cues and task cues prevents the test-anxious student from doing well. The anxious student worries about his or her performance, ruminates over choices open, and frequently becomes fixated in attempts to solve a problem or answer a question. Wine recommends that high-test-anxious students be given intensive practice in dealing with tests, and instructions to focus fully on the task rather than dividing attention between the task and ruminative thinking.

Meichenbaum (1972), following up on the recommendations of Wine, developed a program to help test-anxious college students cope with their anxiety. The program had two components: (1) Students were made aware of their thoughts, self-verbalizations, and self-instructions emitted prior to and in test situations which contributed to poor performance. They developed greater awareness of the internal and external cues which signal anxiety and task-irrelevant behaviors. (2) Each student was asked to visualize imaginary scenes in which he was becoming anxious and tense and then to visualize himself handling and coping with this anxiety by means of slow deep breaths and self-instructions to attend to the task. Students were asked to visualize themselves as clearly as possible performing specified behaviors (studying at night before an exam; taking an exam); and if they became anxious, to visualize themselves coping with this anxiety by means of slow deep breaths and self-instructions to relax and to be task-relevant. They were encouraged to use any personally generated self-statements which would facilitate their attending to the task and inhibit task-irrelevant thoughts.

The group of students exposed to this procedure showed less anxiety and greater improvement in grade-point average than did a control group. These results indicate how very effective in reducing test-anxiety was this cognitive-modification treatment which attempted to make high-test-anxious students aware of the anxiety-engendering self-statements they emit which they can replace with self-instructions and behaviors (such as relaxation) incompatible with the maladaptive behaviors.

A technique very similar to that used by Meichenbaum was also employed by Suinn and Richardson (1971) in an attempt to reduce anxiety. Their technique, called anxiety-management training, involved: (1) the use of instructions and cues to arouse anxiety responses, and (2) the training of the client in developing competing responses such as relaxation or success or competency feelings. It consisted of three steps: (1) a half-hour training in deep muscle relaxation, (2) one-hour training in visualization of a scene which aroused anxiety reactions, a scene which reintegrated competency or success responses, and a scene associated with feelings of relaxation, and (3) one-hour tape-recorded instructions to visualize the anxiety scene, then to immediately terminate the scene through either the visualization of the competency or the relaxation scene. This procedure resulted in the reduction of anxiety in test-anxious students to the level of nonanxious students.

Suggestions for Managing Anxiety and Stress

The findings of the research which has been summarized has implications for anyone desiring to learn to control his or her level of anxiety. The following suggestions which are based on findings made in this study should be helpful to you.

1. Anxiety and fear involve two major elements: heightened arousal and anxiety arousing avoidant images, thoughts, and self-statements. Fear is accompanied by physiological reactions such as increased heart rate, sweaty palms, rapid breathing, as well as psychological reactions such as a feeling of helplessness, thoughts of being overwhelmed, a desire to flee, and so on. Both kinds of reactions are, at least to some extent, under voluntary and conscious control. Therefore you should learn to (a) relax in the presence of stress-provoking cues and (b) develop an awareness of negative thoughts and self-statements that you are experiencing and expressing to yourself.

Slow and controlled breathing makes it easier to relax. You should also carefully review the procedure described in the previous chapter that is recommended for achieving deep muscle relaxation. Since a state of relaxation is incompatible with anxiety and fear, the greater the extent to which you can learn to relax in the presence of stressors, the less the amount of stress you will experience.

Make a conscious effort to list and analyze the images, thoughts, and self-verbalizations that occur when you are in stressful situations. It is very likely that thoughts of panic and feelings of helplessness encourage overt behaviors which are compatible with the emotions you are experiencing. Identify these self-verbalizations that seem to exacerbate the physiological and psychological reactions mentioned. When you develop an awareness of the self-talk, it should be easier for you to take steps to reduce it.

2. Learn to substitute coping self-statements for negative anxiety-engendering self-talk. Being able to relax is the first step in this direction. Relaxation makes it easier to emit positive self-instructions. Develop a set of self-statements for each of the four stages of stress inoculation as described by Meichenbaum and Cameron. These stages include (a) preparing for the stressor, (b) confronting and handling the stressor, (c) coping with the feeling of being overwhelmed, and (d) reinforcing self-statements.

3. Practice employing positive statements in coping with stress-inducing situations. The self-statements can be viewed as cognitive strategems one can employ to deal with the experience of unwarranted anxiety. They should be viewed as strategems designed to alter the way you appraise a situation, the set of expectations, attributions, and self-evaluations.

4. Look for situations which you find stressful (at least to some degree) and practice your relaxation skills and coping self-statements in these situations. Recall that Meichenbaum and Cameron found that the opportunity to practice coping skills in the presence of a stressor resulted in greater reduction of fear.

5. Make sure that you reinforce yourself for having successfully coped with a stressor. This can include additional coping self-statements, a compliment from your spouse, or

a special evening out. This reinforcement should strengthen your coping skills.

6. Make a special effort to find coping self-statements that are applicable and appropriate in a number of situations and that are personally meaningful. This means that much of your self-talk should be of a general nature rather than relevant only to a given situation or condition. Remember that a set of self-verbalizations applicable to more than one situation results in anxiety reduction in more than one situation. It is much easier and more efficient to develop one set of broad self-statements which have general application rather than having to develop specific self-statements for each and every situation which may be anxiety-arousing.

As you develop the ability to implement these six suggestions, you will come to experience less and less fear and anxiety. Like any other skill, your ability to employ the cognitive and behavioral skills of the stress-inoculation procedure will improve with practice. Should you have any difficulty on your own or have questions regarding the use of stress-inoculation training, any therapist familiar with this procedure should be able to help you with any specific problems you may be having.

11/**Anger Control:** Dammit, how many times must I tell you that I am not angry?

There seems to be an ever increasing array of factors in our modern social environment that triggers anger. People become inflamed over such concerns as high taxes, low wages, unemployment, crowded living conditions, educational and political issues, and interpersonal relations. Since it is obvious that not all stress factors can be eliminated from our lives, it behooves each of us to learn to cope with situations in which we are anger-prone. Our failure to do so can be tragic, resulting not only in such physiological consequences as indigestion, headaches, and cardiovascular disorders, but also in social and economic consequences such as the alienation of loved ones and disrupted work performance. The ultimate purpose of this chapter is to help you develop a plan or technique for coping with stressful situations in which anger interferes with your best performance. Let us begin by a review of some of the research which has been done on anger management.

Novaco (1975) undertook a project which involved the development of a program designed to increase personal competence in the regulation of anger and the reduction of its maladaptive concomitants and consequences. This program consisted of a combination of cognitive self-control and relaxation procedures. The cognitive-control procedures were largely derived from Meichenbaum's cognitive theory of self-control and the stress-inoculation technique which he and his colleagues have used with so much success. You will recall that these procedures which incorporated self-instructions were described in detail in Chapter 10 on the management of anxiety.

Functions of Anger

Novaco conceives anger as serving several different functions. It can (1) *energize* behavior by increasing the motivational level, (2) *disrupt* behavior through distraction, agitation, and impulsiveness, (3) *express* negative feelings to others, (4) *defend* against ego threat, (5) *instigate* aggressive behavior which has been associated with the emotion of anger, and (6) *signify* that a learned course of action is necessary for achieving a desired outcome.

Novaco suggests in a forthcoming article that anger is both satisfying and frightening. A difficulty in anger control is that people with chronic anger problems enjoy getting angry. Anger may be satisfying because it serves several positive functions in coping with stress. One of the most obvious functions, as listed above, is that it energizes behavior, i.e., it increases the vigor with which we act. This increased vigor enables us to act more assertively when we encounter provocation or injustice. When our level of arousal becomes too high, however, anger interferes with efficient task performance. When people are agitated, they become impulsive and tend to act before they think. Competence in anger management requires patience, composure, and constructive thought. To the extent that anger can be directed toward issues and tasks, rather than toward other people and their self-worth, a response that can lead to a constructive resolution of the conflict is likely to be found.

The arousal of anger and the thoughts associated with that arousal can instigate aggressive actions. The combination of agitation, thwarted expectations, and hostile internal dialogue serves as a cumulative stimulus for aggressive behavior. The connection between anger and aggression is learned. An aggressive act is intended to change the situation or conditions that have provoked anger.

While the arousal of anger constitutes a state of agitation or tension, awareness of anger can serve as a cue to use coping strategies that will be effective in resolving conflict. Novaco has trained clients with anger problems to use anger as a cue for nonantagonistic coping.

Propositions for Anger Management

One of the first steps in Novaco's program was the development of a set of propositions for anger management. From these propositions a set of self-instructions was generated with the aim of not only mitigating the arousal of anger but also enabling the person to deal more effectively with provocations. The propositions are paraphrased as follows:

1. If one can remain oriented toward the task in a provocation, rather than interpreting it as a personal affront or threat, the likelihood of the arousal of anger is decreased.
2. When faced with a personal provocation, a person with high self-esteem is less likely to become angry than a person with low self-esteem.
3. If a person has developed skills to respond in nonantagonistic ways to a provocation he or she is less likely to become angry than one who does not possess these skills.
4. An awareness of one's own anger arousal increases the likelihood that one can control one's anger.
5. If one can learn to use one's own arousal as a cue for nonantagonistic coping strategies, one is more likely to control the anger.
6. If one feels that one is in control of a situation in which provocation occurs, one is less likely to become angry and more likely to use a positive coping strategy.
7. If one can learn to dissect provocation sequences into stages and use self-instruction techniques that correspond to those stages one is more likely to control one's anger.

8. The successful use of nonantagonistic coping behaviors increases the likelihood that they will be used again because successful coping reinforces those coping behaviors and also enhances self-esteem.
9. Learning relaxation techniques will increase the probability that anger will be regulated.

The thirty-four participants in Novaco's study consisted of both students and staff at Indiana University and some members of the Bloomington, Indiana community. They were first assessed for the degree and extent of their anger reactions by means of an anger inventory, personal interview, and pretreatment laboratory provocations.

Following the pretreatment assessment the subjects were randomly assigned to four groups: cognitive coping and relaxation training, cognitive coping alone, relaxation training alone, and a control group. The treatment within each of these groups is briefly summarized as follows:

Cognitive Coping and Relaxation Training

Small group discussions centered around topics such as the duration and extent of personal anger problems and situational analysis to try to identify particular aspects of provocations that trigger anger. An attempt was made to help participants develop an awareness of self-statements emitted in provocation encounters by having them close their eyes, recall recent anger experiences, and report thoughts and feelings they experienced.

These reported feelings, thoughts, and statements were used in presenting a rationale for therapy. Clients were made aware of the correspondence between anger and the kinds of thoughts they have and the things they say to themselves. In other words anger can be aroused, maintained, and inflamed by the kind of self-talk that occurs in provocation situations.

Novaco's propositions for anger management as well as his analysis of the functions of anger were discussed. Participants were encouraged to develop an awareness of their self-statements during periods of anger, to record their anger-related self-statements, and to do a situational analysis of what triggers the anger response. It was assumed that this experience would increase the clients' self-talk and sharpen their assessment of their own feelings and behavior.

In later sessions clients were instructed in how to view a provocation experience as a sequence of stages including (a) preparation for the provocation, when possible, (b) the confrontation, (c) coping with anger arousal, and (d) a reflective period in which the client can reward himself for coping successfully. Each client was provided with a sheet containing this information (Novaco, 1975):

1. Some of the time and maybe a lot of the time, becoming angry has something to do with doubting yourself, being unsure, or feeling threatened by someone else. It's always important to *remember that you are a worthy person* and that you have many good qualities.

2. Sometimes you get angry because you take things personally when there is no need to do that. But even when someone is being directly offensive to you, you can control and contain your anger by staying task-oriented. That is, the most important thing to do is stay focused and *stick to what must be done in the situation to get the outcome you want*. When you begin taking insults personally, you get distracted from your task and get caught up in an unnecessary combat. Don't let yourself get sidetracked and get baited into a quarrel. Recognize what the other person is doing as a provocation but stay task oriented and issue focused.

3. Sometimes you get angry simply because it is the one thing you have always done in a certain kind of situation. As you learn alternative ways of reacting to provocations that don't involve anger, you will be less inclined to react with anger.

4. One of the most important things you must do to control your anger is to recognize the signs of arousal as soon as they occur. As you become more and more sharply tuned to the signs of tension and upset inside you, you will achieve greater ability to short-circuit the anger process. Heightened anger makes you agitated and impulsive. As you learn to

relax more easily, your ability to regulate anger will improve.

5. Your anger can serve a very useful function and that is it can be an alerting signal for you that you are becoming upset and that effective action is called for, if a positive outcome is to result. *Use your anger to work to your advantage.* Remember, getting angry makes you agitated and impulsive; and *impulsive, antagonistic acts get you into trouble. Stay task-oriented and instruct yourself.*

6. Sometimes you get angry because things look like they are getting out of hand and you want to take charge. Sometimes you are afraid that things will not go the way you want them, so you get angry to control them. You will learn that when you self-instruct and manage your anger, you *are* in control of the situation. *The best way to take charge of a situation can be to not get angry when most people would expect or even want you to be upset.*

7. As you learn to break down provocation experiences into chunks or stages, you will have a better handle on things, which is another way of putting you on top of the situation. You will also learn how to instruct yourself in ways that correspond to these stages.

8. Sometimes you get annoyed, upset, and angry because you have spent more time being problem-conscious than you have been accomplishment-conscious. *You often forget or dismiss the good things* that you do, but you don't let yourself get away with the mistakes and failings. You must *remember to congratulate yourself* when you have succeeded in managing your anger and let yourself feel good about it. (Novaco, 1975, pp. 93-94.) [1]

A sheet of self-statements serving as examples of ways to regulate anger through cognitive controls was also offered to each client. This sheet reads as follows:

1. *Preparing for a Provocation*
   What is it that I have to do?
   I can work out a plan to handle this.
   I can manage this situation. I know how to regulate my anger.

---

1. Reprinted by permission of the publisher from *Anger Control* by Ramond W. Novaco (Lexington, Mass.: Lexington Books, D. C. Heath and Company, 1975).

If I find myself getting upset, I'll know what to do.

There won't be any need for an argument.

Time for a few deep breaths of relaxation. Feel comfortable, relaxed, and at ease.

This could be a testy situation, but I believe in myself.

2. *Confronting the Provocation*

Stay calm. Just continue to relax.

As long as I keep my cool, I'm in control here.

Don't take it personally.

Don't get all bent out of shape; just think of what to do here.

You don't need to prove yourself.

There is no point in getting mad.

I'm not going to let him get to me.

Don't assume the worst or jump to conclusions. Look for the positives.

It's really a shame that this person is acting the way he is.

For a person to be that irritable, he must be awfully unhappy.

If I start to get mad, I'll just be banging my head against the wall. So I might as well just relax.

There's no need to doubt myself. What he says doesn't matter.

3. *Coping with Arousal and Agitation*

My muscles are starting to feel tight. Time to relax and slow things down.

Getting upset won't help.

It's just not worth it to get so angry.

I'll let him make a fool of himself.

It's reasonable to get annoyed, but let's keep the lid on.

Time to take a deep breath.

My anger is a signal of what I need to do. Time to talk to myself.

I'm not going to get pushed around, but I'm not going haywire either.

Let's try a cooperative approach. Maybe we are both right.

He'd probably like me to get really angry. Well, I'm going to disappoint him.

I can't expect people to act the way I want them to.

4. *Self-Reward*

It worked!

That wasn't as hard as I thought.

I could have gotten more upset than it was worth.

> My ego can sure get me in trouble, but when I watch
>   that ego stuff I'm better off.
> I'm doing better at this all the time.
> I actually got through that without getting angry.
> I guess I've been getting upset for too long when it
>   wasn't even necessary. (Novaco, 1975, pp. 95-96) [2]

Clients were encouraged to generate some self-statements of their own and also to analyze their previous dialogues in provocation situations, looking in particular for self-defeating and anger-eliciting self-talk. During these sessions each client was given instructions in techniques for achieving deep-muscle relaxation. These instructions were very similar to those which were presented in a previous chapter.

Cognitive Coping Alone

This group received all of the discussions, instructions, and information as did the previous group with the exception that they did not receive relaxation training, nor was any mention made of the use of relaxation skills as a technique for coping with anger arousal.

Relaxation Training Alone

This group was told that training in relaxation skills would enable them to identify signs of arousal and to substitute a relaxation response for anger. They were taught to relax and encouraged to try to relax in provocation situations. As you can see, this instruction was very similar to that given in desensitization procedures. They received no instruction in self-instruction skills.

Attention Control

This group was told that they were part of an extended treatment project which required that they spend three weeks monitoring and analyzing their anger reactions. No attempt was made at clinical intervention. They were told

---

2. Reprinted by permission of the publisher from *Anger Control* by Ramond W. Novaco. Lexington, Mass: Lexington Books, D. C. Heath and Company, 1975.

that at a later time they would be placed in the treatment condition proving most effective.

Following the treatment period, the clients' reactions to laboratory provocations were again observed. These provocations included a role-play provocation, an imaginal provocation, and a direct-experience provocation. The reactions of the subjects in each group following treatment were compared with their pretreatment performance. Other measures that were compared included an anger-inventory assessment and anger-diary ratings.

Results

The combined treatment of coping and relaxation was most effective in reducing anger and increasing anger management when compared with the control group. Following as a close second was the cognitive treatment alone. Both of these procedures were effective not only in reducing anger but in generalizing the effects from role-playing and imaginal provocations to situations involving direct experience. The cognitive treatment alone was generally more effective than the relaxation procedure alone although the relaxation treatment did produce some measurable effects. The training in relaxation techniques not only provided its group with a means of modifying the tension states that predispose to anger but also helped develop the cognition that they were able to control their arousal states. This realization added to their self-confidence and self-esteem by giving them a sense of mastery over troublesome internal states.

In his discussion of the implications of these findings for the treatment of anger, Novaco puts it this way:

> The results of the project demonstrate that cognitive control procedures can be effectively used to regulate anger arousal. The cognitive control skills that were taught to persons having chronic anger problems involved their becoming educated about their anger patterns, learning to monitor and assess their anger, learning how to alterna-

tively construe provocations to mitigate the sense of personal threat, and instructing themselves to attend to the task dimensions of a provocative situation. Through the making of self-statements, clients were able to influence their perception of provocations ("Maybe he's having a rough day" or "There's no need to take it personally") and to guide their response to the problem situation ("Don't act like a jerk just because he is" or "What do I want to accomplish here"). The use of such covert procedures imparts to the person an explicit sense of personal control which has the effect of diminishing the threat value of the provocation as well as increasing one's response options. Discovering that there are alternative ways of perceiving and responding to provocations plays a major role in the development of competence for anger management. Anger, or even rage reactions, follows from a person (or animal) being "cornered" or "boxed in." We frequently characterize the circumstances of anger arousal as "having reached the end of the rope." As a person acquires coping skills that enable him to resolve provocation situations to his satisfaction, he is less prone to resort to anger as the sole means of influencing the behavior of others. (Novaco, 1975, pp. 47-48.)

Anger Management in Law Enforcement

Novaco (in press) has recently extended his stress-inoculation approach to anger management to police officers. As he points out, law enforcement officers have a uniquely difficult status in regard to anger control. They find themselves in a double bind by not only being thrust into situations having a high potential for antagonism but also being expected to behave in an objective and professional manner. Consequently they are not afforded avenues of emotional release that are granted to other persons.

The procedure which Novaco has developed for the training of law enforcement personnel consists of three steps: (1) cognitive preparation regarding the functions of anger, (2) skill acquisition and rehearsal whereby participants discover the review coping processes through small group exercises, and (3) application and practice of coping techniques during a graduated series of role-play provocations.

As Novaco states: "The anger management strategy is based on the conviction that anger arousal is to a significant extent determined by cognitive factors (i.e. one's construction of a situation, attributions of intent, justifications, and self-statements), and is directed toward the achievement of competence in cognitive self-control skills." The first step of helping participants develop an understanding of the functions of anger as a response to provocation was accomplished by introducing them to a model of anger functions as they relate to police experience. The model specifies five basic types of provocation: annoyances (e.g. "spilling coffee on the officer's uniform"), frustrations (e.g. "a citizen refuses to give assistance"), ego threats ("the officer walks into a bar and someone says 'Here comes super pig'"), assaults ("a suspect being transported spits at the officer through the screen"), and inequity (e.g. "getting a day's suspension for damage to a unit that was unavoidable").

During the second phase participants learn to view anger-arousal incidents as a sequence of interrelated events which include: (a) setting events, (b) cognitive mediators, (c) situational cues, (d) the mode of response, and (e) consequences of the encounter. The provocation experience is seen as a cluster of events which triggers anger with each succeeding event escalating the episode until "one party resigns his needs or copes constructively, or when sufficient coercive power is brought to bear on the antagonist resulting in his capitulation." (Pp. 9–10.)

Setting events include those circumstances which affect one's mood and which prime his reactions, e.g., a patrolman reports for work and finds his cruiser out of gas or in a state of disrepair. *Cognitive mediators* consist of memories, expectations, and self-dialogues which precede or accompany the response to provocation. An officer on patrol, for example, may fret about complaints that he hasn't written enough tickets, or about his failure to get vacation time when he wanted it. This kind of frustration and resulting self-statements can play a major role in shaping emotional reactions and overt responses. *Situational cues* are those stimuli that act as elicitors of the anger response. Profanity, insults, long hair, and so on can elicit and intensify anger reactions of police officers. *Mode of response* to a provocation is the manner in which a person reacts to that situation. Overzealous interrogation and unnecessary roughness by police in response to a personal affront can result in broken bodies including those of the police. *Consequences of the encounter* will determine what further action may result from the episode, i.e., whether it is closed or whether there is further agitation and disruption of performance.

The next step in training consists of the acquisition of a set of skills or methods for self-regulation of anger. The process is begun by having participants describe on index cards some provocation experiences in vivid detail. In small groups each participant presents his chosen scenario for discussion and the group examines such factors as the situational determinants, the variables that might exacerbate or ameliorate the antagonism, and potential situational hazards. The purpose is to generate some potentially useful ways of handling the situations.

Following this experience and additional rehearsal of coping strategies comes a period of regulated exposure to provocative situations in which these skills can be practiced. This is accomplished through role-play situations. An example of a provocation incident used in role-play is presented below:

> While on patrol you notice that a car ahead of you is carrying expired plates. You turn on your lights to pull the car over, but the driver turns at the next intersection and continues on as if he didn't see you. Pursuing the vehicle you hit the siren, and he finally pulls over.
>
> You approach the vehicle and ask for license and registration. The driver states that he has misplaced the registration, so you return to your unit to radio for a records check and while waiting you notice that his left front tire is very worn. When you call his attention to this, he becomes hostile and sarcastic. At that point you request that he get out of the car and open the trunk to show you his spare. With a smirk on his face, he gets out of the car, fumbles

through his pockets, and claims that he has lost the trunk key and cannot open the trunk. (P. 16.)

According to Novaco, the provocative impact of these role-play situations can be increased in intensity and complexity as the scenarios incorporate more ego-threat dimensions such as verbal abuse likely to be encountered in barrooms which "challenge the officer's manhood, question his maternal ancestry, or remark on his wife's occupation" (p. 16). In these role-play episodes other group members can act as observers and help provide support and corrective feedback which facilitates the learning process. Novaco reports that these stress-inoculation workshops have been well received. Both his procedure and the results are most impressive. Although his techniques have been developed specifically for police officers, these principles and procedures could be profitable to anyone with anger problems.

Suggestions for Anger Control

1. Remember that becoming angry may have something to do with doubting yourself or feeling threatened by someone else. Keep in mind that you are a worthy person who has many good qualities.
2. You may find that you become angry because you take things personally. When you find this happening stay task-oriented, i.e., stay focused on the task and stick to what must be done in the situation to get the outcome you want. When you begin taking insults personally, you get distracted from the task and may get caught up in an unnecessary quarrel. Recognize what the other person is doing as a provocation but stay task-oriented and issue-focused.
3. Learn to recognize the signs of anger arousal as soon as they occur. As your awareness of the signs of tension and upset inside you increases, you will achieve greater ability to short-circuit the anger process. If you can learn to relax more easily, your ability to regulate anger will improve.

4. You may become angry in situations which appear to be getting out of hand and you want to take charge. The best way to take charge of a situation can be to not get angry when other people expect or want you to be upset.

5. Get some index cards and describe on them in detail some of the situations in which you have had trouble with temper control. As accurately as you can, recall the dialogue that occurred between you and the other person or persons involved. Either by yourself or with the assistance of another person or persons, examine what happened in these situations. What kind of mood were you in when the trouble started? What cues, such as profanity, yelling insults, threats, and so on, seemed to elicit anger within you? What factors increased the antagonism and hostility? What could have been done to reduce tension and ameliorate the antagonism?

6. Analyze your responses in these situations to see how they could be improved.

7. In addition to overt responses, try to identify your thoughts or self-verbalizations.

8. Analyze these self-statements in terms of the effect they have on your perception of the situation, the other person, and your verbal responses.

9. Make a list of self-statements that are less defensive and hostile than, and that can be substituted for, your previous thoughts or self-talk.

10. From your list of situations that make you angry, have someone role-play the provocation scenes with you. First reconstruct some scene as carefully as you can, with you playing yourself and your friend playing the parts of others involved. If possible, record these role-play situations and listen to yourself as you interact with others. By now you should be able to identify several factors that caused you to become angry.

11. Role-play the same situation again but this time keep in mind everything that you have learned about anger control. Practice your new list of self-statements in-

stead of those you previously gave yourself. Tell yourself to stay task-relevant. Remember that you are a worthy person. Do not take insults personally. See if you are feeling less angry now than before. Listen to the recording of the revised role-play interaction and concentrate on differences in the way you responded to the situation before and after.

12. Congratulate yourself when you have achieved a greater degree of anger control.

13. In additional role-play scenes you may want to get involved in more intense situations and increase your competence in coping with them.

14. Be sure to practice what you have learned in the next situation in which you find yourself inclined to experience anger. Your feelings of success that result from your newly acquired coping skills should be sufficient reinforcement to help you maintain greater control of your anger problems.

As you have been reminded throughout this book, please remember that these procedures have been translated from the research of professional therapists interacting with subjects into this book on self-control. By all means seek professional assistance if these self-help procedures do not work for you.

12/Improving Your Dating Skills: Hey babe, how about a date tonight?

Relating to members of the opposite sex in a satisfying manner is a major need of many, if not most, people. Many of us, especially during adolescence and early adulthood, are confused, bewildered, and discouraged about dating. Martinson and Zerface (1970) found that students are more concerned about "learning how to get along better with the opposite sex than with receiving help in choosing a vocation or learning about their abilities, interests, intelligence, and personalities."

Since our society does not provide instructions in forming male-female relationships, it is not surprising that the rate of dating problems is so high. Most people learn the skills of dating in a haphazard, unsystematic way with the result that they have little knowledge and are often confused about what to do. Only recently have experimental psychologists turned their attention to the problem of developing systematic programs to teach dating skills.

Review of Shmurak's Research

Even with advances in the cause of women's liberation, it remains customary for the male to approach the female when initiating conversation, and so on, rather than vice versa. For that reason emphasis in this chapter will be devoted to the work of Shmurak (1974), who designed and evaluated three dating-behavior training programs for college males. In his review of the literature on the subject, Shmurak concluded that most previous investigators had operated on the assumption that males with dating problems should develop specific skills such as identifying the appropriate time to approach a female, being calm and at ease when with a female, giving and receiving compliments, talking about one's feelings, knowing when to initiate sexual activity, speaking fluently on the telephone, and so on.

Shmurak used a competence approach which began by specifying problematic dating situations instead of required skills. The responses of individuals who handle these situations competently were then studied. Following that, a training program was developed to teach troubled males more competent responses to particular problem situations. The use of this model made it possible to identify and to teach specific responses that had proven effective in dating situations.

According to Shmurak, approaches to alleviating dating difficulties have been based on three different assumptions regarding the root of the problem. They are: (1) males with dating problems have adequate repertoires of appropriate behaviors but do not know the appropriate time to use them; (2) males with dating problems have adequate response repertoires of appropriate behaviors and know when and how to use them. However, in dating situations they suffer from conditioned anxiety which inhibits their enjoyment and effective performance in these situations; and (3) males with dating problems do not have adequate response repertoires and as a result they suffer from realistic anxiety over how they will do in dating situations. This assumption implies that the acquisition of new behaviors or response patterns will both improve their performances and alleviate their anxiety.

In his investigation, Shmurak treated three basic groups of males with whom we are presently concerned. They were as follows: A "response acquisition" group was taught specific dating techniques and skills on the assumption that males do not possess the necessary dating competencies. A "cognitive self-statement" group was taught to make what was felt to be appropriate self-statements on the assumption that dating problems are not the result of lack of adequate response repertoires of appropriate behavior but that anxiety inhibits effective performance and enjoyment in dating situations. A "combination group" was taught basic skills and appropriate self-statements on the assumption that dating problems may be caused by both the lack of adequate response repertoires and anxiety.

Three measures were employed to determine the effectiveness of each of the three treatment conditions. The first was a self-report of the number of dates. The second measure was the rating of each participant's response to laboratory dating situations as role-played on audio tape. The third measure was a report by a female of her reaction, in the form of rating, to phone calls received from the male.

Participants were undergraduate and graduate males from Indiana University, recruited in response to an announcement put in the mail boxes in the men's dormitories. The assignment of the participants to the various groups was at random.

Since the "cognitive self-statement" treatment was found to be more effective than those other methods, we shall now discuss that procedure in greater detail. Remember that this treatment is based on the assumption that males do possess adequate dating skills but that anxiety inhibits effective performance and enjoyment in dating situations. The assumption is also made that this anxiety can be controlled by learning to control your thoughts, i.e., what you are saying to yourself. Students in this group, as you will see, learned to "think" positively rather than negatively. They were presented with an audio tape which: (a) presented the situation, (b) presented a male model who verbalized what the student would be saying to himself if he were actually in the situation. This "self-talk" began negatively, realized the negativity, and switched to positive self-talk; and (c) presented the model giving himself self-talk reinforcement for changing his self-talk from negative to positive. Some examples follow:

1. (a) (Situation) ˙Let's suppose you've been fixed up on a blind date. You've taken her to a movie and then for some coffee afterwards. Now she begins to talk about a political candidate, some man you've never heard of. She says, "What do you think of him?" You say to yourself:

   (b) (Self-talk) "She's got me now. I'd better bullshit her or she'll put me down. I hate politics anyway so this chick is obviously not my type.... Boy, that's really jumping to conclusions. This is only one area and it really doesn't show what type of person she is. Anyway, what's the point of making up stuff about somebody I never heard of? She'll see right through me if I lie. It's not such a big deal to admit I don't know something. There are probably lots of things I know that she doesn't."

   (c) (Self-talk reinforcement) "Yeah, that's a better way to think about it. She's just human, trying to discuss something intelligently. I don't have to get scared or put off by her."

2. (a) (Situation) You have enjoyed your date with this girl and would like to ask her out for the next weekend. Now you are walking her home. There is a silence and you decide this is the perfect time to ask her. You say to yourself:

   (b) (Self-talk) "These silences really get to me. I really want to ask her out but what if she says "no"? Boy, that would really be shitty.... Yeah but it's better than missing my chance. I wonder what she's thinking. Maybe she *wants* to see me again and is just *waiting* for me to ask her out. I *did* have a great time tonight so maybe she did too. I'll just have to plunge ahead."

   (c) (Self-talk reinforcement) "That's it. It's so much better to take the bull by the horns than to do nothing and worry about what will happen."

3. (a) (Situation) You've struck up a conversation with a girl on a bus on your way to a ski weekend. It's been a good conversation and you'd like to spend more time with her over the weekend. The bus is

just pulling up to the lodge. Now is the time to ask to see her again. You say to yourself:

(b) (Self-talk) "Aw, shit. I really want to ask her out but I feel so shaky. Is it even worth the effort? What if I'm politely told where to get off? But she won't ask me first. I've gotta make the first move. We've had a good chat on the bus so far. That's a real good sign—I've really got nothing to lose. If she's busy tonight, I'll just ask her to ski together tomorrow."

(c) (Self-talk reinforcement) "That's it. I really pulled myself together. It really feels good to 'think positive.'"

4. (a) (Situation) Suppose you ask her for a Saturday night date. She says, "Oh, I'm really sorry but I'm busy Saturday night." You say to yourself:

(b) (Self-talk) "She doesn't want to see me! I bet she doesn't have any plans and is just waiting for somebody *else* to call. I haven't got a chance with her; she *must* be dating somebody *else*. Wait a minute, why do I always jump to these stupid conclusions? Maybe she really is busy and would like to go out with me another time. Maybe she's even afraid I won't ask her out again because I don't believe her. Well, I'll never find out if I give up this soon. I have to be turned down at least twice before I give up."

(c) (Self-talk reinforcement) "Hey! I'm really getting good at saying positive things to myself instead of negative. What a difference!"

The students also listened to a tape giving a general introduction to dating problems at their first meeting. The script read as follows:

The purposes for our getting together here today are first to acquaint you with the rationale behind the training program and secondly to give you some idea of what kinds of things you will be doing in the course of our training sessions.

A study has shown that there are almost as many explanations which guys give themselves for why they're having trouble dating as there are guys. You yourself have probably entertained a number of hypotheses to explain your lack of success at dating, for example, being a poor conversationalist or the victim of your mother's domination. To

help you become aware of the explanations you give yourself, let's stop for a minute or so while each of you asks yourself why you have trouble in dating situations. Just relax, reflect back on your experience, and ask yourself, "Why do I have trouble enjoying myself with girls?"
(pause of 90 seconds)

O.K., let's continue now. We have found that most people believe they have dating difficulties for one or more of the following reasons. Some people think they have formed a permanently negative self-image. This self-image is what prevents them from enjoying dating. Some believe they are just "shy." They think that the rest of their lives will be spent withdrawing from contacts with women instead of enjoying them. Some see women as strange, foreign, and therefore dangerous. Others believe they're not handsome enough. Some feel that since they didn't have sisters, they never learned what girls were like, and haven't got the slightest idea how to go about things. Others feel that they've been afraid for so long that they're hopelessly far behind everyone else and would be embarrassed to try for fear that their efforts would be ridiculed by the girl and their peers. Some think they're just stuck with being poor conversationalists. Some fear they will be nervous and that it will show terribly. Some let their doubts about what is proper for a boy or girl stop them. Many, instead of just thinking about what to say to a girl, get preoccupied with the thought that they will fail. Then, since their efforts are not aimed at facing the situation and figuring out what to say or do, they really do fail.

Others are very down on their chance of *ever* doing better. They feel that "Well, I failed in the past, I'll probably fail today too, so why try?" Some are afraid of their feelings being hurt if they are rejected by a girl. Others believe that girls are only attracted to football heroes or guys with a good line. Some believe that girls are always comparing them to others and so feel they cannot be themselves with a girl.

However, it really doesn't matter very much *why* you think you have a problem with dating. *The point is that you think you have difficulty* in dating. Whether you think it's because you're shy, because your parents messed you up, or whatever explanation you may hold, *right now,* through this training program, you can start taking steps to eliminate your problem. This point cannot be stressed enough. Too many guys decide they are just not able to enjoy women for some reason or other. Then they think they have to live their lives like that, just accepting this painful lack. Well, it is just not true that you have to accept this lack.

Students then listened to a tape explaining what cognitive self-statements are. They were told that by thinking negatively one raises the probability of his failing whereas by thinking positively one raises the probability of his succeeding; that to change negative self-statements into positive ones, we must become aware of our negative self-statements and use them as a cue to initiate more positive ones. Here is the script of the tape:

> By learning how to deal with your negative and fear-arousing thoughts and feelings while in problematic dating situations, you can begin to turn them into positive confident ones. That is the basic idea behind this training program. A large part of your problems in dating situations are the result of the negative things you say to yourself. For example, when you pick up the phone to call a girl, does a wave of fear run through your body because you're telling yourself she'll probably reject you? Do you tell yourself that no girl could possibly like you, or that you're going to be awkward and clumsy? In many cases, this negative self-talk may be so habitual that you are unaware that you do it and that you could be talking more positively to yourself. The training sessions will be aimed at making you aware of the negative things you say to yourself. First a problematic dating situation will be presented. Then you will imagine that you are in it and will say what you would say to yourself if you were actually in it. Next, you will hear a model giving his own self-talk in that situation. He will start with negative self-talk, become aware that he is doing that, switch to positive self-talk, and then congratulate himself for doing so.
>
> Then you will practice identifying your own negative self-talk and changing it to positive. We will record your self-talk and play it back to you as many times as necessary to help you learn to catch yourself thinking negatively and change it to positive.

The students participated in several individual sessions which included role-playing situations in which each student engaged in verbal interaction with the experimenter. The interaction centered upon verbal responses to hypothetical dating situations. Following are some of the situations to which each participant made a verbal response. Criteria of a "good response" are also presented:

> This is your first date with Ann, and the two of you are just leaving a movie. Because it is still quite early in the evening, you ask her what she would like to do next. She answers, "I don't know. It's up to you." You say: ...
> A good response would not have repeated the question but would have come up with a suggestion. The suggestion should be offered as a question rather than a statement. E.g. "How about a pizza?" not "Let's get a pizza."
> ....
> You have gone to see your adviser and have been asked to wait in the hall for awhile. You take a seat next to a girl, and would like to interact with her. You say: ...
> A good response might have been to ask her if she's been waiting to see her adviser too. You could ask a question about something she's reading, or a book she's carrying. E.g. "Are you waiting to see Dr. Smith too? I hope he can help me get a good program for the summer."
> ....
> Let's suppose you're having lunch with Jane, a girl you don't know very well. Over lunch you've been talking politics. But every time you express an opinion, she contradicts you. Now you tell her you'd like to see Smith win the election, and she says, "You're crazy." You say ...
> A good response should be one that shows continued interest in the other person. It should not reflect defensiveness or hostility on your part. You should not change the subject. E.g. "Why do you feel that way?" or "You really feel strongly about it, don't you?"
> ....
> Let's suppose you've been fixed up on a blind date. You've taken her to a movie and then for some coffee afterwards. Now she begins to talk about a political candidate, some man you've never heard of. She says, "What do you think of him?" You say: ...
> A good response to this situation would directly express ignorance and also express interest in finding out about him. E.g. "Gee, I don't know; I've never heard of him. What's his position on the equal rights amendment?"
> ....
> You ask a girl to dance and she accepts. You've just succeeded in getting a good conversation going with this girl

when the music stops. You want to continue talking with her. Now as she begins to walk away, she says, "Thank you very much for the dance." You say . . .

A good response should express a desire to continue talking and show pleasure in her company. E.g. "Sure, I enjoyed it too. Let's sit down and talk awhile."

. . . .

You are out for a big night. Your date seems bored and won't tell you what's the matter when you ask. The situation gets more and more unpleasant and you decide you must do something. You say . . .

A good response would express concern for how she feels and show that you want to know what's bothering her. It should show no hostility or effort to make her talk. You could offer to take her home. E.g. "You seem kind of down tonight. Would you like me to take you home and we'll talk tomorrow?"

On the basis of his research, Shmurak concluded that a treatment of modifying cognitive self-statements can result in improvement in actual dating behavior, as well as increasing transfer of learning to laboratory situations on which training has not been given. This transfer of training in dating skills from familiar laboratory situations to unfamiliar situations and to actual behavior did not occur with subjects in the response-acquisition group.

As Shmurak points out, two features of this study suggest that its findings constitute particularly strong evidence for the superiority of the cognitive self-statement position: (1) It is one of the few studies which has demonstrated transfer of the treatment effect from laboratory to real-life situations, and (2) it is the first study of dating behavior in which actual behavior was measured by an observer (the girl who rated the performance of the subject relative to the impression he made in a telephone conversation to her) rather than self-report by the participant.

The superiority of the cognitive self-statement treatment suggests that college males with dating problems really do know what to do and only need to get themselves to do it. It may be that other populations (those with less education or social experience, for example) may not know what to do in a dating situation, but for college students, it seems to be primarily a matter of getting themselves to do what they already know how to do.

These results indicate that cognitive self-statement modification is effective for confidence-building and improved dating performance in college males. The study also lends support to Meichenbaum's 1975 theory of cognitive behavior modification and extends the range of behaviors or problem situations to which this approach has been successfully applied.

Suggestions for Improving Your Dating Behavior

By following the suggested activities listed below you should be able to improve your performance in dating situations. These suggestions are derived from the cognitive self-statement procedures which Shmurak found to be an effective method of improving dating skills.

1. Think of some particular dating situations that have not gone well for you and make a list of them.
2. As accurately as you can, recall the dialogue that occurred between you and the other person or persons involved.
3. Analyze your verbal responses in these situations to see how they could be improved.
4. Have someone role-play these dialogues with you. If possible, record them on a tape recorder and listen carefully as they are replayed. This kind of feedback should be helpful in the identification of specific comments, tone or inflection of voice, and so on, that might have elicited a negative reaction from your dating partner.
5. As you recall and reconstruct these dialogues, try to identify your thoughts or self-verbalizations that occur at the same time as your overt verbal responses. Make a list of the "self-talk" that occurred with each of the above dialogues that you recon-

structed.

6. Analyze these self-statements in terms of the effect they had on your perception of the situation, the other person, and your verbal responses.

7. Make a list of self-statements that are less defensive or hostile that can be substituted for your previous thoughts or self-talk.

8. Rehearse your list of dialogues but substitute your revised list of more positive self-statements and overt verbal responses for those that actually occurred in the original verbal interaction.

9. You might find it helpful to role-play as many situations as you can think of that might arise in a dating situation.

10. If you know a member of the opposite sex as a close friend but have no romantic interest in him or her, you might invite that person to some social activity. You should feel more at ease with the person and be able to exhibit more effectively your social skills without undue anxiety. This kind of experience should serve as a confidence-builder.

11. Make a list of the dating situations in which you feel most competent. It may be a movie or ball game. You may prefer a situation in which the two of you are alone or you may prefer the company of other people. Then invite the girl of your choice to this kind of activity.

12. Remember that success breeds success. If you are successful on one occasion, the next one should be much easier.

13/Tips for Enhancing Interpersonal Relationships: I'll like you if you'll like me

Pause for a few moments and consider a world inhabited only by you. In effect, you would be that much-talked-about last woman or last man in the world. Perhaps the prospect appears inviting. Having no responsibilities or obligations to other individuals, never having to be wary of saying or doing something that would offend someone or cast an unfavorable light on you, and all the other social constraints which seem to bind and imprison each of us at one time or another would be totally absent. The world would be yours —all yours.

But wouldn't your own personal world inevitably become very lonely? Wouldn't you eventually long for at least one other individual to share experiences and to provide companionship? Autobiographical reports of individuals who have experienced social isolation, among them religious recluses, castaways, and prisoners of war (Weissberg, 1951; Anson, 1932), suggest that a solitary existence is a painful one. Indeed, solitary confinement is often utilized as a potent punishment for uncooperative individuals in our penal institutions. Researchers such as Henry A. Murray (1938) and Stanley Schachter (1959) have discussed and investigated the tendencies and apparent need of individuals to affiliate. Although definitive "why" explanations have not been provided, it is generally agreed that individuals both desire and need the companionship of others. As John Donne so aptly stated, "No man is an island."

If I had suggested that you consider a world inhabited only by you and certain other individuals selected by you, the fantasy would have become much more attractive. Pause again for a moment and consider which persons you would choose, and what is most important, *why* you would choose them. You probably have concluded that you would choose those individuals whom you like or love and reject those individuals whom you dislike. But what are the qualities which contribute to a positive appraisal of others, i.e., why is it that you like certain people and dislike others?

Determinants of Attraction or Liking

In discussing the qualities which you would most probably find attractive or likeable in another individual, let us assume that you now have a new neighbor who just moved into the house or apartment next door. One factor which tends to influence attraction is propinquity or physical closeness; thus, the mere fact that the individual lives nearby increases the likelihood that you will become friends. It would be easier to become friendly with the people next door than with those down the street, or with the people in the next apartment than with those on another floor. Propinquity provides opportunities for interactions to occur and for friendships to develop.

The physical appearance of your new neighbor will tend to influence your evaluation of him or her. Our culture strongly values socially acceptable physical appearance and desirable character traits and also promotes a strong alliance of the two qualities. One example of this alliance was provided in 1972 by a group of researchers, Dion, Berscheid, and Walster, who reported that the effects of physical appearance were so prepotent that physically attractive individuals were believed to have greater occupational success, to have more desirable personality traits, to lead better lives, and to be happier than unattractive individuals. Therefore, if your new neighbor possesses physical and personality traits that are appealing, you will tend to like or be attracted to him or her.

Let us suppose that your new neighbor invites you over for coffee, and your conversation covers a wide variety of topics ranging from such subjects as pet preferences to political affiliation. If you and your neighbor hold similar attitudes regarding your discussion topics, you will have a strong basis for developing friendship. Byrne and Nelson (1965) reported that the attraction effect of similarity of attitudes is so strong that it can be described mathematically. Attraction varies as a linear function of the proportion of similar attitudes. The relationship core simply stated is that as the number of similar attitudes increases, so does the attraction or liking for another individual. When someone else agrees with us, consensual validation is provided. That is, agreement provides supporting evidence for the correctness or rightness of our opinions or beliefs. But when someone else disagrees with us, consensual invalidation is provided, and the possibility that our values could be incorrect or unreasonable is enhanced. We much prefer to be correct, and thus we much prefer those individuals who assure us of our correctness.

Getting back to your neighbor, you will have a tendency to be attracted to your new neighbor if he or she does not "crowd" you. Frequent invasions of your privacy or your personal space will cause you to react defensively and negatively toward a perceived intruder. Propinquity can provide opportunities for interactions, but too much physical closeness will be viewed as threatening and very uncomfortable.

The ability level of your new neighbor will also influence your attraction for him or her. You will tend to be more attracted to an individual whom you perceive as very competent and possessing high abilities than to an individual whom you perceive as incompetent and possessing low abilities. But of more importance than ability level or any of the other influences previously discussed is your neighbor's evaluation of you. If you were to accidentally overhear a conversation between your neighbor and someone else, during which your neighbor said several positive things about you, your liking or attraction for your neighbor would tend to increase. Being liked is a very strong influence on reciprocal liking. We are very much affected by positive evaluations from others, *even* if we are fully aware that they are false (Byrne, Rasche and Kelly, 1974). The old maxim, flattery will get you nowhere, has not been supported by research investigations.

Self-Applications

The attractive qualities which have been discussed regarding your hypothetical neighbor can provide helpful hints for improving your own attractiveness to others. If you are interested in forming new friendships, you may be advised to take note of individuals who live nearby, work in the same area, or whom you would frequently encounter under typical circumstances. Propinquity allows for the numerous interactions which may lead to lasting friendships. Begin a casual conversation with some of those individuals whom you meet on a daily basis. Do not push or crowd your new acquaintances by forcing continued dialogue or by discussing personal topics immediately, but do be bold enough to initiate a "Hello, how are you today?" Have a friendly greeting for your acquaintances each day and you may be pleasantly surprised by the outcome.

Certainly it is not possible for everyone to be strikingly beautiful or dashingly handsome, but physical attractiveness does influence liking or attractions. Although we make several noises about not judging a book by its cover and beauty only being skin deep, we are much influenced by "packaging" especially in the initial stages of getting to know someone. Good grooming is essential. Make the most of what you have to offer by dressing as attractively and as appropriately as possible, by finding the most becoming style of hair for you, and by being both clean and neat. The "real" you inside may be of primary importance, but the outside cover is what other people first encounter and is also what research indicates others generally use as one important basis of evaluation. Our opinions of others are strongly influenced by appearances. Not to be cognizant of and appreciate this fact may be to deny yourself many advantages.

Earlier I discussed the strong attraction effect of similarity of attitudes. I would not suggest that you alter any of your beliefs or opinions simply to make them agree with those of select others, but I would suggest that you express disagreement in an open-minded rather than in a dogmatic fashion. Stringently avoid implication of my side is right, thus your side is wrong. Hodges and Byrne (1972) reported that in two experiments dogmatic statements were met with very negative responses from those who held opposing views, but open-minded statements elicited at worst indifference from those who disagreed. Leaving room for disagreement reduces the threat and other negative effects of incongruent attitudes. Saying, "the Democratic Party seems to be the best for me," in preference to, "anyone who has any real political sense would choose to be a member of the Democratic Party," is an example of getting the point across without alienating others. One method of increasing your potential to respond in an open-minded manner is behavior rehearsal, which is much like the play-acting you practiced as a child. Pretend that someone disagrees with you regarding some of your most important attitudes involving such controversial topics as politics, religion, or sex, and practice responding in an open-minded fashion. Practice frequently, alone or with others, in order to foster open-minded habits of responding.

Perhaps you tend to think that the manner in which you disagree with someone is not important. To fully appreciate the negative effects of a dogmatic viewpoint, try a little role-playing. Make a short list of those values, beliefs, or attitudes which are most important to you. Take each item on your list and fervently argue an opinion in direct opposition to your own. Imply that your belief is the only correct attitude and give all the "reasons" why. If you find yourself becoming angry your role-playing has been effective. If your anger is not aroused by the process or if you seem to feel silly arguing with yourself, dogmatically argue an opposing view with members of your family or some close friends. Note their reactions and question their feelings toward you. I am certain that you will quickly be convinced of the negative effects produced by dogmatism and the importance of open-minded disagreement.

As discussed above, one of the strongest influences on attraction or liking is positive evaluations of us by others. Thus, the mere fact that you like other individuals will influence them to reciprocate. Some methods of indicating to another person that you like him or her are effective listening and expressing interest and approval.

Be wary of dominating conversations. Give others opportunities to speak and encourage them to do so. But simply allowing others to speak will not qualify you as a good listener. You should not merely pause, permit someone else to speak, and then continue with whatever you intended to say. You should be an interested listener. You may indicate interest by sitting or leaning forward, looking at the individual who is speaking, and responding frequently by nodding or rephrasing portions of the conversation to illustrate that you understand. Being an effective listener is a very important skill. Too often we hear only portions of what others have to say. We quickly draw conclusions regarding their views. To guard against such negative behaviors, practice being a good listener and observe the behavior of those individuals whom you consider to be effective listeners. Do not interrupt a speaker, listen to *everything* he or she has to say, indicate your interest, and respond appropriately.

Another method of illustrating positive evaluation or liking for others is expressing approval. As suggested earlier, even flattery which is known to be incorrect may be enjoyed, but honest approval will be regarded even more highly. Take care not to express approval inconsistently or too frequently. T. L. Huston (1974) suggested that a response to approval is determined by the perceived accuracy of the basis of the approval, and by the sincerity or authenticity of the positive evaluations. Generally, honest appropriate approval will be well received by others and will serve to increase the attractiveness of the approver.

Lasting Relationships

Some of the influences which determine initial attractiveness also occupy a very significant role in lasting relationships. Attitude similarity is an example of a potent influence in both the early and later stages of interpersonal relationships. Close friends and marriage partners tend to resemble one another in attitudinal characteristics (Winslow, 1937; Byrne, 1971). Terman and Buttenweiser (1935) reported that happily married husbands and wives exhibited greater similarity of preferences and attitudes than did unhappily married or recently divorced couples. Not only are the attitudes of happily married husbands and wives more similar to each other than those of unhappy couples, happily married husbands and wives tend to overestimate attitude similarities or assume a greater similarity than actually exists (Byrne & Blaylock, 1963; Levinger & Breedlove, 1966). One explanation of this phenomenon is illustrated in the following figure:

Figure 13.1. Diagram Showing How Husband and Wife Who Feel Positively toward Each Other Can Either Agree or Disagree on an Issue

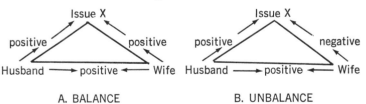

A. BALANCE   B. UNBALANCE

In "A" of Figure 13.1 the husband and wife feel positively toward each other and toward issue X; thus, the situation is balanced. In "B" of Figure 13.1 the husband and wife feel positively toward each other but disagree concerning issue X; thus, the situation is unbalanced. One relatively easy method of balancing the situation is for the couple to assume that they actually do agree regarding the controversial issue. Byrne (1971) suggested that assumed similarity may actually be an index of the positiveness of a marriage relationship.

Lasting relationships such as marriage may also be viewed as exchange or bartering situations in which the quantities for barter may range from agreement, as in the above example, to time spent engaging in certain activities. Each individual seeks to maximize his or her reward or gratification while minimizing cost or expense. In happy or successful marriages and friendships the partners enjoy a mutually rewarding relationship. In the above situation in which the partners disagree regarding an issue, they might tend to assume that similarity existed because past consensual validations had led them to expect balance and agreement rewards. Misperceiving or assuming similarity is much easier for a husband or wife than altering personal attitudes or attempting to modify those of a spouse. Assuming similarity may also be a more attractive alternative than tolerating unbalance or dissimilarity. But if the relationship is basically a very positive and rewarding one, dissimilarity will be tolerated in order to preserve the valuable original exchange.

Dealing with Conflicts

In many friendships and marriages the exchange or bartering ratios become unbalanced. The parties no longer participate in a reciprocal relationship with each member equitably sharing rights and duties. Each member attempts to minimize his or her costs and has little expectation of reward. Each partner may learn to give as little as possible of such things as affection, time, interest, and so on, if he or she learns to expect nothing in return. The parties in the relationship may begin to attempt negative types of control such as withdrawal and coercion. That is, husbands and wives may begin to use such tactics as pouting, violent displays of temper, drinking excessively, or even physical abuse in order to control the relationship. If the unbalanced situations continue, each spouse will provide a high ratio of costs to rewards, the total value of the relationship will become negative, and the original exchange will no longer be valuable.

It would appear, as evidenced by the ever increasing divorce rate, that many unbalanced marriages result each year. During this coming year if trends continue, 4.5 million individuals will marry and 1.8 million will divorce. The cost of divorce is generally staggering economically and emotionally. Elliot Aronson (1969) has suggested that those persons who have in the past been very close to us possess the greatest potential to hurt or punish us. The emotionally devastating effects of divorce may occur in part because husbands and wives learn to expect love, affection, favors, and approval from each other, and withdrawal of such rewards can promote a marked loss of self-esteem. Attempts can be made to reestablish reciprocity in which each partner will dispense rewards with the confidence that he or she will be compensated in a like manner in the future. Positive control must replace the negative unsuccessful type of control if unbalanced marriage exchanges are to achieve balance and remain valuable.

Each partner must recognize that impressions of the other partner are based, not upon a global immutable personality, but upon specific behaviors exhibited by that individual which can be altered or modified. But each partner must also be willing to initiate and be committed to changing the relationship. As long as each spouse is determined to let the other "make the first move," the relationship will remain locked into defeating interaction patterns.

One method of beginning a program of positive change is for each member to list three *specific* behaviors which he or she would like to see the other partner accentuate. Increasing positive behaviors rather than decreasing undesirable behaviors quickly helps to alter the negative emphasis of past problematic interaction patterns. A next step might be to work out a series of exchanges for the desired behaviors. For example, a wife could agree to attend a movie of particular interest to the husband. Desired exchanges (add only one exchange per week) should be revised on a weekly basis. Set aside a time period each week for revising the contractual agreement, make certain that both partners sign it, and post the agreement in a conspicuous place for easy and frequent reference. Signing the behavioral contract is an essential task which emphasizes the sincerity and dedication of the partners, and conspicuous posting of the document provides an important reminder of the new procedures. Adhering to new positive contingencies should allow each individual to begin to maximize his or her gratification and permit the relationship to move toward becoming a balanced and valuable exchange.

Additional Hints

By establishing a contractual agreement, consequences of specific behaviors are emphasized. The partners' methods of dealing with each other begin to be translated into contingencies of reinforcement. In addition to the specific behavioral exchanges in the contract, each partner should carefully observe when desirable behaviors of the other partner occur and *immediately* reinforce such behaviors with recognition and approval. If your husband, wife, or close friend does something which pleases you, say so. Praising or acknowledging desirable behaviors is termed social reinforcement and can be a very potent influence on human behavior.

If certain desirable behaviors do not occur, you may be able to foster them through a social modeling process. For example, if you wish that your husband, wife, or close friend would not interrupt you while you are speaking, take care to always allow him or her to stop talking before you respond. Humans are strongly influenced by social models, and he or she may take the hint. If and when he or she does allow you to complete a thought, even a small one, immediately acknowledge the courtesy. Over a period of time you may slowly raise the criterion of reinforcement by demanding completion of longer ideas without interruption before offering approval. You will discover that such positive techniques will be far more effective in promoting desirable behaviors than negative types of control such as "shouting over" an interrupting speaker.

Another skill which is very important in successful marriages or friendships is the offering of constructive as opposed to destructive criticism. Destructive criticism attacks the entire person and leaves him or her no room for escape. Some examples of destructive criticism are: "You're a slob," and "You're dumb." But constructive criticism focuses on behaviors which can be changed or improved such as: "That was a stupid thing you did," and "You have very bad table manners." The aim of criticism should be directed toward improving offensive or undesirable behaviors, and only constructive criticism aids in achieving this goal.

One final essential quality to successful interpersonal relationships is empathy, which is the ability to put yourself in someone else's shoes and to actually see their point of view. A very effective method of experiencing empathetic understanding is to play the role of the other person. An example of changed attitudes as a result of role-playing procedures was reported by Clore and Jeffery (1971). In their study, college students played the role of an accident victim, and crossed their university campus in a wheelchair, taking a cup of coffee at the student union. After their experience, the students found that their attitudes toward increasing funds for aiding disabled individuals were much more positive. Tolerance for the attitudes of others is greatly increased when each member in a relationship is able to be empathetic and perceive an issue from the point of view of the other individual. Often a role-playing experience is necessary to fully appreciate a different perspective.

Your attractiveness to others and your ability to maintain lasting successful relationships depends upon your value as a reinforcing or rewarding agent. The determinants of attraction discussed above such as physical attractiveness, positive evaluations, similar attitudes, and high-ability level are all indications of your reward potential for other persons. Maintaining successful relationships and dealing with conflicts require the establishment of balanced exchanges in which your reward value for an interaction companion exceeds your costs. I hope that after completing the preceding discourse your awareness of significant factors influencing interpersonal relationships and of the importance of recognizing consequences of specific behaviors will allow you to enhance and improve your interactions with others.

14/**Learning to Control Pain:** It doesn't hurt anymore

Pain is an unpleasant sensation which we all experience from time to time, but some people seem to be able to tolerate it more than others. The intensity of pain also seems to vary with the setting in which that pain is experienced. A headache, for example, seems to hurt worse if you think about how it is hurting. If you get involved in some other activity, however, the pain may seem to subside. The purpose of this chapter is to help you to become more familiar with the nature of pain and to develop skills to cope with it whenever it occurs.

Some very exciting research on pain control is now underway at the University of Waterloo, in Ontario, Canada. This research was initiated by Turk (1975), who incorporated Meichenbaum's stress-inoculation procedure in a skills-training treatment to experimentally induce pain. The pain was produced by a blood pressure cuff inflated around the upper left arm of each person who participated in the experiment. The participants were asked to tolerate the pain as long as possible. Next they were made aware of some strategies for developing greater pain tolerance. These strategies included:

1. Physical and mental relaxation and attending to slow, deep breathing.
2. Focusing attention on things other than induced pain, for example, doing mental arithmetic or attending to

environmental cues, such as counting ceiling tiles, studying one's clothes, and so on.

3. Focusing attention on bodily processes or bodily sensations including the pain, for example, watching and analyzing the change in the arm or hand.

4. Changing or transforming the experience of pain by means of fantasy. One might imagine lying on the beach; imagine the arm is only cold and not painful; think of the arm as being numb as if injected with novocaine; or imagine that one is a spy who has been shot in the arm and is being chased by enemy agents in a car down a winding mountain road.

The participants were encouraged to develop a plan to deal with the pain, selecting from the strategies described above and adding any additional strategies that they desired. They were then asked to imagine themselves in stressful situations, including that of pain. They imagined how they would use a variety of coping techniques (self-statements, relaxation, and the other strategies). Initially they verbalized aloud the sequence of strategies that they were imagining; but, as proficiency increased, verbalizations were faded until the imagery process was engaged in without verbalization.

In order to consolidate the coping strategies, the participants were asked to role-play, giving advice to a novice on how to cope with stress, specifically the experience of pain. Then came the postassessment phase of the test of pain tolerance. Those receiving the stress-inoculation training increased their pain tolerance from an average of seventeen minutes on the pretest to an average of thirty-two minutes on the posttest. Turk stresses the fact that this fifteen minute improvement takes on particular significance when compared with that of Smith, Chiang, and Regina (1974), who found that subjects' tolerance for experimentally induced pain was prolonged by only five to ten minutes following the administration of ten milligrams of morphine per seventy kilograms of body weight.

The methods of pain control described in this chapter have been developed in the treatment of experimentally induced pain. They are, therefore, most applicable in circumstances involving relatively short term, delimited pain, such as childbirth and painful medical procedures.

Pain as a Private Experience

One of the most common things for a person experiencing pain to say is, "You don't *know* how painful it is. I just can't tell you how much it hurts." Not only is it hard to say how *much* it hurts, it is practically impossible to describe exactly *how* it hurts. We have words such as "burning," "pricking," "searing," and "tearing" that attempt to define the sensations of pain, but sometimes they don't seem quite adequate. Although some of the outward signs of it may be visible and describable, pain is a private, individual experience.

And because it is so private, no two people undergo exactly the same feelings of pain from the same source. Many factors besides the intensity of the stimulation contribute to the experience of pain. On two different occasions you may experience quite different "pain" from exactly the same external stimulation. Think of receiving a minor wound to your face during an active game, such as football or hockey. You would probably not even notice the cut, and would go on playing, feeling little, if any, pain. However, if you had received exactly the same degree of injury while working around your home, or shaving, or some such activity, you would probably immediately notice the cut, take steps to stop the bleeding, and find it uncomfortably painful. (It is only *after* the football or hockey game that you are likely to find that the wound causes you some discomfort.) Or, consider cutting your finger on the edge of a magazine that you are reading. During some active game you would not likely notice much pain from a minor cut like this.

Still another example: In several primitive tribes women

in labour apparently experience no pain. They simply stop their work to have the baby and return to work immediately afterwards. (In Canada the average hospital stay after birth is from five to seven days.) But in these primitive cultures the husband stays in bed with "labour pains" while his wife is having the baby (Kroeber, 1948). Perhaps the men are not really experiencing the pain of labour (they say they are!), but, in any case, the women certainly can't be undergoing the intense, debilitating pain that is usual in our culture. Obviously, pain is influenced by many things.

In this chapter, we will examine various techniques for reducing pain. These originated in studies that examined how people cope with pain—why the experience differs from one person to another, from one situation to another, and from one culture to another. Almost everyone attempts to control pain through some means or other, although he may do it quite unconsciously, without giving it much thought. Rarely is anyone completely passive, both mentally and physically, in the face of discomfort—and even passivity is one way of dealing with pain.

Often, people try such things as "thinking about something else," or "just trying to relax," or "telling myself it will be over soon," in order to put up with or reduce feelings of pain. You probably can think of many other such methods. It makes some sense that if people use such mental or physical activities so frequently, almost instinctively, then it is likely that they really work. Under the right circumstances such things actually do work, if they are well learned and practiced. Studies such as this one have helped to expand and refine these methods so that they are more successful. What it amounts to is that everyone has the potential for dealing with pain effectively. Learning pain management is mainly a matter of developing this potential.

As we have said, the purpose of this chapter is to help you learn more about pain for your eventual benefit when you have to undergo painful experiences for one reason or another.

There are three aspects of pain that must be considered

in a pain-management program. They are (1) sensory input: the actual intensity of the stimulation at the point on your body at which it is received; (2) direction of attention: the attention that you pay to the stimulation you are receiving; and (3) interpretation of sensations: situational, social, and cultural determinants of a painful experience.

Sensory Input

A very effective means of affecting the sensations of pain is through relaxation (Bobey and Davidson, 1970; Harris, Katkin, Lick, and Haberfield, 1976).

The Effects of Relaxation on Pain

How can you actually reduce the physical sensations that you feel? One suggestion comes from methods of natural childbirth, that is, childbirth with the aid of few, if any, drugs (Lamaze, 1958). An *essential* ingredient in these methods is *complete relaxation*. Physical tension—the tightening of muscles—makes you feel more anxious and upset, and it increases physical sensations, i.e., pain. And pain tends to cause tension. This sets up a vicious cycle; pain leads to more tension, and so on (Dick-Read, 1959).

How do you stop the pain-tension-anxiety-pain cycle? By relaxing. The woman attending her first childbirth class has the same response to this suggestion that you may feel now: "Sure! Relax! That's easy to say. Just try to relax in severe pain. Relaxing is the *last* thing you feel like doing. All you can do is tense up and try not to scream." It isn't usually quite so simple to just "relax" under adverse circumstances.

It isn't simple, but it is *possible*. Witness to this fact are the thousands of mothers-to-be who take childbirth preparation classes each year, and who report much less pain from labour than those women who do not engage in the training. Further evidence is provided by the popularity of this approach, which is growing by leaps and bounds every year. Classes are being held in hospitals everywhere, and doctors are routinely suggesting that patients attend. So *it is possible* to relax, even under circumstances that are normally as uncomfortable (or downright painful) as childbirth. And, most importantly, it has been found that this relaxation *lessens the actual sensations of pain,* despite the fact that these sensations have a clear-cut physiological origin (Coger and Werbach, 1975).

How Does Relaxation Work?

It does several things. (1) Muscle tension increases painful sensations. Anyone who has experienced a charley horse or muscle spasm needs no convincing of this. Relaxation is incompatible with tension—you cannot mentally and physically relax and at the same time tighten your muscles. Therefore, *relaxation reduces the amount of pain that is directly caused by tense muscles.*

(2) When you are experiencing a painful stimulus, it takes a lot of concentration to stay relaxed. You can learn specific techniques (Jacobson, 1962) to stay relaxed under these circumstances, but they do take considerable effort. As a result, while you are concentrating on relaxing, you are *unable* to devote much attention to the experience of pain. To illustrate this process you can consider your brain as capable only of paying primary attention to one thing at a time. You know, for instance, that you cannot concentrate on doing very many tasks at once without getting rather confused. If you are filling all of your brain's capacity for attention with one kind of information, you cannot accept much information from other sources. This is precisely what happens when you are concentrating very hard on relaxing. While you are taking up a great deal of your powers of attention with staying relaxed, you have little attention left over to experience the pain, except on the edge of your awareness. You will probably still "feel" the painful stimulation to some extent—that is, you will be aware that it is there. Women well-prepared for labour sometimes speak of knowing the pain is there but finding that it is not overwhelmingly important; they are concentrating on the

relaxation-breathing techniques so much that the pain is merely in the background, and no so "painful." Thus, *by occupying your attention with something else, relaxation reduces the amount of pain you experience.*

(3) When you are relaxed you are not as anxious as when you are tense. You probably have experienced anxiety as an interference during an examination. Anxiety is also detrimental in other kinds of circumstances. Specifically, it tends to lead to muscular tension, and this, of course, leads to an increase in the pain. Rachman (1967) concluded that a major component in relaxation is mental relaxation. A method of achieving relaxation, such as by the precedure prescribed in detail in Chapter 9, will help you attain a calm, relaxed mental state, as well as physical relaxation. *Relaxation reduces your feelings of anxiety in a situation and therefore reduces your pain.*

Relaxation reduces pain, then, in three main ways: (1) it reduces muscular tension, thereby alleviating some pain; (2) it occupies your attention, pre-empting most of the discomfort; (3) it reduces anxiety and encourages mental relaxation, which further help reduce tension.

Controlling Attention

The next technique that is useful in control of pain is a set of strategies for controlling your attention. Let's illustrate why attention is important and how it can be controlled. You can monitor your attention to see where it goes.

For a moment, stop reading and notice where your attention wanders. You may have noticed that your attention seemed to move about from one thing to another, almost involuntarily. Your attention is just naturally drawn to things in your environment that are most obvious at the moment. For instance, if there is a sudden loud noise or bright light in the room, you are almost certain to pay attention to it. In the same way that you tend to focus on this kind of perceptual stimulus, normally you are strongly drawn to attend to other intense stimulations, including painful ones. Notice, as you read the following paragraph (Stevens, 1971), how you can direct your own attention.

As you are reading this realize that your awareness is like a searchlight. Things on which you focus your attention are pretty clear, but other things and events tend momentarily to fade out of awareness. If you right now direct your attention to your own breathing—the sounds, the feelings, the movement of your chest and stomach—you are mostly unaware of the sensations in your hands. As you read about your hands, your attention probably moves there, and you become aware of the sensations there, and the awareness of your breathing has probably faded away. As you can see, your awareness can shift from one thing to another quite rapidly, *but you can only be fully aware of whatever is the focus of your attention at the moment.*

As you read the previous paragraph you directed your attention to several different things. You can also control the direction of the searchlight yourself. After you have finished this paragraph, try the following exercise. Just relax for a minute and notice where your awareness goes. Be aware of what thoughts or images come into your mind— pay attention to these thoughts and notice that it is not easy to just stop them and think about nothing at all. (As you have probably experienced before, telling yourself "Don't think about it" is often difficult if you don't intentionally think about something else.) Then, instead of just trying to stop your thoughts, simply focus your attention on your breathing. Whenever you realize your attention has wandered to thoughts or images, just refocus your attention on the physical sensations of your breathing. Don't struggle. Just notice when you become preoccupied with words and images, and then return your attention to your breathing. To make sure you feel comfortable with this exercise, reread this paragraph once now, and then try sitting back and focusing on your awareness in this manner for a minute.

The attention direction that you just tried is commonly used as a means of coping with pain or other kinds of stress. You probably can recall at some time trying to "think about something else" in order to get rid of an unwanted thought or feeling. "Thinking about something else" is much easier than just trying to "stop thinking" about the unpleasant thing. You cannot completely focus your attention on more than one thing at a time, so if you consciously direct your attention to something reasonably involving, then you cannot attend fully to anything else.

Some Strategies to Direct Attention

Although you probably do some kinds of attention-diverting things already, it will probably be helpful to outline and practice several sorts of such activities. Then you will be able to pick and choose from a wider assortment, and to change from one thing to another when you find it necessary.

Imagery

One of the most commonly used means of diverting attention from an unpleasant stimulus is imagining a pleasant scene (Turk, 1975). "Think about something nice," the mother tells her child who is receiving an injection. Emergency room doctors have learned the very useful technique of attention-diversion. Asking an adult to talk about something that interests him and asking a child to pretend he is watching his favorite TV program are two such strategies used routinely in performing painful emergency procedures when it is not possible to use anaesthetic. The more involved the image is, the less attention you can give to other stimuli and, therefore, the less pain you will experience.

The kind of imagined scenes that are useful are ones that are involving and vivid, like some particularly clear daydreams that you may have had. You may sometimes daydream about an incident so vividly that you completely forget what you are doing. Boring lectures are particularly conducive to this sort of thing. Although you may not frequently experience such an image, it is possible for everyone to do so with some practice.

Try involving yourself in the following image right now,

and see just how vivid you can make it. Just sit back and relax in your chair and read this passage slowly, pausing now and again to dwell on the image (Horan and Dellinger, 1976).

Imagine a pure white plate with a lemon on it, resting on a table. You can clearly see the glossy yellow of the lemon's skin against the whiteness of the china plate. You can see the texture of the lemon rind, clean and fresh looking. There is a knife on the table, next to the plate. Now imagine that you're picking up the knife. You hold the lemon with one hand, and with the other, using the knife, you cut the lemon in two. As the keen edge slices easily into the lemon, the juice runs out onto your fingers and onto the plate. The citrus odor immediately hits your nose: sharp, clean, pungent, delicious, invigorating. Now you pick up one of the lemon halves, with the juice still dripping onto your fingers and onto the plate. Using the knife again you cut a wedge from the lemon half; raise the wedge to your mouth and touch your tongue against it gently. Every taste bud in your tongue is drenched with the tangy lemon juice as your mouth puckers instinctively. A shiver goes up and down your spine, and your shoulders shake involuntarily. Now sit back, close your eyes, and picture for a moment the lemon, the cutting, the tasting.

Good. Was your image very vivid? It does take practice to develop imagery skills, but everyone has the potential to imagine a vivid scene, given the right subject matter. Try one image now (Horan and Dellinger, 1974).

Once again, make sure you are comfortable in your chair, and *read the passage slowly, pausing from time to time to think about the image.* Visualize yourself standing by the shore of a large lake and looking out across an expanse of blue water and beyond to the far shore. Immediately in front of you stretches a small beach and behind you, a grassy meadow. The sun is fierce and very hot, bathing the landscape in a shimmering brightness. It is a gorgeous summer day. The sky is pale blue, with great billowy clouds drifting by. The wind is blowing gently, just enough to make the trees sway and make ripples in the grass. Feel the wind on your cheeks. It is a perfect day, and you have it entirely to yourself, with nothing to do, nowhere to go. You have a blanket, towel, and swim suit, and you walk off through the meadow. You find a spot, spread the blanket, and lie down on it. It is so warm and quiet. It's such a treat to have the day to yourself to just relax and take it easy. Think about that warm, beautiful day. You change into your suit and walk towards the water, feeling the soft lush grass under your feet. You reach the beach and start across it. Now you can feel the hot sand underfoot. It is almost too hot to stand on, but not quite. It's just very warm and very nice. Now visualize yourself walking out into the water slowly, up to your ankles, on to your knees. The water is so warm it's almost like a bath. The water is so warm, so comfortable, as the wind continues to blow. You splash it up around you and feel the wind, now cooling on your wet skin. Look around. You are still all alone. You still have this lovely spot all to yourself. Far across the lake you can see a sailboat, tiny in the distance. It is so far away you can just make out the white sail jutting up from the blue water. You take another look around and decide to return to your spot to lie down and enjoy the sun, across that warm sand to the grass. Now you feel the grass beneath your feet again— deep, soft. You can feel the hot sun warming your skin. It must be ninety degrees, but it is clear and dry. The heat isn't oppressive; it's just nice and warm and comfortable. You lie down on the blanket and feel the deep, soft grass under your head. You're looking up at the sky, seeing those great billowy clouds floating by, far, far above. In the distance you can hear the rustle of the water against the beach. You can hear the sound of a bird gently singing in a tree nearby. You can even smell the sweet grass around you. You can feel the gentle breeze in your hair and on your skin. You are very comfortable, quite complacent, and totally relaxed. Take a minute or two to sit back, close your eyes, and continue the image on your own.

How do you feel? Was this image involving for you? If

it wasn't, either try repeating one of these images or try one of your own that you think might involve you more.

Such an image can be very useful in an unpleasant situation. Focusing your attention on some images like these can take your mind away from unpleasant sensations that you are experiencing.

Pleasant Images

Both of the images described above were images that included only pleasant things and excluded any unpleasant feelings that you might be experiencing while imagining them. You can probably think of many more examples of these, from imagining yourself skiing down a fantastic ski run to imagining yourself at an enjoyable party or thinking of spending a good time with someone. If you *focused* your attention on any of these scenes, you would experience any ongoing unpleasant stimulus differently: you would notice it less, it would bother you less, and you would feel more control over your own sensations.

You can focus your attention fully on only one thing at a time. And you can *choose* what you will focus upon. Your attention may wander from time to time, and you may, for example, occasionally find yourself dwelling upon unpleasant sensations. But you can voluntarily *bring your attention back to an image* when you notice that it has wandered.

Imagining a Change of Situation

On the other hand, you could use an image that actually involved feeling an unpleasant sensation, but in a far different situation. For example, one person who had a pain in his arm imagined that he was James Bond, agent 007, and that he had been shot in the arm as he was being chased by some counter-agents. He was fleeing from them in his car down an incredibly dangerous, winding mountain road and was concentrating intensely on keeping the car on the road and traveling as fast as he possibly could. Under these circumstances the pain from the imagined bullet in his arm was the least of his worries, and it faded into the background, although it was still there.

The particular image that you use in coping with painful stimulation is not the most important thing. More important is that you be involved in the image so that you have little attention left to pay to the discomfort. You may still be somewhat aware of the uncomfortable or painful feelings, but these are more in the background as your attention is primarily focused on something else.

Changing Images

Something to keep in mind when you use such images is that there is no reason for you to feel "locked in" to any one image. If you find the scene that you are using to be ineffective or that it becomes less vivid after a while, you can easily switch to another scene. Beef up your images: there is no limit to what you can include. Any sensations will be useful—you can include eating, dancing, arguing, sex, running, skydiving—anything that will occupy your attention. They are fantasies—throw in unexpected things that will keep your attention. Experiment, and with the experimentation you can discard things that don't work and switch to things that are more effective. Sometimes you may find that you can maintain one, very detailed or involving image for a long time, and at other times, you may jump around from one image to another and back again constantly, or you may find images merge and blend into one another. Plan ahead so that you have choices readily available, but don't feel locked in to your plans. Use as many senses as possible—smell, taste, touch, and so on.

Mental Activities

These are other means of diverting your attention (Turk, 1975). For the sake of clarity, we can divide these into three main classes: attending to the environment, focusing on a train of thought, and focusing on sensations in your body. Each will be discussed in that order.

(1) *Attending to the environment.* To occupy your thoughts with something other than unpleasant stimulation, you can attend carefully to your physical surroundings. You can engage in such activities as counting floor or ceiling tiles, examining the construction of a piece of furniture in the room, or carefully looking at a garment you are wearing.

(2) *Focusing on a train of thought.* You can engage in mental activities other than images. Making a list of things to do before the weekend, or planning a day's activities, are things that some people have previously used to control attention. Remembering and/or singing the words to a song is another example. Mental arithmetic, such as counting backwards from one hundred by sevens, is also attention demanding.

(3) *Focusing on sensations in your body.* Analyzing the sensations in one part of your body and perhaps comparing them to another part, analyzing the intense stimulation as if you were preparing to write a biology report regarding the sensations experienced (heat or cold, pressure, tingling, etc.), comparing the sensations to feelings you have experienced before—all these are means of directing your attention away from the unpleasant feelings themselves. You may allow yourself to experience discomfort, but you can control the context of that discomfort, so that it is no longer simply pain, but rather is of some "scientific" interest—you are more "objective" about it, not so much experiencing the sensations as observing them. You may choose to rate your pain on some scale and watch how the pain changes. Notice that pain does not always remain at the same level. On the other hand, you may focus on another part of your body exclusively, so that the painful portion is not in the forefront.

Thought Stopping

A strategy that can be very useful in stopping unpleasant thoughts is called "thought stopping" (Cautela, 1969; Rimm and Masters, 1974). It is such a simple technique that it may seem like an unusual thing to do, but it can be quite helpful. If you find yourself thinking about pain or having other unpleasant thoughts, you can simply yell, very loudly, "Stop." This forceful action on your part interrupts whatever you were doing and gives you time to substitute another activity. You can either yell "stop" aloud, or you can "yell" it silently or in a whisper, to yourself. Aloud, it is probably more forceful, but it also works when it is "in your head." Once you "yell" the word and the unpleasant train of thought is interrupted, immediately begin to use one of the strategies you had planned.

Interpretations of Sensations

Imagine cutting yourself during an active game such as hockey or football and cutting yourself while you are home doing some relatively uninvolving task, such as shaving, reading a magazine, or slicing onions. Although the physical injury may be the same, in the active game you are likely to ignore the cut, perhaps even be completely unaware of it; but at home, during a more leisurely pursuit, you are likely to react more strongly, washing it and applying a Band-Aid, perhaps some first-aid cream, and so on. Most importantly, in the second situation you are almost certain to find the injury *more painful*. Why should just the setting have such an influence if the degree of injury is exactly the same? Let us take a few moments to explore this problem, for it can lead to another very potent means of controlling pain.

As powerful as pain can be, it is actually a delicate sensation. Pain intensity is very susceptible to change. One of the most powerful influences on pain is emotion. A few examples will help illustrate.

Consider the person who one evening develops an intense and persistent pain in the chest. "Indigestion" may be his first thought. When the discomfort is stronger and more persistent than he has experienced before, he will probably become more upset and start thinking about the possibility of a heart attack.

At this point the pain serves a useful function. It acts as a signal that something is wrong with the body and encourages a person to take precautions. In this instance he will probably seek a doctor's diagnosis. Until he has that diagnosis, however, the uncertainty about what is wrong will increase his anxiety and cause the pain to feel even worse. He will probably attend directly to the painful sensations. His uncertainty and fear of the worst contribute to the painfulness.

The patient is told by his doctor that he is experiencing an attack of toxic gastritis and inflammation of the stomach from contaminated food. The removal of uncertainty will likely then cause the pain to subside somewhat. His relief at the news that he has a much less serious problem than a heart disorder and the new interpretation of the sensations in his chest make the discomfort less intense and less bothersome, even if it lasts for a few days more.

This example demonstrates the effects that attitude toward a pain-inducing situation may have on the experience of pain. Sometimes the effects of attitude on pain may be more complex than those in the example, but they are usually no less important.

Another example showing how one's reactions to sensations determine pain intensity comes from a study done during World War II (Beecher, 1946). Soldiers seriously wounded in battle were compared with civilians who had surgical operations that resulted in less tissue injury than the soldiers suffered from their wounds. Only one-quarter of the soldiers (who had not received any medication for pain) requested pain-relieving drugs. On the other hand, 83 percent of the civilians asked for pain-relievers. The difference between the two groups lies in their emotional interpretations of physical sensations. The soldiers had been in constant battle, under severe fire, their lives in danger for weeks. As a result they saw their injuries positively, as a chance for relief, as an honorable means of saving their lives. For the civilians, however, the surgery was generally a depressing, traumatic experience, filled with worry and anxiety about the future.

Clearly, the physical stimulus is not the only, or even the major, determinant of the amount of pain one feels. How one appraises or interprets the pain, what his attitude toward it is, how he interprets the sensations—all these play a major role in the experience of pain.

It is possible intentionally to change our interpretation of a physical sensation sufficiently to reduce or increase our experience of that sensation. We do it all the time, although we are not usually aware of it. Whenever we experience some unpleasant sensation—whether it be pain or sorrow or disappointment—we tend to attempt to change our own feelings about it, to lessen its impact.

If, for example, you fail to get something you very much wanted—perhaps a good mark on an exam—your first reaction will probably be disappointment. You may moan and groan over your misfortune and become quite upset and depressed by your mark. Notice that in this instance you are viewing your poor mark as something important, perhaps a significant sign that you can't succeed in the course, or are likely to flunk out, or just aren't measuring up to the standards you set for yourself. These thoughts contribute to the bad feelings you have about your mark.

Although this pattern may ring familiar to you, so might a different response to a poor exam grade. On occasion you may have started out with the disappointment and unhappy appraisal described above, but then realized that you were just getting more and more upset by such thoughts about the mark. It is as if the unpleasant thoughts themselves serve a useful function: they call your attention to the cycle of depressing thoughts leading to feeling lousy, leading to more dwelling on unpleasantness, leading to more depression or anxiety, and so on. Once you become aware of this cycle it is natural to attempt to stop it. One way that you may have occasionally tried to stop it is by simply changing your thoughts concerning the event. In the case of the poor exam mark, you might begin telling yourself that you just didn't study hard enough and you will work harder next time, or that the exam wasn't really a fair one, or that for one reason or another you don't really care about that mark or perhaps don't care about the course (or about school, period!). You won't always be successful in this attempt at self-convincing, but often you will at least begin to change your interpretation of the event and thereby lessen the unpleasant feelings.

Of course, you may often have quite different reactions to a grade than either of these and may not have actually experienced the process described. The example is intended merely to illustrate that how we react to an unpleasant sensation such as disappointment is influenced by our interpretations of events. Furthermore, a negative train of thought can act as a cue that leads us intentionally to attempt to alter our interpretation by substituting different thoughts.

The point is that you can affect your own feelings in a fairly direct, intentional fashion. You "said to yourself" the things that would encourage change. You "told yourself" that the test didn't matter or that you could do better next time. *You are consciously influencing your thoughts by a sort of internal monologue—an ongoing series of statements to yourself*—in which you tell yourself what to think and to believe, and even how to act (Meichenbaum, 1977).

We use these same "self-statements" not only when we are faced with a disappointment, but also when we are experiencing some other unpleasant feeling such as pain. We think, for example, "Just relax and keep calm—it will be over soon," or "Don't think about it; think about something else that's pleasant" (using an imagery technique). It is possible, then, to use *intentional self-statements* to help yourself to deal with a painful experience. Such self-statements can alter your interpretation and feelings about the sensations and can thereby reduce their painfulness. Moreover these self-statements act as plans for handling future problems, as when you go over or "rehearse" in your head a future event, thinking about how you would react to different occurrences.

Preparation

The first stage in a stressful situation is the time before any unpleasant sensations occur and also the time before the stress becomes very severe. The *preparation* stage gives you the opportunity to prepare yourself for the intense stimulation before it becomes too strong.

View the task as a challenge—as a problem to be solved. That is, see yourself as making the decisions, planning ways to deal with the situation—*actively* influencing your own sensations.

Some of the ideas to call to mind during this initial phase are listed below, along with sample self-statements to "cue" the ideas. *You do not need to memorize these.* Instead, a thoughtful and careful reading, together with rewording and adding to the items to suit your own style, will enhance your understanding and therefore the usefulness of this method of coping with pain.

Some Coping Ideas and Self-Statements Preparation— preparing for the intense stimulation before it becomes too strong.

(1) Remind yourself that you have a problem to solve, a situation that you have to deal with. The idea is that you *reject a helpless attitude* and instead determine to *work at coping, develop a plan.* You may need to remind yourself of this if you find yourself feeling helpless or apathetic. What sorts of statements to yourself would summarize this idea so that you can use them as reminders? Some suggested self-statements follow. Alter their wording and/or add to the list so that there is at least one that you would feel comfortable using.

(a) I can deal with this task. Let me actively prepare.
(b) I must just think about what I can do to deal with this. Think about a plan for future events.
(c) At this point think of other self-statements that you might find useful to remind yourself of this idea.

(2) Aim to maintain a positive attitude. Discouragement, anxiety, apathy *may* occur. But when you keep alert to such feelings you can counteract them if they crop up.

Catch yourself when you are thinking negative thoughts. Stop them, and *redirect your attention to coping ideas.*

Again, read over the following examples of self-statements aimed at this purpose. Then change the wording and/or add to the samples. The goal is to have at least one statement that feels perfectly natural and is meaningful to you.

(a) Stop worrying. Worrying won't help anything. What are some of the helpful things I can do instead?

(b) I'm feeling anxious—that's natural. But that's no reason to give up. Let me just breathe deeply and relax.

(c) Can you think of negative self-statements that you could replace with positive ones? Remember that the negative self-statements can serve as reminders to switch to coping self-statements.

Confrontation

Now that we have considered some of the coping things that you can say to yourself during the preparation stage of a stressful situation, let us proceed to the second stage. As the unpleasant sensations begin to increase in severity, you are directly confronted with the intense stimulation and have the challenge of dealing with it. This *confrontation* stage is the one in which you begin to employ the strategies that you have planned to use.

Following are some of the self-statements that you could use during this stage to help you handle the situation. Once again, picture yourself using them. Try to recall some of the negative thoughts you might have had and substitute coping ones for them. There is no need for rote memorization—just slow, careful reading.

Coping Ideas and Self-Statements Confrontation—confronting and handling the intense stimulation.

(1) Now you will want to make full use of the coping

strategies available to you. When you feel the need, you should call to mind the various possibilities that are open to you.

A general self-statement can serve to remind you to use a strategy when you need one. Some examples follow. You aren't locked into any strategies and can switch whenever necessary. Change wordings and add to the list to suit yourself.

(a) All right, I'm feeling tense. That lets me know that I should take some slow, deep breaths as I relax more, and switch from the strategy I was using to another one.

(b) I won't get overwhelmed. I'll just take one step at a time. Let me just use my skills to handle a bit at a time.

(c) Stop these negative thoughts. Let me just concentrate on one of the strategies to do something positive.

(d) Think of any other statements that would help you to begin using strategies when you are feeling the stress.

(2) You can use self-statements to call to mind the various possible strategies. "IRMA" can be used as a cue word to remember the kinds of techniques: it stands for Imagery, Relaxation, and Mental Activity. Of course there are many possible specific techniques in each of these categories. The following self-statements, and similar ones, can serve as reminders of ways that you can cope with unpleasant feelings and sensations.

(a) This pain is getting to me. Wait! Remember IRMA: Imagery, Relaxation, and Mental Activity. OK, let me develop a good Image (or Relax, or use a Mental Activity).

(b) Relax. Just breathe deeply and relax. Concentrate *fully* on breathing and relaxation.

(c) I won't think about any pain. I will focus my attention on remembering details of the movie I saw last night.

(b) Add here some self-statements that you could use to call to mind these specific techniques, for example, some specific images, or thoughts, or things in the environment that you could attend to.

Remember that these lists are not intended to limit the choice of what you can say to yourself. Instead, they are illustrations of the sorts of positive, helpful things people have used in the past in similar situations and which you might find helpful. But self-statements are useful only if they express ideas that you find helpful. The lists, plus your additions to them, can serve as a cafeteria-style offering from which you can choose the most helpful things as you prepare for and experience a stressful situation.

Critical Moments

During a stressful situation there are times when you find that the sensations seem particularly bad or that you can't go on anymore. At such critical moments you are particularly prone to negative thoughts, which make the situation worse and can lead to your feeling the sensations much more acutely and perhaps stopping the procedure. You may remember such times from your experience with the blood-pressure cuff and from other stressful situations. You need to recognize these times and actively direct your thoughts to coping skills.

It would be unreasonable to expect to totally eliminate feelings of pain in a severe situation. Rather, you can attempt to keep the pain manageable and stop yourself from over-reacting and increasing the unpleasantness.

As you read through the next section of self-statements to help you deal with this critical stage, imagine yourself interrupting any negative thoughts you may have had and substituting for them these positive thoughts. Picture to yourself how they would help you to more successfully deal with the stimulation.

Coping ideas and self-statements critical moments—dealing with the thoughts and feelings that arise at critical moments.

(1) You know that you will feel some intense stimulation. It is only realistic to expect some discomfort. But at the same time you do not want to magnify the intensity of the sensations—just keep them manageable. You can use such statements as the following to represent this "realistically manageable" idea.

(a) When I feel a lot of pain, I should just pause, then focus again on a strategy for dealing with it.

(b) I won't attempt to eliminate the pain totally. I just need to keep it manageable.

(c) I know the sensations would rise. But I can keep them under control.

(d) Think of any other statements you could use.

Critical moments most often involve the wavering of your attempts to cope. At the time you may feel you are overwhelmed by unpleasant thoughts or feelings. You may think you "can't go on" or "can't cope any more." Since these thoughts in themselves make the situation worse, your task is to stop them whenever they occur and substitute coping thoughts so that you can deal with the situation more effectively. Unpleasant thoughts definitely won't help; pleasant or coping ones may.

Some of the possible ways of stopping the unproductive thoughts and changing to pain-management techniques are indicated in the examples below. Change wordings to suit yourself, and take the time to add to the list the ways you would find most useful.

(a) Things are going pretty badly. I can't take any more —no, wait—just pause. I shouldn't make things worse. I'll review any planned strategies to see what I can switch to.

(b) My arm looks terrible. Things are falling apart. No. I'll stop that. Relax. I will focus my attention on something else. That's better, I'm regaining control. Just a slow, deep breath.... Good.

(c) I can't get my mind off this pain. The image won't work. I'm going to have to stop. NO! Wait a minute! I planned for this. Stop the negative thoughts. Let me use a strategy and I'll get over this difficult time. OK, let me relax, relax, breathe slowly and deeply, and sing that song I heard this morning.

(d) Think of other critical-moment self-statements to cope with thoughts that are headed in the wrong direction.

Don't forget to give yourself a "pat on the back" when you are doing well. It can only help to say to yourself that you used a strategy well, or handled a rough spot successfully, or otherwise to praise yourself a bit.

Summary

In this chapter we have been concerned with a means of influencing your own appraisal, your interpretation of the sensations and feelings you experience as a result of pain. By that influence you can change how you feel about the whole situation. You can help make it less unpleasant, rather than more unpleasant. We have divided a stressful experience into three parts (although they may overlap): preparation, confrontation, and critical moments. This breakdown helps prevent you from feeling overwhelmed and makes the situation more manageable. The experience is now three phases, and you have specific self-statements that you can use in each phase. You don't have to worry about what is to come because you have things to do at each stage. You can keep yourself occupied by using the self-statements to direct your attention to the positive techniques you have.

One other point should be noted here. At various levels of pain, or different stages, you may find particular coping strategies more effective than others. For example, early in the stressful situation relaxation and imagery may be very useful. As the sensations mount the more active mental strategies, such as mental arithmetic, humming a tune, or thought stopping, may be more useful. The rhythmical nature of some techniques helps you to hold your attention. Or just carefully focusing on your slow breathing may be best at this stage for you. Once again, there is no reason that you shouldn't try anything at any time. But you may find that not all strategies are uniformly effective during the whole stressful situation.

15/Controlling Other Behavior Problems: Now I can deal with all of those disturbing problems

The self-management techniques discussed thus far in this book can be applied to any kind of behavior that you wish to change. This chapter includes suggestions for exercise programs and impulsive buying behavior.

Developing an Exercise Program

Most of us are aware of the need for more exercise but for one reason or another, we just never seem to be able to find a convenient time. For years I had intended to start a regular physical fitness program but had not gotten around to it, except on a sporadic basis, until one of my colleagues invited me to join him in a daily jog. At the time of this writing I have been exercising on a regular basis for almost ten years. Following is a list of suggestions which have been helpful to me:

1. Find another person who is also interested in developing a regular exercise program. There may be times when you would skip a workout alone but you do not want to let the other person down. Two people can also be a source of reinforcement for each other.

2. Gradually work into your program so that you do not become too fatigued or sore in the early stages. These conditions may make exercise so unpleasant that you are tempted to quit.

3. Schedule a workout session as a part of your daily activity. Do not consider your day's work completed if you have not gone through your exercise routine. You should eventually reach a point where your day is not complete without a workout.

4. Make desired activity contingent on the completion of your daily exercise program. Do not permit yourself to eat the evening meal or watch TV, for example, until you have had a workout.

5. While doing your exercises think such thoughts as: "I'll feel so much better now," "How much better I will look as I become more firm and muscular (or slender)," "I shouldn't have to worry about heart problems after doing this," or "I may be adding years to my life through exercise." Think every positive thought that you can while engaged in your routine workout.

6. If you miss a workout without good cause think about how soft and flabby you feel, how much weight you are putting on, or how you are letting yourself down. Imagine that your health is deteriorating when you do not do your exercises.

7. Compete with your previous performances but do not push yourself to the point where exercise ceases to be fun. If you can jog faster or farther than you have done previously, you have reason to be elated. You are making progress. Do not become discouraged, however, if you cannot run a four- or even a five- or six-minute mile. Compete only with yourself rather than judging your performance against that of some superathlete.

8. Discuss your performances with another person—preferably someone else who also has a regular program for physical fitness. It is satisfying to tell someone else about your accomplishments.

9. Set a minimum amount of activity to be completed during each workout. Exceed that minimum if possible. Raise your minimum standards when you feel you are capable of reaching new heights in performance.

10. If you are also trying to lose weight, weigh after

each workout. While eating a meal, imagine yourself on the scales trying to get down to a given weight. This will help you reduce your intake of food.

11. The longer you continue your program the more satisfying it is and the more you miss not exercising. You will actually reach a point where you feel sluggish if you miss a workout. You have now reached a point where your routine is self-reinforcing. At this point you should be able to forget about contingencies involving more enjoyable activities following exercise. The opportunity to exercise provides sufficient reinforcement to maintain that behavior. It has now become a habit.

I realize that for some people (traveling salesmen, for example) maintaining a regular workout schedule may be difficult. Even if you are unable to maintain a formalized program, there are steps that you can take to increase the amount of exercise you get.

1. When driving, park the car a distance away from your destination rather than driving to the entrance. This will increase the amount of walking you do.
2. Climb stairs rather than ride elevators or escalators.
3. When traveling short distances, walk rather than drive.
4. While standing around, stand on your toes and raise yourself up and down. This will strengthen leg muscles.
5. When seated, squeeze a rubber ball or find some arm exercises to strengthen the upper extremities.
6. When you feel tense or anxious, run in place or engage in some other form of exercise. You may find it helpful to get a punching bag for such occasions. This kind of activity should not only relieve your tension and anxiety but also increase your physical fitness.

Reducing Impulse-Buying Behavior

All of us buy articles that we do not really need and cannot afford. We buy them simply because they strike a seemingly irresistible chord in us. Impulse buying can be approached like any other behavior problem. We first need to know the extent of the problem and to create an awareness of it. These suggestions are recommended:

1. Make a budget for a month at a time. Keep an accurate record of all that you buy for an entire month. If you're shocked to find where your money has gone, you will have acquired greater awareness of your spending behavior.

2. Establish reinforcement contingencies for staying within your budget. You might set aside a small amount of money to spend in any manner you choose when you stay within your budgeted expenditures.

3. Pay for what you buy in cash. You can write a check or use a credit card and never be aware of how much you are spending. When you count out the cash it makes you aware that you are spending money. Do not carry much more money than you will actually need.

4. Shop from prepared lists. If you see something such as a coat or a pair of shoes that you feel you cannot resist, never buy them on the spur of the moment. Wait a day or two and see if the article is still irresistible. By then it may have lost some of its appeal and you will have saved a considerable amount.

5. Do not window shop. You are less likely to want what you do not see.

6. Stay away from places where you have made impulsive purchases in the past. Find out what your weakness is and avoid that kind of store.

Final Comment

Remember that the principles and techniques included in this book can be applied to any kind of behavior that you are interested in changing. By now you should be able to formulate a program without difficulty. It is my hope that by this time you have already begun a self-control program and are experiencing success. Should you want to change some behavior and find the material presented here either inadequate or too difficult to comprehend, any behavioral psychologist should be able to provide the assistance that you seek.

References

Chapter 1

Bandura, A. Foreword in *Behavioral Self-Control*, Thoreson, C. E., and Mahoney, M. J. New York: Holt, Rinehart & Winston, 1974.

Herenden, D. L., and Shapiro, M. M. A within- and between-subjects comparison of the effects of extinction and DRO on salivary responding. Paper presented at meeting of the Midwestern Psychological Association, April 1971.

Herenden, D. L., and Shapiro, M. M. Classical and DRO discrimination of salivary responding. Paper presented at meeting of the Western Psychological Association, April 1971.

Lunde, D. T. Our murder-boom. *Psychology Today*, July 1975, *9*, 35-42.

Mahoney, M. J., and Thorensen, C. E. *Self-Control: Power to the Person*. Monterey, Calif.: Brooks/Cole, 1974. Pp. 71-72.

Miller, N. E. Learning of visceral and glandular response, *Science*, 1969, *163*, 434-453.

Pavlov, I. P. *Conditioned Reflexes*. London: Oxford University Press, 1927.

Chapter 2

Deci, E. L. Effects of externally mediated rewards on intrinsic motivation. *Journal of Personality and Social Psychology*, 1971, *18*, 105-115.

Guthrie, E. R. *The Psychology of Learning*. New York: Harper & Row, 1935.

Jones, M. C. The elimination of children's fears. *Journal of Experimental Psychology*, 1924, *7*, 382-390.

Maslow, A. H. *Motivation and Personality.* New York: Harper & Row, 1954.

Penick, S. B., Filion, R., Fox, S., and Stunkard, A. J. Behavior modification in the treatment of obesity. *Psychosomatic Medicine,* 1971, *33,* 49-55.

Premack, D. Toward empirical behavior laws: I. Positive reinforcement. *Psychological Review,* 1959, *66,* 219-233.

Rimm, D. E., and Masters, J. E. *Behavior Therapy Techniques and Empirical Findings.* New York: Academic Press, Inc., 1974.

Wolpe, J. *Psychotherapy by Reciprocal Inhibition.* Palo Alto, Calif.: Stanford University Press, 1958.

Chapter 3

Boudin, H. M. Contingency contracting as a therapeutic tool in the deceleration of amphetamine use. *Behavior Therapy,* 1972, *3,* 604-608.

Cautela, J. R. Treatment of compulsive behavior by covert sensitization. *Psychological Record,* 1966, *16,* 33-41.

Ferester, C. B., Nurnberger, J. I., and Levitt, W. B. The control of eating. *Journal of Mathetics,* 1962, *1,* 87-109.

Fox, L. Effecting the use of efficient study habits. *Journal of Mathetics,* 1962, *1,* 76-86.

Franklin, B. *Autobiography of Benjamin Franklin* with introduction by Verner W. Crane. New York: Harper & Brothers, Publishers, 1966.

Harris, M. B. Self-directed program for weight control: A pilot study. *Journal of Abnormal Psychology,* 1969, *74,* 263-270.

Homme, L. E. Perspectives in Psychology, 24: Control of coverants, the operants of the mind. *Psychological Record,* 1965, *15,* 501-511.

Jackson, B. and VanZoost, B. Changing study behaviors through reinforcement contingencies. *Journal of Counseling Psychology,* 1972, *19,* 192-195.

Levinson, B. L., Shapiro, D., Schwartz, G. E., and Tursky, B. Smoking on cue: A behavioral approach to smoking reduction. *Journal of Health and Social Behavior,* 1971, *12,* 108-113.

Lindsley, O. R. A reliable wrist counter for recording behavior notes. *Journal of Applied Behavior Analysis,* 1968, *1,* 77-78.

Mahoney, M. J. Self-reward and self-monitoring technique for weight control. *Behavior Therapy,* in press. Cited in Thorensen, C. E., and Mahoney, M. J. *Behavioral Self-Control.* New York: Holt, Rinehart & Winston, Inc., 1974.

Mahoney, M. J., Maura, N. G., and Wade, T. C. The relative

efficacy of self-reward, self-punishment, and self-monitoring techniques for weight loss. *Journal of Consulting and Clinical Psychology*, 1973, *40*, 404-407.

Mann, R. A. The use of contingency contracting to control an adult behavior problem: Weight control. *Journal of Applied Behavior Analysis*. 1971, *12*, 107-113.

McGuire, R. J. and Vallance, M. Aversion therapy by electric shock: A simple technique. *British Medical Journal*, 1964, *1*, 151-153.

Mees, H. L. Sadistic fantasies modified by aversive conditioning and substitution. *Behavior Research and Therapy*, 1966, *4*, 317-320.

Miller, M. M. Treatment of chronic alcoholism by hypnotic aversion. *Journal of the American Medical Association*, 1959, *171*, 1492-1495.

Nolan, J. D. Self-control procedures in the modification of smoking behavior. *Journal of Consulting and Clinical Psychology*, 1968, *32*, 92-93.

Penick, S. B., Filion, R., Fox, S., and Stunkard, A. J. Behavior modification in the treatment of obesity. *Psychosomatic Medicine*, 1971, *33*, 49-55.

Rhem, L. P., and Marston, A. R. Reduction of social anxiety through modification of self-reinforcement: An instigation therapy technique. *Journal of Consulting and Clinical Psychology*, 1968, *32*, 565-574.

Rimm, D. E. and Masters, J. E. *Behavior Therapy Techniques and Empirical Findings*. New York: Academic Press, Inc., 1974.

Shapiro, D., Tursky, B., Schwartz, G. E., and Shnidman, S. R. Smoking on cue: A behavioral approach to smoking reduction. *Journal of Health and Social Behavior*, 1971, *12*, 108-113. Reprinted in M. J. Mahoney and C. E. Thorensen, *Self-Control: Power to the Person*. Monterey, Calif.: Brooks/Cole, 1974.

Stuart, R. B. Behavioral control over eating. *Behavior Research and Therapy*, 1967, *5*, 357-365.

Watson, P. L. and Tharp, R. G. *Self-directed Behavior: Self-modification for Personal Adjustment*. Monterey, Calif.: Brooks/Cole, 1972.

Chapter 4

Ball, M. F. Seven major hazards for obese patients. In Stare, F. J. (Ed.) *Obesity: Data and Directions for the 70's*. New York: Medcom, Inc., 1974.

Decke, E. Effects of taste on the eating behavior of obese and normal persons. Cited in S. Schachter, *Emotions, Obesity and Crime.* New York: Academic Press, 1971.

Homme, L. E. Perspectives in psychology, 24: Control of coverants, the operants of the mind. *Psychological Record,* 1965, *15,* 501-511.

Morganstern, Kenneth P. Cigarette smoking as a noxious stimulus in self-managed aversion therapy for compulsive eaters. *Behavior Therapy,* 1974, *5,* 255-260.

Nisbett, R. E. Taste, deprivation, and weight determinants of eating behavior. *Journal of Personality and Social Psychology,* 1968, *10,* 107-116.

Penick, S. B., Filion, R., Fox, S., and Stunkard, A. J. Behavior modification in the treatment of obesity. *Psychosomatic Medicine,* 1971, *33,* 49-55.

Schachter, S. Some extraordinary facts about obese humans and rats. *American Psychologist,* 1971, *26,* 129-144.

Stuart, R., and Davis, B. *Slim Chance in a Fat World: Behavioral Control of Obesity.* Champaign, Ill.: Research Press, 1972.

Chapter 5

Berecz, J. Modification of smoking behavior through self-administered punishment of imagined behavior: A new approach to aversion therapy. *Journal of Consulting and Clinical Psychology,* 1972, *38,* 244-250.

Cautela, J. R. Treatment of compulsive behavior by covert sensitization. *Psychological Record,* 1966, *16,* 33-41.

Cautela, J. R. Treatment of smoking by covert sensitization. *Psychological Reports,* 1970, *26,* 414-420.

Elliot, R. and Tighe, T. Breaking the cigarette habit: Effects of a technique involving threatened loss of money. *Psychological Record,* 1968, *18,* 503-513.

Haddock, R. (Ed.) *Warning: The Surgeon General Has Determined that Cigarette Smoking Is Dangerous to Your Health.* Nashville, Tenn.: Southern Publishing Co., 1973.

Homme, L. E. Control of coverants, the operants of the mind. *Psychological Record,* 1965, *15,* 501-511.

Nolan, J. D. Self-control procedures in the modification of smoking behavior. *Journal of Consulting and Clinical Psychology,* 1968, *32,* 92-93.

Powell, T. R., and Azrin, N. The effects of shock as a punisher for cigarette smoking. *Journal of Applied Behavior Analysis,* 1968, *1,* 63-71.

Roberts, A. H. Self-control procedures in modification of smoking behavior replication. *Psychological Reports,* 1969, *24,* 675-676.

Shapiro, D., Tursky, B., Schwartz, G. E., and Shnidman, S. R. Smoking on cue: A behavioral approach to smoking reduction. *Journal of Health and Social Behavior,* 1971, *12,* 108–113.

Winett, R. A. Parameters of deposit contracts in the modification of smoking. *Psychological Record,* 1973, *23,* 49-60.

Chapter 6

Beneke, W. M., and Harris, M. B. Teaching self-control of study behavior. *Behavior Research and Therapy,* 1972, *10,* 35-41.

Bowman, J. The 7 C's of note-taking. Unpublished paper, Department of Reading, East Tennessee State University, 1975.

Elliot, Chandler. *The Effective Student.* New York: Harper & Row, 1966.

Goldiamond, I. Self-control procedures in personal behavior problems. *Psychological Reports,* 1965, *17,* 851-868.

Jackson, B. and VanZoost, B. Changing study behaviors through reinforcement contingencies. *Journal of Counseling Psychology,* 1972, *19,* 192-195.

Jackson, B. and VanZoost, B. Self-regulated teaching of others as a means of improving study habits. *Journal of Counseling Psychology,* 1974, *21,* 489-493.

Kanfer, F. H. The maintenance of self-generated stimuli and reinforcement. In A. Jacobs and L. B. Sachs (Eds.), *The Psychology of Private Events.* New York: Academic Press, 1971, Pp. 39-59.

Marston, A. R., and Feldman, S. F. Toward use of self-control in behavior modification. Paper presented at the meeting of the American Psychological Association, Miami, Florida, 1970.

Moor, John A. *How to Study.* New York: Rinehart, 1970.

Robinson, F. P. *Effective Study.* New York: Harper, 1970.

Spache, G. D., and Berg, P. C. *The Art of Effective Reading.* New York: Macmillan Co., 1966.

Zimmerman, J. Applications of productive avoidance to the problem of accelerating "productive" behavior in humans: Rationale, some data, and some speculations. Unpublished paper, Indiana University School of Medicine, 1970.

Chapter 7

Ashem, B., and Donner, L. Covert sensitization with alcoholics:

A controlled replication. *Behavior Research and Therapy,* 1968, *6,* 7-12.

Avant, S. S. A note on the treatment of alcoholics by a verbal aversion technique. *The Canadian Psychologist,* 1967, *8,* 19-22.

Cautela, J. R. Covert sensitization. *Psychological Reports,* 1967, *20,* 459-468.

Cautela, J. R. Treatment of compulsive behavior by covert sensitization. *Psychological Record,* 1966, *16,* 33-41.

Franks, C. M. Conditioning and conditioned aversion therapies in the treatment of the alcoholic. *The International Journal of the Addictions,* 1966, *2,* 61-98.

Miller, E. C., Dvorak, B. A., and Turner, D. W. A method of creating aversion to alcohol by reflex conditioning in a group setting. *Quarterly Journal of Studies on Alcohol,* 1960, *21,* 424-431.

Raymond, M. J. The treatment of addiction of aversion conditioning with apomorphine. *Behavior Research and Therapy,* 1964, *1,* 287-291.

Sobell, M. B., and Sobell, L. C. Individualized behavior therapy for alcoholics. *Behavior Therapy,* 1973, *4,* 49-72.

Voegtlin, W. L., and Lemere, F. The treatment of alcohol addiction: A review of the literature. *Quarterly Journal of Studies on Alcohol,* 1942, *2,* 217-803.

Chapter 8

Ellis, Albert. *Humanistic Psychotherapy: The Rational-Emotive Approach.* New York: Julian Press, 1973. Pp. 1-17, 55-59.

Ellis, Albert, and Harper, Robert A. *A Guide to Rational Living in an Irrational World.* Englewood Cliffs, N.J.: Prentice-Hall, 1961.

Homme, Lloyd E. Perspectives in Psychology: 24, Control of coverants, the operants of the mind. *Psychological Record,* 1965, *15,* 501–511.

Johnson, W. G. Some applications of Homme's coverant control therapy: Two case reports. *Behavior Therapy,* 1971, *2,* 240-248.

Lakein, A. *How to Get Control of Your Time and Your Life.* New York: Peter H. Wyden, Inc., 1973.

Mahoney, Michael F., and Thorensen, Carl E. *Self-control: Power to the Person.* Monterey, Calif.: Brooks/Cole, 1974.

Watson, David L., and Tharp, Roland G. *Self-directed Behavior: Self-modification for Personal Adjustment.* Monterey, Calif.: Brooks/Cole, 1972.

Williams, Robert L., and Long, James D. *Toward a Self-managed Life Style*. Boston: Houghton Mifflin, 1965.

Chapter 9

Bugg, C. A. Systematic Desensitization: A technique worth trying. *Personnel and Guidance Journal*, 1972, *50*, 823-828.

Carrol, H. A. *Mental Hygiene: The Dynamics of Adjustment*. Englewood Cliffs, N.J.: Prentice Hall, 1969.

Davidscn, G. C. Elimination of a sadistic fantasy by a client-controlled counter-conditioning technique: A case study. *Journal of Abnormal Psychology*, 1968, *73*, 84-89.

Goldfried, M. R. Reduction of generalized anxiety through a variant of systematic desensitization. In M. R. Goldfried and M. Merbarum (Eds.) *Behavior through Self-Control*. New York: Holt, Rinehart & Winston, 1973.

Homme, L. E. Perspectives in psychology, 24: Control of coverants, the operants of the mind. *Psychological Record*, 1965, *15*, 501-511.

Johnson, W. G. Some applications of Homme's covert control therapy: Two case reports. *Behavior Therapy*, 1971, *2*, 240-248.

Meichenbaum D., and Cameron, R. The clinical potential of modifying what clients say to themselves. In M. G. Mahoney and C. E. Thorensen. *Self-control: Power to the Person*. Monterey, Calif.: Brooks/Cole, 1974, 263-290.

Morris, L. W., and Thomas, C. R. Treatment of phobias by a self-administered desensitization technique. *Journal of Behavior Therapy and Experimental Psychiatry*, 1973, *4*, 397-399.

Paul, G. *Insight vs. Desensitization in Psychotherapy*. Stanford, Calif.: Stanford University Press, 1966.

Rimm, D. E., and Masters, J. E. *Behavior Therapy Techniques and Empirical Findings*. New York: Academic Press, Inc., 1974.

Stampfl, T. G., and Lewis, D. G. Essentials of implosive therapy: A learning theory based on psychodynamic behavior therapy. *Journal of Abnormal Psychology*, 1967, *72*, 496-503.

Suinn, R., and Richardson, R. Anxiety management training: A nonspecific behavior therapy program for anxiety control. *Behavior Therapy*, 1971, *2*, 498-510.

Thoresen, C. E., and Mahoney, M. J. *Behavioral Self-control*. New York: Holt, Rinehart & Winston, 1974.

Watson, P. L., and Tharp, R. G. *Self-directed Behavior: Self modification for Personal Adjustment*. Monterey, Calif.: Brooks/Cole, 1972.

Wine, J. Test anxiety and direction of attention. *Psychological Bulletin*, 1971, *76*, 92-104.

Zimmerman, J. If it's what's inside that counts, why not count it?: Self-recording of feelings and treatment by "self-implosion." *Psychological Record*, 1975, *25*, 3-16.

Chapter 10

Meichenbaum, D. Cognitive modification of test anxious college students. *Journal of Consulting and Clinical Psychology*, 1972, *39*, 370-380.

Meichenbaum, D., and Cameron, R. Stress inoculation: A skills training approach to anxiety management. Unpublished manuscript, University of Waterloo, Waterloo, Ont., 1973.

Meichenbaum, D. Toward a cognitive theory of self-control. In G. Schwartz and D. Shapiro (Eds.), *Consciousness and self-regulation: Advances in Research*. New York: Plenum Press, 1975.

Meichenbaum, D., and Turk, D. The cognitive-behavioral management of anxiety, anger, and pain. Paper presented at the Seventh Banff International Conference on Behavior Modification, Banff, Canada, 1975.

Suinn, R., and Richardson, F. Anxiety management training: A nonspecific behavior therapy program for anxiety control. *Behavior Therapy*, 1971, *2*, 498-510.

Wine, J. Test anxiety and direction of attention. *Psychological Bulletin*, 1971, *76*, 92-104.

Chapter 11

Novaco, R. W. *Anger Control*. Lexington, Mass.: Lexington Books, 1975.

Novaco, R. W. A stress inoculation approach to anger management in the training of law enforcement officers. *American Journal of Community Psychology* (in press).

Novaco, R. W. The functions and regulation of the arousal of anger. *American Journal of Psychiatry* (in press).

Chapter 12

Martinson, W., and Zerface, J. Comparison of an individual counseling and a social program with non-daters. *Journal of Counseling Psychology*, 1970, *17*, 36-70.

Meichenbaum, D. Toward a cognitive theory of self-control. In G. Schwartz and D. Shapiro (Eds.), *Consciousness and self-regulation: Advances in Research.* New York: Plenum Press, 1975.

Schmurak, S. Design and evaluation of three dating behavior training programs utilizing response acquisition and cognitive self-statement modification techniques. Unpublished doctoral dissertation, Indiana University, 1974.

Chapter 13

Anson, F. P. *The Quest of Solitude.* New York: Dutton, 1932.

Aronson, E. The gain-loss theory of interpersonal attraction. In W. Arnold and D. Levine (Eds.), *Nebraska Symposium of Motivation.* University of Nebraska Press, 1969.

Byrne, D. *The Attraction Paradigm.* New York: Academic Press, 1971.

Byrne, D., and Blaylock, B. Similarity and assumed similarity of attitudes between husbands and wives. *Journal of Abnormal and Social Psychology,* 1963, *67,* 636-663.

Byrne, D., Rasche, L., and Kelley, K. When "I like you" indicates disagreement: An experimental differentiation of information and affect. *Journal of Research in Personality,* 1974, *21,* 512.

Clore, G. L., and Jeffery, K. M. Emotional role-playing, attitude change, and attraction toward a disabled other. Paper presented at the meeting of the Midwestern Psychological Association, Detroit, May, 1971.

Dion, K., Berscheid, E., and Walster, E. What is beautiful is good. *Journal of Personality and Social Psychology,* 1972, *24,* 285-290.

The high cost of divorce in money and emotions. *Business Week,* Feb. 10, 1975, pp. 83-90.

Hodges, L. A., and Byrne, D. Verbal dogmatism as a potentiator of intolerance. *Journal of Personality and Social Psychology,* 1972, *21,* 312-317.

Homans, G. C. *Social Behavior: Its Elementary Forms.* New York: Harcourt, Brace & World, 1961.

Huston, T. L. *Foundations of Interpersonal Attraction.* New York: Academic Press, 1974.

Lazarus, A. A. *Behavior Therapy and Beyond.* New York: McGraw-Hill, 1971.

Levinger, G., and Breedlove, J. Interpersonal attraction and agreement: a study of marriage partners. *Journal of Personality and Social Psychology,* 1966, *3,* 367-372.

Liberman, R. P. Behavioral approaches to family and couple

therapy. *American Journal of Orthopsychiatry*, 1970, *40*, 106-118.

Lindgren, H. C., and Byrne, D. *Psychology: An Introduction to a Behavioral Science* (4th ed.). New York: John Wiley & Sons, 1975.

Murray, H. A., and collaborators. *Explorations in Personality*. New York: Oxford, 1938.

Schachter, S. *The Psychology of Affiliation*. Stanford, Calif.: Stanford University Press, 1959.

Stuart, R. B. Operant-interpersonal treatment for marital discord. *Journal of Consulting and Clinical Psychology*, 1969, *33*, 675-682.

Terman, L. M., and Buttenwieser, P. Personality factors in marital compatibility. *Journal of Social Psychology*, 1935, *6*, 143-171, 267-289.

Weissberg, A. *The Accused*. New York: Simon & Schuster, 1951.

Winslow, C. N. A study of the extent of agreement between friends' opinions and their ability to estimate the opinion of each other. *Journal of Social Psychology*, 1937, *8*, 433-442.

Chapter 14

Beecher, H. K. Pain in men wounded in battle. *Annals of Surgery*, 1946, *123*, 96-205.

Bobey, M. J., and Davidson, P. O. Psychological factors affecting pain tolerance. *Journal of Psychosomatic Research*, 1970, *14*, 371-376.

Cautela, J. Behavior therapy and self-control: Techniques and implications. In C. M. Granks (Ed.), *Behavior Therapy: Appraisal and Status*. New York: McGraw-Hill, 1969.

Coger, R., and Werbach, M. Attention, anxiety, and the effects of learned enhancement of EEG alpha in chronic pain: A pilot study in biofeedback. In B. L. Crue, Jr. (Ed.), *Pain: Research and Treatment*. New York: Academic Press, 1975.

Dick-Read, G. *Child-birth Without Fear*. New York: Harper & Row, 1959.

Jacobson, Edmund. *You Must Relax*. 4th edition. New York: McGraw-Hill, 1962.

Hannington-Kiff, John G. *Plain Relief*. London: Heinemann, 1974.

Harris, B., Katkin, E., Lick, J., and Haberfield, T. Paced respiration as a technique for the modification of autonomic response to stress. *Psychophysiology*, 1976, *13*, 386-391.

Horan, J., and Dellinger, J. "In vivo" emotive imagery: A preliminary test. *Perceptual and Motor Skills,* 1974, *39,* 359-362.

Kroeber, A. L. *Anthropology.* New York: Harcourt, Brace & Company, 1948.

Lamaze, F. *Painless Childbirth: Psychoprophylactic Method.* London: Burke Publishing Co., 1958.

Meichenbaum, D. *Cognitive-Behavior Modification.* New York: Plenum Press, 1977.

Rachman, S. Systematic desensitization. *Psychological Bulletin,* 1967, *67,* 93-103.

Rimm, D., and Masters, J. *Behavior Therapy: Techniques and Empirical Findings.* New York: Academic Press, 1974.

Smith, G., Chiang, H., and Regina, E. Acupuncture and experimental psychology. Paper presented at Symposium on Pain and Acupuncture, in Philadelphia, Pa., April, 1974.

Stevens, J. O. *Awareness: Exploring, Experimenting, Experiencing.* Moab, Utah: Real People Press, 1971.

Turk, D. C. Cognitive control of pain: A skills-training approach. Unpublished Master's thesis, University of Waterloo, 1975.

Author Index

Subject Index